The
Power
to
Transform

The Power *to* Transform

A Field Guide to Building a Human-Centered,
Tech-Enabled Work Culture

LARRY McALISTER

With Lisa Fitzpatrick

Foreword By George Kurian

BONUS FEATURES

As you embark on this transformative journey with *The Power to Transform: A Field Guide to Building a Human-Centered, Tech-Enabled Work Culture*, I want you know there is more to learn. Unlock exclusive bonus features by scanning the QR code below. Access our complimentary training program for a deeper dive into "Section 5: Thrive: The Core Strategies." Enhance your understanding with a video on "The Rise of the Tech Augmented Leader," and seize the opportunity for a free 30-minute consultation with me.

These features have been crafted to facilitate a seamless implementation of the book's concepts. Effortlessly empower your business towards a more human-centered, tech-enabled future.

Scan the QR code below and embrace the
Power to Transform:

The Power to Transform
A Field Guide to Building a Human-Centered, Tech-Enabled Work Culture

©2023 Larry McAlister

All Rights Reserved. Printed in the United States of America

Paperback ISBN: 978-1-947276-41-3
eBook ISBN: 978-1-947276-40-6

Publishing and Design:

EP◆C AUTHOR
P U B L I S H I N G

Ordering Information: Exclusive discounts for quantity purchases.

Contact: 561-601-9871 | info@epicauthor.com | EpicAuthor.com

First Edition

For my mother, Hope. May her spirit soar.

TABLE OF CONTENTS

FOREWORD

A ll change provides an opportunity to revisit how things have been done before—and build anew. In our case, it was time to tell a new story around what NetApp stood for, and where we were going. Our business transformation set the stage for a radical, but necessary, HR and work culture transformation.

This story began because our business needed to change with the industry transformation happening around us. And we realized that the people part of that change was the hardest, but most important part—especially for an institution that had been successful but whose entire approach around the market, talent, and organization as a whole needed to change. We needed to stop resting on past successes and commit to learn again.

We sought to shift more towards technology and data-driven decision making but also to rid ourselves of old-fashioned notions around how we deal with one another as humans. To facilitate these transformations, we steadily advocated for a *growth mindset*. We're not going to lie, embracing a growth mindset can be challenging. But without it, many end up defining everything by a single story. Everything we say or think or believe carries the heavy weight of universal truth. Opening our minds through experience and hearing others' perspectives can be incredibly enlightening—and provide for opportunities and solutions we could not have previously foreseen. And that's the beauty and fortitude in rebuilding from a strong foundation. So to us, how we approached transformation at NetApp was all about advocating for these ideas around change—and appreciating that we are all learners, not knowers.

The story behind *The Power to Transform* proves work communities can adapt quickly and en masse, particularly when we work together as a coordinated team to bring these changes about. No small feat for any enterprise, but we have now shown it's possible. In recent years, we worked constantly on embracing new opportunities and creating new capabilities in our business. For what it's worth, innovation is scary and uncertain. As company leaders, it's often presumed we have all the answers. We certainly did not, and needed to admit that we were learning along the way as well; what we did do was to fervently pursue the tough questions. And we learned to accept failure as an inevitable step on the road to success. And that's what we worked to teach our company. That we had to take risks. And try new things. To turn change into opportunity. "*We won't get everything right,*" we told them. "*And that's okay.*" We committed to our curiosity and a shared vision of the future; to a growth mindset. The culture of NetApp today is a testament to our adaptability and desire to keep "at pace" with what was happening in the talent space during this workplace cultural transformation.

What it comes down to is the stories we can tell. The stories that we can share reflect the pride of what NetApp stands for—what we do, how we do it, and who we are. And how NetApp is helping each employee to grow as an individual. We all want to feel like we are growing and adapting and changing together for the betterment of our company *and* our own growth. We maintained faith that we could do both—and we showed that, as a team, this was achievable. And we are most proud that this was a collective effort; created, sustained, and nurtured by all of our team.

But the effort, and the story, never ends. At NetApp, we have a wonderful story, inside and out. Not only are we proud of what we accomplished, we are proud of the manner in which we pursued accomplishing it. A story you'll hear more about in the following pages.

—**George Kurian**
CEO, NetApp

What is Transformation?

Growth comes from feeling uncomfortable about
taking the risk, and taking it anyway.
—George Kurian, CEO, NetApp

For many, the terms *business transformation* or *cultural transformation* can seem like scary words. And stats don't lie—a lot of leaders want it. Nearly 40 percent of all CEOs believe their organizations would be more economically viable if they did one thing: transform.[1] Without context and a good game plan, transformation may seem like a steep challenge for even the most seasoned and progressive senior management team. But it doesn't have to be. With this field guide, our "case study," if you will, you'll be armed with the tools needed to build your own human-powered, tech-enabled work culture.

So, what exactly is transformation? Most of the time, when faced with tough business challenges—and without necessarily knowing what the fix needs to be—companies will outsource their issues to large global management firms and then write them a big fat check. Consultants such as these can bring a host of resources and traditional theoretical thinking, but even with outside support, the truth is that most of these efforts don't cut it. Over 70 percent of organizational transformations fail.[2] There are many potential contributing reasons for this, many of which we'll discuss in detail. For me, a key one is the human factor.

Ultimately, transformations may *occur* in a business, but they *happen* to the people who work there. This speaks to questions such as: What happens to all the people who continue working in this newly transformed company? Were their needs, questions, and concerns addressed? Their doubts and reservations? Were their opportunities clearly presented, and were they informed about the new frameworks and updated expectations? More often than not, employees aren't brought along for the business transformation ride. But they should be! More than any other definition you'll come across, transformation is, at its most essential, systematically changing *behaviors* for long-term business success. Companies are made up of people, and for transformations to be successful and endure, employees must transform as well—and for that, they need help and support.

Let's talk for a second about what transformation is NOT. It's not change management—or at least not *just* that. It's something more systemic, more global and more long term. It's a bigger change—and requires more time. You want to change a product line or switch out some software? Altering a series of policies or restructure a department? Sure, you could call that change. But changing the culture? That's a whole other process, and one that doesn't happen overnight. Transformation, with a capital "T," is not just procedural or transactional. It's not something you can manage with a three-day offsite or a training session. At its core, transformation comes down to people. It's human-powered. That's why transformation is not just change. It's true transformation. At the *human* level. We're talking about changing methods, behaviors, and systems that have been the status quo, maybe for years. Possibly decades, as in NetApp's case.

"*In most organizations,*" shares OC Tanner in their 2024 Global Culture Report, "*change management strategies have fallen behind the pace of change. Catching up requires a people-centric approach that elevates employee voic-*

es, empowers leaders at all levels, and builds a healthy, transparent culture."
Work culture is an ecosystem—and that's what transformation both disrupts and builds anew. That's why any transformation you want to embark upon must include the *atomic level,* as Alexi Robichaux, CEO of BetterUp, refers to it. It's got to be an individual, human-level transformation. It's about business, but it's also deeply personal. Because we bring our whole, mentally fit selves to our work. Companies are comprised of individuals, and transformation is about shifting people's behaviors, mindsets, and skills to help your workforce tap into its full potential.

The purpose of any work-based transformation is to help the business thrive. There are many layers to this and perhaps just as many ways to go about it. But you need a strategy and an *action plan.* And these days (to state what may be increasingly obvious), expect to include artificial intelligence (AI). Meaning AI-enabled tech. You can find books to guide you, and there are plenty of theoretical approaches out there that a leader such as you can try. I encourage you to arm yourself with as much research and study as you can handle, but that's not what this book is about. Nor is this book exclusively for human resources (HR) professionals. This book is for any leader in business, from CEOs to HR—anyone looking to make big, bold, and systemic changes within their company. I'm here to tell you how to *fly the plane,* and in a very un-convoluted, non-business-ese kinda way. In this book, you'll be drawn a map that your team, leaders, and company want and need. You'll learn what to pack, how to write your flight plan, and how to share your strategy with others in a way that they can easily follow. So, strap in as I help you gain the altitude you need quickly because, as we know, getting from the runway to above the storm clouds is the hardest part.

Now, many don't consider *transformation* part of their job description. It certainly requires a change in perspective regarding what your leadership role consists of. But the truth is, to be in business is to be in transformation. Constantly and perpetually, whether you know it or not. Consider the pandemic. Didn't we all just go through the biggest transformation most of us have seen in our lifetimes?! (And with the advent of Generative AI, we are arguably about to enter the biggest transformation humanity has ever seen.) At COVID's apex (and long after), we all saw dips, fits and starts, and some ill-conceived choices. We might have even made a few of our own. If only we'd had a playbook… For us, COVID hit just as our NetApp transformation was in its first year. Because of all the prep work we'd done, we were, perhaps, more prepared for the changes than most and could respond quickly when circumstances demanded it. You never know when a transformation might be forced upon you, whether by a worldwide pandemic or market pressures. That's why the ideas here are not of the "one-and-done" variety. The tactics we deployed, and the mindset we applied to all of it, were designed to make NetApp more nimble, long term, and, ideally, future proof. It worked for us.

I wrote this book (which is a little bit about Equinix but primarily centers around NetApp) to talk about our transformation and how we did it ourselves. We didn't go hire any large management consulting firms. We did it with our bare hands. And my message to you is, *You can do it too.* I'll tell you how. To jumpstart your transformation or to simply spark some ideas. I'll talk about what transformation is, my way of looking at things, and then we'll get to how I did it. Meaning what I was up against and how I attacked it.

This is not your typical business book. It's not about leadership development or just about my wheelhouse of HR. It's about business transformation as a whole and how to set up your own transformation team to help your business be successful. How to use branding, technology partnerships, internal advisors, and more to tie it all together into one all-encompassing strategy.

When starting a business transformation, consider what's at its core: the human factor. It's human transformation that equips your workforce with the skills, capabilities, and mindsets to stay flexible, build resilience, and make smart, strategic decisions in the face of a large, complex change. A human transformation at the cultural level must include a broad array of strategies (including tech) deployed simultaneously and supported by clear and consistent messaging about the outcomes you and everyone will be after together. Simply put, it's best done as an inside job. Consultants will never know your culture the way you do.

Now, you may still be tempted to go the consulting route. They're presumably the experts, and they'll take a lot of pressure off you and any other employees you'll need to pull in to manage the sweeping changes underway. Why not outsource? Here's why: Consultants will come in and lay out a big plan for you. Notice how one of the first orders of business on their plan will be to cut money in your company here and there so you can pay their bills, right? And then it's left to you to take over from there—or you can continue to re-up their contract for years to come. *You don't have to do that.* I'm saying if you have the right mindset and approach, you can, beginning with the existing internal resources available to you, make all the changes that need to be made. You can transform without outside assistance. We did it at NetApp, and you can too. That is the essence of this book: to make the "how" as seamless and accessible as possible for you, the reader.

But first, I'd like to introduce a few key concepts to orient you to my way of thinking. They include *authenticity, human-centric, democratization*, the *Golden Thread*, and *enablement*.

Authenticity

The first book I thought I might write was *The Power of Authenticity*. I still may. The more I ponder the idea, the more I realize how much it runs through all my work and thinking. What does authenticity have to do with transformation? A lot. In fact, I'd argue you can't succeed without it. In business—and as we all likely know, in life too—authenticity creates the groundswell for trust and well-oiled teams. Transforming to a growth organization, moving faster than your industry peers, securing higher engagement and performance numbers, and having teams who are not scared of change all require honesty and having the best quality conversations possible. We'll get into the details in the section on Quarterly Conversations (and teams that evaluate their own Pulse Survey results), but the short of it is, by getting rid of all the artificial scaffoldings HR has kept in place for the past forty years, we were able to make it far easier for employees, managers, and teams to collaborate directly and more truthfully.

As a change agent or transformation expert for your organization, you (or whomever you assign) will, in many ways, be the face of it. And if people don't buy that you really mean what you're saying, it won't matter how much the marketing department helps you with your campaign. With culture and values, you've gotta take it off the walls and into people's lives. Posters broadcasting *Trustworthiness* and *Pride* will never cut it. If you're not living it, if your company's community isn't embodying these principles day-to-day, no aspirational mission or values slogan is going to matter. But if they are, and a healthy culture exists, or the effort is being made to create one, employees will know the difference. All the latest data backs up this principle and how it translates to real world business results.

Being authentic also means being true to yourself, and if you've built a transformation strategy you and your team really believe in, that will come across. That translates into my approach to leadership training as well. I don't advocate for leadership competencies. Every person is different, as is every situation. Each leader needs to decide for themselves how they're going to operate—and when done with authenticity, that leader has a better chance of building the kind of loyalty and rapport everyone welcomes from their staff.

There's another aspect of this idea of authenticity, and that's *transparency*. I recommend you take the time to present your full strategy and your plans to everyone so they all can come along for the transformation ride. You want to give everyone a chance to be a part of it—versus having it be something done *to* them. I don't want to be seen as a leader coming down the mountain with all the perfect answers. This "radical" transparency applies to any and all challenges. When you hit road bumps and obstacles (such as those revealed by AI-enabled survey data), by sharing the problems with everyone, you make them part of the answer as well.

Of course, the tone of any community, business or otherwise, is often set at the top. We'll discuss how to make wise choices in terms of corporate culture and what helps provide fertile ground when considering or preparing to embark on a transformation. In our case, at NetApp, there were qualities to CEO George Kurian's leadership style that set him apart and, I believe, set the stage for such seemingly radical changes (for a corporate entity) in such a short span of time. He endorsed both a *growth mindset* and a kind of *radical empathy* that gave us room to take risks. A member of my team recounted a situation that exemplifies what I'm talking about: "*I was around when the [formal handoff] between the departing CEO and the new one [George] happened…at an All Hands, and people were CRYING. The way that they handled that transition? From both an outsider and a communications perspective, I thought it was really well done. The previous CEO and George were on stage together, hugging and that kinda stuff. And even though the transition happened very quickly, it was done very graciously and in a very classy manner. It was done in a very human way too.*" When asked if George expressed concern for the employees, one of my team members replied, "*Oh, yeah. He [tells us] he cares for us all the time.*"

Human-Centric

When I was exploring the possibility of calling my consultancy the *Corporate Humanist Consultancy*, some laughed at the irony. Corporate *humanist*? But to me, that reinforced the need, the necessity even, to do so. It's been a lifelong career quest of mine to bring more humanism into the workplace. To be honest, though, when the term was first suggested to me, I had to look it up. Here's what Merriam-Webster says it means (the part that resonated with me, anyway): *a devotion to human welfare; an attitude, or way of life, centered on human interests or values, especially a philosophy that stresses an individual's dignity and worth.* Need I say more? I've never not wanted to put more *human* back in human resources. More soul and care, generosity, empathy, and humor! And I feel the world is finally catching up. These are exciting times! Where we can have real conversations about being more people-oriented than process-oriented, offer challenges, not grades, and focus on cultivating better working relationships instead of the mountain of artifice that, until relatively recently, so dramatically cluttered up our business systems with checklists and never-ending paperwork.

Being human-centric also means removing the expectation that the way things *have* been was inherently right or even helpful. I'll discuss terms such as *whole person*, *well-being*, *resilience*, and *growth mindset* and the once radical idea that we get to be fully human in the workplace. With the advent of AI, new stats from neuroscience, and the tragic catalyst of COVID, we've gained an opportunity to reinvent the very idea of what workplace culture is and can be. The opportunity to transform is good for employees, yes, but what's exciting is to understand that this type of people-focus is terrific for business too. As one of our tech partners says, "*When your employees are thriving, so does your organization. It just takes a little dose of transformation.*"

Democratization

As you read this book, you'll begin to notice that I reference the term *democratize* quite a bit. What I really mean by that term is access and *enablement*. A two-way highway for information. Communication and the sharing of knowledge fuels ideas and growth. Democratization is a way to break silos, pollinate ideas, and spread buckets of village wisdom across an organization. Traditional management training says, "*Let's just focus on the leaders, and that'll make everyone better.*" I say, "*Let's just make everyone better.*" In business, we should democratize talent strategies and our decision-making processes *and* provide each employee with a voice.

The Golden Thread

The virtuous circle. Weaving interconnected strands. An ecosystem. There are a lot of metaphors around this idea, but basically, it means that, strategically, I don't believe in one-offs. If you're embarking on…well, anything… such as firing up a project or licensing a piece of software, and it's not propelling the entire strategy, there's a pretty good chance it will fail. So, don't do it. Bringing a piece of technology that's not tied to anything means you won't get the adoption or the ROI that you want. That's the lesson of the Golden Thread. My axiom for *"We don't do anything by itself."*

Enablement

Enablement is my response to what's traditionally referred to as *corporate talent training and development.* Both address the question: *How do you grow your employees?* Where traditional training offers one solution, enablement provides an array of opportunities. In my view, our role isn't to enforce but to unleash that talent and opportunity—and provide the conditions for both. My role is not to develop but to *enable*, which is why I changed the title of Talent Development to Talent Enablement (TE). This was a watershed moment, and NetApp has not looked back. TE encompasses not only traditional training but also extends beyond it by providing resources, tools, new mindsets, and a broad array of communication channels designed to foster continuous growth, innovation, and well-being. The model is designed to create an environment that surrounds employees with ways to grow faster and better. I'm not developing the workforce; I'm enabling employees to do for themselves. Simply put, by enablement, we mean *"allowing you to do for yourself."*

PART I

The Year of Execution

Rebuilding an Organization for the Future

E ver since I was a little kid, I loved designing worlds for others to play in. I remember, as a teenager, having the first Apple II computer on our block. With it, I bought software and made up a baseball league for everybody in my neighborhood. Whether it was the Dungeon Master role in *Dungeons and Dragons* or putting together basketball tournaments out on the court, I was always creating environments for game play. It was a childhood passion, and I had more fun watching others get into the game— and team up with me to keep making it better—than I did playing myself. This passion kept evolving for me. I love creating worlds for people to play in, and eventually—or inevitably—I found ways to express this profession-ally.

1 · Humanizing the Corporate World

Out of necessity, while at the Citibank in Vegas, I built my own trainings. I was the youngest director in the history of that site and was told *"You are now the director of learning and development, but…you have no budget."* So, I had to self-create—and I loved every minute of it. I was in my natural habitat! I started training others how to train their groups, and then I got to see them take that material and keep it going. My core happiness is seeing these self-generated ideas, built with everybody's sweat and inventiveness, populate out. Even more exciting is making the next iterations better and better over time. When I work, I feel like an HR version of a game developer or world builder. NetApp's transformation was just another version of that. Now, after my most recent implementation (and largest in scale to date), I can look back and see how it all started—with my neighborhood friends and my family. I'm so grateful for them. Those early successes gave me the confidence to feel I was on the right track as I made my career choices going forward. It's been a lifelong goal to upend traditional performance manage-ment approaches and bring more humanity back into the workplace.

And more than traditional performance management (which I've always found doesn't serve the business either), the spirit of gameplay has informed my talent management philosophy. Whether it's a single player game, such as golf, or a team sport like basketball or baseball, there's still the spirit of camaraderie, of respect for the importance, the necessity even, of each individual player that defines that world. Or business. Or corporation. That's why I named my consultancy the Corporate Humanist Consultancy. To bring this kind of humanization to the corporate world.

No matter how large the organization, it's still made up of individuals. Just as on a football field, where the offensive line enables the quarterback to shine, every role is critical. One can't exist without every other. Not only because they affect themselves, of course, but also because their betterment directly affects the whole. All boats rise. I don't subscribe to a "command and conquer" mentality in leadership. Or to zero sum. I believe business success arises when each employee is inspired. When the company supports each of its members. No exceptions, no exclusions. I am a committed advocate for the idea of each person succeeding. Not just for their own sake. It creates a better outcome for everybody. That individual and the business. While activating the transformation at NetApp, I talked a lot about democratization and enablement with my people. This all culminates into a transformation, a talent strategy, and an internal brand we call *Thrive*.

Like a game developer, if you see that your job is to create the *best* possible environment for people to work together, to grow and get there faster? If you see *that* as your role? Then you're beginning a transformation journey. And embracing a more progressive management philosophy. It's not performance management in the way we once understood it. This kind of role encompasses an entirely different way to approach Talent Development and a comprehensive talent strategy. It's a different muscle than what we've known historically. It's a democratization of management. It's about enablement, authenticity, and appropriate responsibility. It's also a different approach for HR—as primarily a business division. A business unit. In the following pages, you'll learn about the transformation which took place at NetApp. Our story (along with other accounts following our travels in corporate HR at Equinix, Citibank, and elsewhere) will help you take the steps necessary to enact this progressive performance management philosophy, no matter what sphere of business you function within.

The Building Blocks

A lot of people in my role come in and focus on leadership and leadership development per se. And they'll say specifically, *"I'm here for the leadership."* It's natural to want to work with the top of the organization, starting with the CEO and the key leaders. And it makes a lot of sense. It can feel like the most important work in an organization, and sometimes, it is. I certainly couldn't have accomplished as much without CEO buy-in. I needed leadership to believe in my plan and fund it. As my partners in transformation, they were going to have to stand on a stage with me and tell their teams: *"We're doing this."*

But you can't stop there. My approach isn't for them alone. At NetApp, it wasn't about traditional leadership development or doing some trainings. As you'll see, I believe that top-down alone doesn't work. In this case, I went to the CEO and leadership and said, *"I'm here for everybody."* It's not that existing NetApp talent managers were opposed to the idea or hadn't considered it before, but their lack of bandwidth meant I was the first person at NetApp to hoist the banner high for democratizing the organization. The timing was right. And the changes we ended up making were for leadership as well but were done by way of focusing on every single employee. Specifically, the focus was on the employee-manager relationship, which, hands down, is the most important one in any company. To improve the trust, function, and performance of this working partnership, I needed to democratize the message, the actions (such as putting Pulse Survey results into the hands of the individual teams), and the individual growth. I always had to get CEO staff and managers involved, but the masses were—and will always remain—my focus.

It's certainly not the easier path. It's much more difficult to think about every employee as an individual who needs individual growth. It involves a complicated web of interconnected strategies—the Golden Thread. The Golden Thread of Thrive. No one piece will produce the enduring results you're looking for. It's not about launching a single program; it's about delivering on an all-encompassing strategy deployed across the entire organization—simultaneously and continuously. All the players need to be on the field before the games can begin, and it's through working in concert that they will move the company forward.

Leading with Soul and Care

I am a passionate advocate of the idea that a strong *employee experience*[3] leads to a better customer experience. When employees are happy, aligned to the business, feel motivated, and enjoy their work (and enjoy who they're working with), it translates into all kinds of benefits. Many studies have proven this to be true. Increased productivity. Better collaboration. Better innovation. Better customer engagement. Ultimately, better business results. Overall, better communication—and a view toward what can be done—leads to better business outcomes.

Companies will suck your soul if you let them. It's not intentional or anyone's fault; it's just by design. And humans, by nature, give everything that they can to the company. So, in my heart, what I also really wanted to do was put soul and care back into the way employees are treated. It's a more human-centric approach. From the very beginning of introducing Thrive, I knew that the way to accomplish this was ALL about building and re-humanizing the relationship between the manager and the employee. Because I knew that's where the action was. And from there, where fundamental, enduring change could begin.

In Year Two, our *Year of Technology*, I brought in a transformative coaching company called BetterUp. Among many services, they offer scalable, whole person behavior change. Its founder/CEO, Alexi Robichaux, and I agree on many points, but especially this one. He refers to it as the *atomic level*.

*All this work in business transformation... what we found is there's
a layer that is often missing. Are you actually optimizing...the individuals themselves? Change can be...replete with opportunity? [But]
that's really hard to do when we're burnt out....When we're stressed...
When we feel like our employer doesn't care about us. You have all
these firms that work on the systems level, and what we realized...
is we haven't actually optimized the atomic unit, which is the people
themselves wanting to change. And having the skills, the mindsets, and
the psychological resources to actually capacitate that change.*

There's so much research out there showing that a positive employee experience—and employees being engaged—translates to higher revenue. But
what do businesses DO with these research results? How can you actually,
practically, make changes happen? Hire out a solution? Insist existing leadership become transformation experts? Of course, there is no one definite
path; every situation is unique. But most outside playbooks don't consider
the current or aspirational culture. But if you *start* with the aspirational
culture and follow this book to make the transformation plan yourself with
your executives and your team, you can get there. As NetApp did.

Your Own Path Forward

To be clear, I'm not talking here about going after policies. I know that's
where many people start a transformation. I wanted to change the *people*.
I went after how leaders and employees worked together. I wanted to show
people how it helps them day to day. That was the structure I was focused
on. I didn't go after any *governance structure* because I know how that goes.
Sure, governance and accountability gaps are always plain enough to see.
But going after those takes a long time. It's not without good reasons (and
only incremental gains) that many, many battles have been lost on that bat-
tlefield. And the focus is usually about the top, which wouldn't get at what
I would need to tackle first. As I've been saying, I wanted to go after both
employees and leaders and transform how they work *together* into a much

more growth-oriented culture. My targets were mindsets, technology, and building an ecosystem for growth. To get people motivated, inspired, and working better together. You can get a lot more done much more quickly when you're attacking those elements. Which, again, is not an easy thing to do. I'm not saying it's a simple process, but the more traditional option leaves a lot of scar tissue on governance, such as policies and internal controls, in its wake.

My goal here is to offer you some examples for a path forward. Methods you and your business can take on by yourselves. You may occasionally want to bring in consultants or experts to contribute to your larger, internal discussions and offer other voices as needed, but they won't necessarily have to be part of the critical path.

NetApp didn't continue with McKinsey for this. All of us did it. Barehanded. No matter what kind of business leader you may be, whether within HR or not, you can make a radical transformation in your company. It is achievable. We'll offer you a detailed blow-by-blow of how we tackled it. In NetApp's case, it was all upside, and that's why I'm so excited to share our story with you.

Eventually, I think we could say we transformed HR at NetApp, but what we really transformed was the way that employees, managers, and leaders grow, talk to each other, see their careers, and have a *voice* in the strategy. And that all came about because of what we did.

2 • A Vision of Transformation

Transformation is not a one year gig. Change might be, but transformation is not. To build the necessary momentum, to get from zero to one, you've got to get out of the pull of gravity, or you'll never reach altitude. You've also gotta go fast. With *velocity*, meaning speed *and* direction. You must be targeted and have specific endpoints in mind long before you pull the trigger. And you must make sure you are all aiming in the same direction, moving together as a team at an appropriate speed. That's why your team's gotta be tight. No loose ends. No half-in/half-out situations. And for that, you need a vision of transformation. Why? Because you can't *pilot* transformation.

Now, we may pilot, say, an AI-enhanced coaching tool because if you can show some data, which may increase the investment. But you don't pilot a transformation. That's my view. Some people take the other route. They'll test pilot a transformation in a group. But here's the problem with that: If you do something in one group, it'll just get swallowed up by the rest of the organization. So, I said to leadership, "*We're doing this transformation, including no performance ratings, none of the old school stuff for* everyone *at the same exact time.*" You've got to be all in, and your team's gotta be too. What's more, your leadership's gotta be supportive. We'll get into all the strategy, the vision you'll need to make it happen, but for starters, the will needs to be there. And the courage and drive to see it through.

The NetApp leadership team was well aware that its existing HR model, though still widely used in the industry, was archaic. No question it needed to be transformed. And the teams had grown more siloed, less agile, slow to evolve, and risk averse. The policies had served NetApp at the time, but it was time for a transformative approach. Leadership wanted to build a culture that would attract and keep the best talent. What was critical path for them was performance, and that meant building high-performing teams. They also sought people and cultural transformation to support the creation of those teams, which would exist, ultimately, to support and cement the ongoing business transformation (which was well underway as NetApp was moving from a storage company to a cloud company). The challenge for NetApp was, that's where consultants often drop you off—after the business transformation. Market forces had pushed NetApp to think more broadly and inclusively about talent and productivity in the workplace. That's when I got a call.

The Thrive Ecosystem

My answer to this challenge was Thrive. Let me explain. Thrive is an idea. It's not just an HR transformation but also a culture and growth model (symbolized by a four-quadrant wheel), a story of change, and a new performance management philosophy. The Thrive Ecosystem for High-Performing Teams is also the journey we started at NetApp. We picked the ball up where the consultants dropped it on the field. Thrive is a full ecosystem of interconnected programs, technology, and tools to enable a culture of high performance and enhanced employee experience. It's how NetApp high-performance teams were built—quickly, in real time and on the job. It encompasses a new approach to Talent Enablement, one that embraces technology and democratization. And it's an entire ecosystem of working on the individual, your team, and the enterprise while always focusing on the future. And that vision began with what my team affectionately called the *Wheel*. Which was comprised of *"Cutting edge technology, tools, and programs to activate powerful employee experiences throughout the life cycle."* The Wheel graphic below (Image 1) details the four different quadrants of aspirations we wanted to accomplish: *Activate Yourself, Activate the Team, Activate the Enterprise*, and *Activate the Future*.

For my team, because they'd had so many false starts and unrealized projects in years past, I called Year One the *Year of Execution*. The second was the *Year of Technology*, and our third was the *Year of Growth*. The fourth, as the pandemic seemed to wind down (but then didn't), was called the *Year of Well-Being*. At the time, I was also referring to this with my team as the Golden Age of HR Technology, but the rapid growth of AI has taken this to even greater heights. In the end, at NetApp, the way each employee looked at their own growth, their career, and their voice was all completely transformed for everyone. But while we may have transformed mindsets, the ultimate beneficiary was (and is) every employee in the company, and therefore, the business.

Put Your Own Oxygen Mask on First

To be clear, at NetApp, the focus was on both HR transformation and cultural transformation. A double whammy. This was the ask and the problem we were hired to solve. If we'd tried to drive a cultural transformation with-

FY21 Focus & Beyond — Activate the Ecosystem for High Performance Teams

Growth Mindset
Inclusive Leadership

01
Activate Yourself

- Quarterly Conversations
- Thrive Rewards
- BetterUp Coaching (IC)
- Mosaic

02
Activate The Team

- Thrive Pulse Survey
- BetterUp Coaching (Managers)
- Thrive Talent (Enablement)

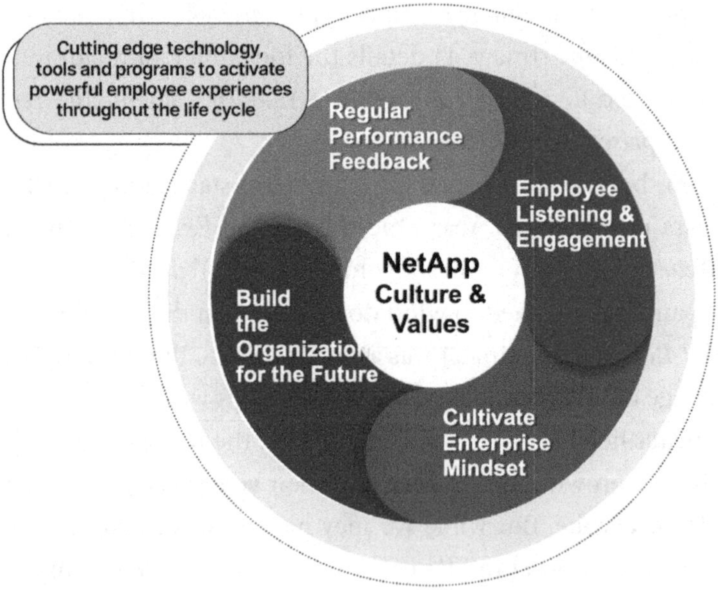

Cutting edge technology, tools and programs to activate powerful employee experiences throughout the life cycle

Regular Performance Feedback

Employee Listening & Engagement

NetApp Culture & Values

Build the Organization for the Future

Cultivate Enterprise Mindset

03
Activate The Future

- Thrive Talent (Talent Acquisition)
- Global Hiring Process, Horizons, Early in Career
- Internal Marketplace/Mosaic

04
Activate The Enterprise

- Breakthrough Leadership Program
- Thrive Talent Career Week

Image 1. The Thrive Wheel—Version 3 (later edition, 2021)

out also transforming NetApp HR, it may not have proceeded as success-fully. NetApp HR needed to first make sure the plane was reaching altitude, was sky worthy and state-of-the-art because, as an established international corporate business, their operations had been on the slow side. That's why this transformation could not just be a change. It required true transforma-tion. Elaine-Marie Bohen, my right hand and NetApp Director of Talent Enablement, said it well: *"There were times when we would literally challenge ourselves, 'Is that old thinking?' It's like the oxygen mask analogy. Put the mask on yourself first before you try to help others. HR supported the business for three-plus years in its transformation journey before realizing, uh, if we don't change, we can't help take the org through the next wave."*

Enable, Not Enforce

For those working in HR today, as you embark on this particular journey, you have to realize that it's consultative, not mandatory. HR is not here to police. We're here to unleash talent. This is about shifting the culture, which is fundamentally about changing behavior. Our focus now becomes finding the best possible ways to promote growth for both the employees and the company—and to show everyone how these two things are fundamentally intertwined, not mutually exclusive. It's about solutions, not pushing people into a box. That's where the trends are taking our profession, and people are realizing that although HR originally existed to control and regulate humans as a resource, now, it's really more about talent *enablement*. Devel-oping your people, not managing them as a cog in the business machine. Providing the conditions for them to succeed will inevitably mean the busi-ness succeeds. We're *enablers*, not enforcers. I appreciate that this is a new way of thinking, but for those in HR, think of yourselves as enablers and partners and less as people ticking off a list.

At NetApp, we transformed HR at the same time we transformed the way every employee grew in this company. And how every employee related to their manager. And how we could build the muscles for working accord-ing to a larger strategic picture, within which we would introduce new technologies to allow teams to function at peak optimization, all while starting to work with more cross-functional accountability and planning. We also shared with everyone how the democratization of data is not a threat but creates the foundation for a more robust workforce, armed with greater knowledge and greater long-term potential. We showed managers how to learn to use that data to their best advantage—and take more of the guess-work out of long-term planning. And, finally, we strove to give employees a voice in the business conversation—and talked about why this was good news for everybody.

Future Proof

One truism in business: In order to have a future, you need to learn to be constantly looking out into it. Both Equinix and NetApp are in a rapidly paced industry when it comes to the acquisition and development of new technology—and the ongoing necessity to acquire state-of-the-art technical skills. (Although I'd argue this is true for most industries, fast-paced or not.) For companies such as NetApp, the shelf life of technical skills required to service these new developments continues to decrease. You're a master of today's tech one year; the next, that could be completely uprooted by the next newly emergent one. It's not (just) about the skills—it's about build-ing a better system within which those skills can operate and continuously evolve. That strategy remains no matter what the technology is. Even with AI, tech doesn't drive vision—it's always the other way around.

Not to say new innovations won't radically alter the course of events, for better or worse, but management should never cede its strategic focus to a machine, even as Generative AI is poised to have a faster and more dra-matic impact on society than the internet (more on that later). All of which means leadership needs to maintain a perpetual future focus. The market is always growing and evolving. When introducing new products, leading to new go-to-market strategies, new acquisitions, and new company heads... leadership has to constantly be asking, *What's coming? What's the next wave of change?* And *How do you get on top of that? How do you build out the right strategic roadmap, the right direction, invest in the right talent? How can you predict the high-level skills most of your employees will require?*

NetApp lost market share because it had missed the boat on some key technology shifts. And it did not move quickly enough to see and adapt to what was coming. They eventually course-corrected but again, to have a future, companies need to stay ahead of market trends, especially in tech.

3 • The Stories We Tell

The corporate example I'm laying out here represents the culmination of a lifetime in leadership, and my ideas continue to evolve. With NetApp, I was in my dream job. It provided me the opportunity to double down on the focus I felt was most important—the individual and that most essential employee-manager relationship. We built out a three-year strategy. COVID threw us some curveballs, but we found ways to make them work for us because we had our strategy already in place. And so, we kept going.

It's powerful if you can get people enthusiastic about your vision, but they've got to believe in the strategy first. And to do that, it's important to share your entire idea—even if it will take years and multiple stages to implement. (That also means you need to work out at least a full, first draft beforehand!) It's okay if you don't have every answer for every step at the outset. The Thrive Ecosystem didn't. It evolved. It was an inspiration to an aspiration, as in, "*This is where we're headed.*" I laid out a path. "*See how individuals lead to teams, which leads to enterprise, which leads to the future?*"

What matters most is whether your audience can see that there's a method behind your initiatives, that there's a bigger picture involved, a Golden Thread of intertwining strands. It will go a long way toward enlisting those early supporters you will require. And ultimately, you're not going to get people excited about a tool or a five year plan set in stone. It's my belief that there's too much emphasis on process and not enough on story and authenticity in leadership today. You've got to help your audience believe in the story. Their story. The company story. The plan for change—and that it not only involves them, but it's also *for* them.

4 • The Zero Point

At that point, the question became, if going from zero to one is the hardest thing to do, how do we tackle Year One at NetApp? When you're starting from a blank whiteboard, what are the right first steps? We'll get to this story (and we eventually got to one), but first, let me tell you a bit more about what zero looked like.

What's NetApp?

NetApp, Inc. is a publicly traded, US-based hybrid cloud data and data management software company servicing commercial enterprises in various industries all around the world. Ranked on the *Fortune* 500 list every year since 2012, NetApp was founded in San Jose in 1992 by three self-described "hippies": David Hitz, James K. Lau, and Michael Malcolm. The company quickly rocketed to over $1B in annual revenue and went public three years later (1995). Today, the corporate headquarters of this cloud-led, data-centric software company is part of the firmament of Silicon Valley. NetApp boasts twelve thousand employees, a net revenue of $6.33B, and over fifty-two offices around the globe. For every major developed country market, NetApp has either employees or customers.

As far as companies go, NetApp was the most tenured one I'd ever worked in. Many of the staff had been there for years if not decades. Before joining, I'd been told it was a "nice" company. A familial, kind place to work, and not typical corporate America. In my experience, all this proved to be true. For many, these qualities remain its long-term appeal.

Clouds on the Horizon

While NetApp's legacy storage business, its "core business," still generates the largest revenue, its margins are slim. But the margins for cloud—now the latest, biggest advantage in the world—are crazy. The race has been on for a bit, and the three big hyper-scalers (Amazon Web Services, Google

Cloud, and Microsoft Azure) are way ahead of the pack. They're the apex players everyone wants to compete with, cooperate with, or sell to. NetApp has enjoyed long-standing partnerships with all of them, but at that point, it was ready to compete with them head-on as well and carve out their own fraction of the seemingly endless cloud market.

But for this kind of growth, you need the people—and expertise—to run it. Cloud engineering and engineering services are the hottest, most in-demand jobs on the market today, and the race to hire and keep them is fierce. After NetApp made its play, its internal head counts in cloud sales and engineering began to mushroom and has yet to stop. In 2022, they hired nearly two thousand more people.

The trajectory from NetApp's "on-premises" hard drive business to today's hybrid cloud services was not predetermined, or inevitable. Some early missteps in speed-of-light storage tech innovations, such as the cloud—and Flash before it—hit this legacy company hard. They were behind and hemorrhaging. They'd lost market share. The whole world was moving to the next iterations of storage and threatening to pass NetApp by. But that was all about to change.

Beginning in the late aughts, the rise of these existential threats forced the board to consider massive, all-encompassing transformations, first to the business (from 2015–2018) and then to both HR and its culture (2019 to present). The latter is the focus of this book, and by its end, I hope you'll feel you have the tools to embark on your own transformation.

In Walks George...

In June of 2015, the NetApp George Kurian inherited as interim CEO was, to use his own metaphor, on life support. The company'd not hit a single quarter's target for nearly two years. It was bad.

And yet, during his first All Hands company meeting, George had a bold ask: *"Have faith in me."* Known for his inspirational brand of leadership, his way of seeing opportunity in the latest swirl of tech advancement within the hyper-competitive race to cloud, attracted a new generation of modern leadership and the opportunity to successfully reinvent this well-liked, highly rated, legacy storage firm into a long-term player in the astronomically profitable future of cloud-based services.

The identical twin of Thomas Kurian (current CEO of Google Cloud), George had been promoted from executive VP of product operations with a do-or-die mandate: *Turn this tech company around and transform the core software business to the cloud.* George's first directives to his team were "*We need to stop the hemorrhaging...and see what's going on.*" He brought in former colleagues from McKinsey to start looking deep under the hood. Their analysis revealed a few issues. "*Consistently, the sense was we had the right strategy,*" remarked EM, but what they uncovered was self-sabotage. NetApp had become "*...feature-frenzied,*" proclaimed George, making it impossible to scale.

About this transition into cloud, Emily Miller, NetApp's VP of Brand, recounts, "*What's guided the company through over the last ten years is the pure joy of the technology and making it work, loving a challenge and solving client's problems...almost to a fault.*" And so, this congenial, global, legacy storage enterprise launched a business transformation throughout the next three years. Much of that early cost-cutting financed the army of consultants who came in to provide guidance on how to make these changes happen. In the end, they called for more operational rigor and more focus, among other mandates. Layoffs began. Overall, this transformation was done in a kind of ripping-it-out-from-the-studs-and-starting-over kind of way. There was budget slashing, there was some challenging reflection, and there were tears.

Transforming from Within

Concurrent with the McKinsey-driven belt-tightening, all future investments in talent, management, and infrastructure were singularly focused on simplifying the service and being all in on the cloud. The "*Profitable Clouds Run on NetApp*" tagline was launched. Fake it 'til ya make it, right? Most analysts, however, were still predicting that NetApp was "*gonna get killed"* by cloud. (*"It's still an on-prem data center company, isn't it?"* they insisted.) A number of organizational shifts at the top reflected some new, transformative thinking, and the main question on everybody's mind was *How do we go to cloud?* Most new hires were in cloud engineering and cloud sales. And the company began to make heavy bets on leadership positions, including those for president (the one to run all the "go to market") and new leaders for cloud and core.

But what would be the point of all this high-level re-architecting if no one looked at the culture of the company at large that it was designed to support? Any investment in the business is always also about the organization. Its people. If the product and sales fronts of NetApp were going to transform, all aspects of the company needed to upgrade with them. Leadership started asking, *"How do you manage, recruit, and retain the best talent? And can we do it with the HR structure and culture currently in place?"* The answer to the latter was no. This company was transforming from within, and it was time for HR to undergo a transformation too. It was, in fact, the last business function to *be* transformed. If NetApp was going to achieve its goals, it would need a modern HR leader—one with a track record for producing genuine and lasting transformation. And that was what George wanted—so, on the heels of the current Chief Human Resources Officer's retirement, he recruited my old boss from Equinix, Debra McCowan, to run the new HR-to-be.

WANTED: Modern HR Leadership

Throughout their business transformation, NetApp's existing HR department had been in a supporting role across the entire organization, including managing layoffs. There'd not yet been time to really look internally at HR and ask: *What do we need to do differently?* But that's what George began to do. He wanted to know, *"What does HR for a transformed, more modernized organization look like?"* It was time to transform—not just change—HR from the inside.

It's not that NetApp hadn't tried before. As things got underway, there was some hesitation in CEO staff conversations. Questions were asked such as, *"Is this the right direction? What if the changes don't stick, and we have to backpedal later?"* The then HR leadership talked about past attempts at some degree of change. *"We had a lot of planes in the air,"* he reported. *"We just weren't landing any of them."* So, there was a little bit of latent expectation over the idea, heard in such skepticism-filled responses as, *"Well, we've tried this before…"* What was going to be different this time? For any transformation, you need executive sponsorship and readiness at the highest level. And George, the current CEO, was ready.

5 · We're Not Babysitters

Most people who spend any time in the corporate world will likely hear (or experience) the old-time critiques of HR. You know what I'm talking about. "Compliance police," "babysitters," "bureaucratic," "dysfunctional," "out of touch with the reality of what businesses need to do," "mired in paperwork," "bogged down by regulatory issues, mandatory training," and the like. HR's gotten a bad rep. These criticisms could be lobbed at most businesses, in every industry, in every company large enough to have an HR department. Hardly unique to NetApp, but NetApp didn't escape some of these entrenched ways of doing things either.

Not to make excuses, but this lack of progress has a lot to do with how human resources departments came about in the '50s and '60s or even earlier. Many long-time NetApp employees described their HR department as being a bit *"stuck in the past"* with some antiquated, old school ways of approaching things and *"operating on a 1980s model."* Vicky Koutsis (Organizational Development Consultant and change expert), who had been working with NetApp for ten years, described it to me this way: *"I was advocating for [change] even when I was an employee. I <u>knew</u> that the leader that is gonna come needed to be a transformational leader. They needed to evolve HR to meet the needs of the future."*

For many, it was systemic frustrations that weren't any one person's fault—or responsibility. It was the systems themselves. When Emily Miller joined in 2009, for example, customer data was still being kept on an Excel spreadsheet. No human capital management (HCM) system! Performance management was still being done on paper (as was the case with several other companies at the time). Talent Development didn't have any cross-functional training programs or any other method for recruiting talent internally. And on the recruiting talent front, which, by definition, needs to be modern, progressive? Elise Graziano, former head of talent acquisition, described it this way: *"In recruiting, you can't be stagnant. You have to be progressive and ahead of what's happening in the market. We don't have to be Google, but we need to keep a growth mindset, be open to trying new ways of doing things and trying new technologies."*

NetApp would regularly lose out to the big three hyper-scalers. Understandable. But how do you attract top talent when your onboarding tool for new employees is homegrown, decades old, and isn't run by any one department? And once a person is hired, there are few pathways for career advancement? Newbies and established employees alike were on their own—and it was not uncommon to remain in the same role, with the same title and same salary, for many years. *"[And] as far as performance management,"* comments Vicky, *"it needed to be a little bit more humane."* All in all, HR certainly wasn't being used in the best way, and if NetApp leadership and the business were modernizing and dramatically transforming, HR needed to catch up.

6 · The Magic of Equinix

I'd worked with Debra before. A super bright ball of energy and confidence, Australian-born and raised Debra McCowan is a forceful visionary in the HR space. We complement one another well in the workplace, with a successful five-year run in creating *The Magic of Equinix* cultural transformation across the globe. Like NetApp, Equinix is a digital infrastructure business, but it's different in that it's the largest data center company in the world. For us, it was like a rocket ship. They were building or acquiring data centers all the time. Revenue was growing. Profits, people, real estate…all growing. When I left, it was during the fiftieth straight quarter of top-line growth. As of this writing, they may be up to sixty-five. On *every* front. They were buying property, building out the infrastructure, and bringing on the people to manage all that—while making more money in the latest quarter than last quarter and more last quarter than the one before that. We went from three thousand to nine thousand employees in two years. We were busy.

In her new role as Chief Human Resources Officer (CHRO) at Equinix, Debra gave her executive recruiter (and a former employee of mine) a mandate: "*I need two VPs. One for talent acquisition and another for talent development.*" This recruiter and I had remained friendly over the years. So, she called me to say, "*You gotta come meet Debra. She wants transformation. I know you want transformation. I know you couldn't do it at the place where we worked together, but I know you wanted to get that going.*" At the time, I was working as the CHRO for a company called Glu Mobile. I'd been there less than a year but was reporting to the head of finance and realized pretty quickly that we weren't aligned on many of the larger scope HR changes I was itching to make. I'm not one to leave a company so quickly, but I could see where Equinix was headed and, well, to be presented instead with a leader who gets it? *"Bye, Glu Mobile!"*

Alignment and Air Cover

Doing proper due diligence during the interview process will come back to you tenfold in positive ways, I promise. Only once was I blinded by the size of the role and salary, and it was the worst experience of my working life. I quickly realized my boss and I were not aligned. She did not provide me air cover and hung me out to dry with my peers and internal customers. I don't blame her. That was just who she was. I blame myself because I walked blindly into a work situation that did not fit my style, skills, or ambitions. Leaving that company literally changed the way I viewed myself, my work, and the companies I wanted to work for. I started focusing on HR technology and then on transformation. Although it was a dark time in my career, it propelled me into an even more rewarding one.

Having learned this valuable lesson, I went into the Equinix opportunity with a very different mindset, and the interview process I had with Debra was a great example of that. She's a griller when it comes to interviewing. She asks a lot of tough questions and really wants to see that you can deliver on what you're saying. I respected and appreciated this. Having been in that seat as CHRO three times myself, I know how critical those key hires can be. Debra met my criteria as well—and I could see right away that we were well-aligned in terms of experience, perspective, and risk level. I understood where she was trying to head, and I was excited to work with her to get Equinix there. We had the same concerns about traditional HR roles and agreed not only on practical changes that could be made but also on strategy. As a senior leader and her first direct report, we worked side by side in a successful culture transformation, The Magic of Equinix, that remains intact throughout the global enterprise to this day. We made a good team, and that transformation became a living, breathing part of the company. I remain very proud of the culture work we did.

7 · Joining NetApp

George brought in Debra, his modern HR leader, as the Executive Vice President and Chief Human Resources Officer (CHRO) in the fall of 2018. And she immediately began to build out her team. I knew George and his brother from Equinix. They'd spoken at our senior leadership meetings about the future of cloud and how Equinix played into that. They were incredibly likable, down-to-earth guys—and tech business geniuses. When Debra first asked if I wanted to join NetApp, I asked her about him. She said, *"Oh, you already know George. He really is like that."* Which was quickly followed by, *"And I need help to do another transformation. Are you up to do it again?"*

During our early discussions about this new position, Debra shared NetApp's current circumstance and George's mandate. That they were in the midst of a business transformation, building up the cloud, and he'd told her, *"I need people and culture transformation. Period."* I'd done my due diligence. I knew where NetApp was headed. I knew that they needed help on the people side. I also knew that in recent years, there'd been financial ups and downs, but it was clear to me that if they could get this cloud thing working, they'd start hitting their numbers. I'm always fine coming into a company that has potential—you get that first stock grant at a low price! I was also happy to be asked to team back up with Debra after our successful transformations at Equinix. But first, I had a request. *"Lemme talk to George."*

The Right People

I'd been through enough companies to know that you can have all the greatest plans in the world and the experience to deliver on your promises, but if you don't have the right people around you to accomplish your preset agendas, they will never get off the ground. A dispiriting waste of time. Been there, done that. Happily, during my conversation with George, what I heard instead from him was just the kind of puzzle I love to solve.

"*We need to have high-performing teams,*" said George, "*who run at the speed of cloud. We need to bust down silos. We need to move faster. We need better leadership.*" Check, check, check. I was down for all that. To which he added, "*And we need to do this quickly. We're in this major transformation, and some people are gonna make it. Some people aren't. But we have to change the mindset of how this company operates.*" The need for me was to look at how the organization worked. *Do we need to rebuild? Do we have the right culture, the right team-based approach to run this next generation of this high-tech global enterprise?*

That was George's main priority. "*Look. We're in the cloud, which is the newest, biggest advantage in the world. Everyone's in the cloud. So, we are moving to the fastest, most dynamic business. And how do we get employees to catch up to that? How do we increase the speed of how we make decisions, how we work together? And how do we grow people?*" I shared that I'd done much of this at my last company. And he knew Equinix, obviously. Then I went into some detail about my ideas, including, "*Sounds like you want to transform into a growth organization and remove the barriers to achieving that. But it's not just about what's taken away, it's what do you replace it with?*" And so, that was my pitch at that point. I then continued, "*If you wanna move at speed and have higher engagement and productivity and people who are not scared of change? You have to be as honest and have the best conversations possible.*" And then I got one of George's "*Correct!*" responses. And when he says *correct*, that means he believes in it. He didn't necessarily know what he wanted to tear down. I told him what *I* wanted to tear down. He just wanted to move faster and have better, more engaged employees who would lean into this new business model. He knew if NetApp couldn't get there quickly, if they couldn't ship to the cloud as fast, they'd still be dragging behind.

I Musta Messed Up

Debra had warned me early in the interview process, "*We have a double challenge when you come to NetApp. Not only are we doing a complete business revolution, we also want to do an HR transformation simultaneously.*"

That takes a lot of effort and a lot of time." It's all well and good to be aligned (as Debra and I already were), but for a senior position such as the one I was up for, you also get interviewed by all senior management, and your pitch (in this case, how I pitched the change) is the ultimate harbinger of whether you get the green light or the Veruca Salt treatment. When interviewing with the CEO staff, they echoed George's mandate: "*We now need to do an HR transformation. We need to transform the people and the culture.*"

They didn't know what that meant, but they knew that "*We're not moving fast enough.*" When a company realizes they are stuck in several places, it's a sign for major change. Some companies don't see those signs or pay heed. NetApp had the foresight and fortitude to start a transformation journey. (Enter Debra and me.) And they understood enough about how very transformative it was going to need to be. "*This is bold,*" they said. "*This is a bold decision to make this transformation.*" Next, I talked to the Executive Vice President WW Field and Customer Operations (the head of go-to market) and some of the other execs, including in cloud. These were smart folks who were making sense to me. So, a little while later, when I finally sat down with everyone and said, "*Here's what I would do,*" they universally replied, "*Oh, yes, please come and do that.*"

At some point, it became the chief technology officer's turn, who simply asked, "*What would you wanna do in your first year?*" So, I pitched what I was thinking, which included transforming the way HR and the business and employees interact with each other and grow together. I talked about topics such as Quarterly Conversations (QC), getting data into employees' hands, and democratizing the data, to which he replied, "*Okay, thanks,*" and left. Naturally, I was thinking, "*Oh, I musta messed that up,*" because I'd only talked to the dude for, like, fifteen minutes, tops. I walked out, called the recruiter, and said, "*I think this just went sideways.*" He replied, "*No, he recommended to hire you.*" "*Okay!*" I replied. "*I wish all my interviews were fifteen minutes.*" It was hysterical. It also reassured me that there was a deep willingness at least for change if not transformation. They might not have been aware of everything that was going to happen, and that change wasn't necessarily going to be easy, but they were clearly aware that how they were doing things wasn't working.

TA-TE Combo

There were many reasons Debra and I worked well together, but two really key ones were: (1) we both had a high tolerance for the risk of failure, but even more effective for us was (2) we could see the future and frame it so that everyone else could see it too. From the beginning, we spoke broadly together about transforming HR. This started during the interview process for my new position when she asked me, "*Do you wanna come and run Talent Development or Talent Acquisition?*" Traditionally, in HR, Talent Acquisition (TA) and Talent Development (TD, or Learning and Development, or Talent Management, or various other titles) are usually two separate groups. My response to her about the Equinix opportunity was "*Why would they be separate? It's the complete employee journey. We have to plan together for the complete employee journey.*" I also have passion for these two roles, so that's what we did. We agreed, and I said, "*Let's combine them, and I'll do both.*"

So, I joined Equinix as the Vice President of Global Talent. We were among the first to adopt this idea, to break the invisible Chinese wall between TA and TD (or what I've since called Talent Enablement, or TE— more on that later). Today, you're starting to see the trend move in that direction, but back in 2014, this idea of the *complete employee journey*, this more holistic approach to the entire employee life cycle from prospect to alumni, was rare. In my case, at Equinix, I was overseeing branding, interviewing, hiring (which used to be TA only), and then onboarding, development, and career growth and culture (which used to be TD only). We took the same approach at NetApp, and again, now you're starting to see more and more global talent people cover both. I joined NetApp in January of 2019 as President of Global Talent—a position in which TA and TE were already bundled, providing a good head start in our work to help develop a transformed HR mindset around the complete employee journey.

8 · New Leadership

I want to talk to you now about why your relationship with your boss matters and how you can utilize that relationship to make transformation happen.

The Executor and the Futurist

Debra and I both took the Meyers-Briggs personality test once. Amazingly, many of our type descriptors were precisely the same, but where she's the *influencer* and *executor*, I'm the *futurist*. And that was where we clicked right there. In practice, these identifications proved both useful and true. As a work team, we hit each other's blind spots. We were opposites. Two ends of a shared brain with a shared vision. Together, we'd frame the future, and I'd get out there and talk to everyone about it. I'd put the pitch to it, work to get everyone on board, and she'd provide me with air cover. When we picked back up at NetApp, we had a shorthand that enabled us to begin to execute on some of our ideas very quickly. We butted heads at times to be sure, but I challenge you to find two people who have created more from zero, twice in eight-and-a-half years, than us. And that's why making sure the alignment is there from the beginning is so powerful. Why it helps to have a partner who matches up with your vision and protects you when needed. And why two heads working as one can be so transformational.

The Face of Change

Everybody thinks that if the CEO says it, it'll get done. That's only partially true. Same thing with the CHRO. The CEO can set the course (or approve the course you set), but there's the message and then there's the *messenger*. The company heads can help deliver the message because leadership has to believe in it, support it, and be a communicator of it, but somebody's gotta be the face of the change. You can't just depend on the CEO. There are way more things to do, way more visibility, and way more meetings, and way more answering questions, and selling into the organization than the CEO is EVER gonna have time for. And it's not really their job.

Yes, it has to start from the top. Absolutely. But you can't just drop it at the CEO's doorstep. And if I'm the one advising you, I'm going to tell you that you need someone who is steeped in these ideas. Who eats, breathes, and sleeps transformation. The messenger. Because it's a campaign—and it's not a sprint, it's a marathon. The CEO won't be the one out there running it. Anne Fulton, founder/CEO of Fuel50, puts it this way: "*You need a strategic influencer that's a powerful communicator. A visionary. A futurist… That's a key capability that you need to enthuse and engage and bring a lot of people along with your vision. Unless you can bring people on that journey, it's not going to be effective.*" So, step one, get the CEO to say it; step two, pick your change leader who'll build their team to make transformation a reality. Again, to really make that change, you need someone to be the face of the transformation. Someone's got to be the messenger and the driver. And that could be anyone—at NetApp, and at Equinix before, that happened to be me.

Who's This Guy?

So, how does that work, practically? In our case, George hired Debra and me to implement the HR and cultural transformation. And he was always incredibly supportive. Anything I asked him to do, he did. I wouldn't have gotten anything done without him. But he was not going to tell us *how* to get it done—we brought the strategy. We had several approaches that we continued to use very effectively, first at Equinix and then throughout my time at NetApp.

At Equinix, Debra and I were always together, her as head of HR driving transformation, and me, the face of this culture change. Remember, broadcasting the message is just the first half of the equation. If people don't buy it, if they don't believe the messenger, it won't matter how much support you get from marketing. They have to know you mean it, or there's no reason to bother. Authenticity is tough to fake, and it's essential if your transformation, whatever form it takes, is gonna stick. So, the reason she and I clicked is because we were dreaming the same dream and genuinely believed we could make those dreams come true. We shared a yes mindset. And tactically, we both had the skills to frame the story and the future.

We were thick as thieves planning together every day, traveling together all the time, on our The Magic of Equinix world tour in London, Paris, Amsterdam, Singapore—where all our big city hubs were located (and where most of the world's data is stored). But if she hadn't been all-in? I wouldn't have been as successful. If she hadn't been willing to put in all the time with me and all the travel? It wouldn't have been successful. You have to partner with someone who has a Debra on the inside. A backer in the C-Suite. And again, everyone immediately involved, the team, has to have the same high level of tolerance around the risk of failure. If I had come in saying, "*I'm doing this. I'm going for it,*" and my boss responded with, "*Okaaaaaaay...It's never gonna work.*"? Not good. She has to be as willing and as likely to say, "*We made a mistake,*" or "*That didn't work out,*" and yet be confident we'll still recover from whatever misstep occurred. If your boss doesn't have the same risk tolerance as you, you're gonna trip.

So, I would come to her with my plans. We'd also develop plans together, using storyboards or other development tools, as necessary. It all depended on which audience we were targeting. We got into a routine. I'd go to Debra with a game plan that my team and I had built. She would offer her feedback and upgrades. Once we agreed on the goals we were looking to achieve, we'd then go to the CEO and say, "*Hey, we're about to go in and talk to your direct reports. What are you concerned about? What role are you gonna play? This is what I need you to say. This is what we need to have come out of it.*" So, the three of us would later go into that next meeting aligned. Let's say you didn't set up this partnership and went in cold. If they just invited me once in a while to pitch to CEO staff, they'd probably just look at me like, "*Who's this guy?*" It was Debra's idea to ensure the CEO was on board before we walked into that room because the head of the company had to be our ally in there.

Second, I had to account for the fact that she wouldn't be in the room as my partner. In my past two jobs, she said, "*I'm going to bring you into the CEO staff meeting, and you're going to tell the story. I'm going to be there as a CEO staff member, but you'll be the one presenting. And if it starts going sideways, I'll jump in."* She'd prep me beforehand with, *"Okay, this is how this executive staff is going to report that...but I don't wanna be in the room as your partner. I'm sitting around the table that you present to."* So, day of, I knew I'd be flying solo. And when I'd go into that roundtable and say, *"Here's my game plan, my budget, and what I want to do,"* she'd be busy working to make sure our agenda continued to go our way. That worked because we were aligned. It was two HR people strategizing, not two HR people pitching.

Unlike at Equinix, at NetApp, we didn't have to plan as hard together because we already had a process in place. But there were a lot of different elements. And more trust. More of the sentiment: *"Just go give them that pitch."* We were able to get many of our initiatives off the ground right away because we followed these strategies, to great effect, for the length of our partnership. And once we'd get the green light on a budget or program, whatever it was, I was off to the races.

Wind Me Up

Looking back at my last five leaders, three of them had very similar characteristics: Wind me up, let me go, and give me air cover. Inspiration. Enablement. Air cover. And fortunately for me, Debra had qualities that enabled me, personally, to thrive. I carried these leadership themes into my teams, for them directly but also as we looked to spread these principles across the organization—the key one being enablement. And the main question I was always asking was *"How do you operationalize this transformation and the culture? How do you get it off the walls and into people's lives?"*

Having a change management focus with your boss, locking in that trust and common understanding, is the first, most essential step in making transformation happen. But again, like the CEO, my boss's role was not in execution. DOING it was not Debra's role. I was her guy for that. She'd set me up, and I'd break it down for everybody, tell them how it was going to work.

As the corporate face of this transformation, I'd put the pitch to it, inspire others, and then build it all out—execute, communicate, and do all the change management. That way, if anyone asked, *Who's the Thrive guy?*, they'd be pointing not at multiple people but squarely at me. The face of the NetApp HR and cultural transformation. I was the one on stage, the one hosting meetings, and getting invited to other meetings to talk about it. If someone was not believing in it or needed to know more? I was in that meeting. If I hit resistance, Debra'd provide air cover. We were kindred spirits on the framing and execution aspects of our plan. If you're in it together, it's easier to take the stress from the doubters. And I would take all the arrows and protect my team like Debra did for me.

As with Debra and George, I could not have done it without my staff, my change management unit. So, as you look to embark on your own internal transformation, look for that person. Allow them to build out their dream team to make your aspiration a company-wide reality.

9 · Driving Transformation

Our Year One mantras came from an article I'd found online. For my first offsite with the new team, I went searching for inspiration and landed on the website of an old colleague of mine, Mark Efron. Formerly of Aon Consulting, he's now president of The Talent Strategy Group. I was already familiar with his book, *One Page Talent Management*. This latest article from him, "*The Three Reasons HR Transformations Fail (and how to make sure yours doesn't)*"[4] got me inspired. As soon as I read it, I yelled, "*This is totally true!*" These maxims completely resonated with how I approach transformation. The steps are: First, clarify the vision. Second, increase talent quality. Third, move faster. I adopted these steps and reframed them as the three elements that *drive* transformation. The worst things you can do when embarking on transformation of any kind, anywhere, of any size, are to be unclear about your messaging, involve whomever, and go too slow, right? Any one of these is a transformation killer. All three? Pretty tough to overcome. The better way is to have the clearest vision, get the right people on your team, and go fast using not just speed but also direction.

Clarify Your Vision

There are millions of reasons why change efforts fail. In fact, there's a whole genre of books, workshops, and consultants dedicated to just this kind of challenge. Alexi Robichaux, founder/CEO of BetterUp, the Human Transformation Company, distills the concept down to its very essence: "*Transformations are about change, at their core. And what we know is, for the most part, people don't like change...[We] know, whether you read Kegan and Lahey's* Immunity to Change, *or whoever you read, there is this resistance to change because it breaks our habits, our patterns.*" People often resist even without realizing it. "*We've been doing the same thing for thirty years. Why change?*" or "*Why now?*" And even among those tasked with a transformation, you may get some pushback. "*How are we gonna get people to move?*" And that's where people fail. They just can't see the end, can't envision the end of the rainbow. If you can't imagine the future, how can you ever hope to get there? So, it gets murky. You feel like you're not making progress. And then people stop believing it's gonna happen. Or even *that* it can.

So, for those who can see the future, your responsibility is to share that vision and outline how much better for everyone the new normal, at the end of the rainbow, is going to be. You'll be presenting before/after scenarios (the *from-to*, I call them) that inspire people to willingly come along, and you'll be using a host of other strategies too. Look at it this way: If you're daring to embark on a radical transformation, clearly explaining what you're trying to accomplish is an essential first step.

Mind you, when you start out, you're pitching a dream. You haven't delivered anything yet. It's just an idea. A vision—ideally, a clear one. Debra has a great quote on the subject—one of my favorites of hers: "*In our last two companies, we showed up selling vapor in a bottle.*" So true. At both Equinix and NetApp, that's exactly how we started out. We were saying,

"I promise, at the end, something's gonna be in this bottle. This is gonna be something someday. I swear!" When we went around the world for Equinix, pitching our vision, we'd hear, *"Boy, you guys are asking questions that are very difficult and futuristic."* WE knew where we were going, and so, we just kept repeating the same messaging: *"This is what it's gonna be!"* Of course, some would respond with, *"All right. That SOUNDS great. But I, right now, sitting in my seat, Larry, don't know how you're gonna get there."* That's when we would reach for our change management tactics and tools and lay out our plan. But to begin, you have to be a little bit brave. If you wait to get all the pieces in a row, I dare say, you'll never get the momentum you need to even get this journey started.

Get the Right People on Your Team

When I first came to NetApp, I collected a handful of like-minded people who were just doing various jobs across the company. I built 'em all up and built a common change function underneath me. My talent enablement, my change team, and me—the internal group I had pieced together—became the mechanism to make all the change happen.

Speed

Go ahead, break glass. In my early pitches, I worked to prepare the CEO staff for what was coming next. I let them know, *"Hey, we're gonna break some glass, and some, we're not gonna pick up."* Meaning transformations are imperfect, but speed is more important than perfection. It's true in all instances, but it was especially so in the NetApp case, where we were aiming for *high-functioning teams to move at the speed of cloud* with which to aid the ongoing business transformation. That was the real reason behind the change: to support the business—this highly competitive tech business (already heavily biased towards speed). Momentum and early wins are significant milestones you're gonna want to aim for. And if you hear rumblings like, "*Oh, something-something didn't work*," just keep going. That doesn't stop the transformation.

Velocity means speed *and* direction. To be truthful, you need both. When Alice told the Cheshire Cat she didn't know which fork in the road she wanted, the cat replied, "*Then, it doesn't matter…*" which way you go. But it does matter, and that's where clear vision comes in. Your North Star. Your team's North Star and your company's. Once you know where you're going, head there with laser-like focus and keep everybody moving along with you. In our case, this mandate came directly from George. He wanted to get to high-performing teams at the speed of cloud.

SECTION 3
Building the Team

I talked, they built.

When Debra and I initially joined NetApp, a lot of our focus that first month was assessing what was going on. What were the priorities, what were people working on, and which team members were no longer needed? What about the top talent? Who was going to be recruited to join our transformation team?

10 · The Re-Org

And then we began planning the re-org. This was no consultant-based re-org—quite the opposite. And yet, it was still quite doable. What prevents many business leaders, or internal HR leaders, from managing these changes themselves is how large the task *seems* to be. "*It's too big,*" many say. "*I need a consultant to come in and do it.*" That may be true—but they also often drop the plan about fifty feet above your head. You still have to do a lot of work to pull it down the remaining distance. Taking the reins yourself may require a change of mindset of what a role like this is or can be. So, who is the best fit for this job? Leaders with the right experience, passion, and vision. And the best among us also know how they're going to get there and how to inspire people to follow along.

Debra and I met with existing HR staff. After canvassing the remaining talent, we presented our assessments to the leadership team. I still had a hundred recruiters on the TA side (and a much larger budget), but for my change team, I could only support a handful. Each member needed to count. More than anything—more than tenure, more than skill and experience, they had to have an aptitude for change. And genuinely find joy in shaking things up. If you can find smart, enthusiastic people, willing to support your vision? That's gold.

The true path of transformation happens through breaking glass and ruffling feathers…and I certainly had my detractors. (But I also had Debra.) Opposition can happen when you're working to give employees an active voice in the company conversation. A voice designed to help influence change. Crowd-sourced, AI-enhanced points of view versus a few senior executives in a room opining about how the staff are doing and what the staff are thinking. If you're not breaking glass, you're not making real change. Sometimes we pick that glass up, and sometimes we don't. So, I stress-tested every candidate, asking them, "*Are you okay with that?*"

First Offsite

Within a month of my start date, I pulled together a small group of twelve or fifteen people (including some from the India team) for a two-to-three-day offsite. I dubbed that group the *Employee Engagement Team* or something like that—a loose assembly of organizational development with some change management people.

During our time together, I mentioned the critiques I'd heard from leadership and understood that NetApp was ripe for transformation. Instead of focusing on Best Place to Work awards, I told them, let's actually *make* it the best place to work! I invited them to be vocal and run with ideas. "*Take full ownership!*" I was the one leading the charge, sure, but that didn't mean my ideas were untouchable. It's rare that a vision goes from one idea to execution unchanged—certainly none I've ever been involved with.

One thing I did *not* say was that this work would be easy or quick. Or that anyone could phone it in. My central message to them was "*Going from zero to one is the hardest thing to do. It will take all our effort, but it's not impossible.*" Lisa kindly reflects back on these conversations. "*When we went into that meeting, what stood out to me was, Oh! We finally have some strategy here. I think it was clear in that room, in that first conversation, that we were all on the same page about where we thought the company should go.*"

So, we launched in a Sunnyvale headquarters conference room with a whiteboard months before we ever landed on the brand name Thrive, or

Ecosystem for High-Performing Teams, or the tagline *People Powered, Data Driven*, or the full spectrum internal branding that continues to carry on throughout the company. Like most things, our global corporate transformation began as a conversation. I delivered my nameless vision and all the changes that would be required to implement it. We talked about Thrive before it got a title. I shared my ideas for NetApp's HR and cultural transformation. On what the end of the rainbow would look like. The birth of Thrive really began here. As I drew a "stick figure" circle on the board in black marker, the framework for what we affectionately called—and still refer to as—the Wheel began to take shape.

During those few days, I split the team up into sub-units to work on various specifics based on what later became the four quadrants of the Wheel. Toward the end of our time together, I'd narrowed down the attendees to those I called my "keepers." I told a few right then that I wanted to bring them on full-time. Lisa shares this about it: "*That offsite really gelled the people who needed to be involved. And who was interested in working on it. We were all inspired to move it forward.*" For those who remained, those few days really brought us together. In our subsequent years working as a team, everyone often referred back to this first offsite. Including me. It was a seminal moment when we all got into a room and really started planning and strategizing. For all of us, it remains the day when it all began. And it's for them, in many ways, that this book exists.

Global Talent Enablement Team

My handful of keepers came from disparate parts of the enterprise, and these smart, talented professionals had all been at NetApp for years. Elaine-Marie (EM) Bohen, Director, Talent Enablement, was my ultimate Thrive partner. A master facilitator, EM was my direct report. She was an invaluable counterpoint to my core skill sets, and we made a great team. A change management expert, Vicki Koutsis has a background in industrial organizational psychology and a PhD in industrial/organizational psychology. As my internal change person and a key strategist, Vicky's contributions were invaluable.

Lisa Melsted was our communications specialist. Our keeper of the Golden Thread. Having spent her PR/communications career in the technology space, she brought a deep knowledge of the company and its corporate history.

Like TA and TE, I brought change management (Vicky) and communications (Lisa) together. We dubbed it *Change and Comms*. Together, Lisa and Vicky spearheaded this team. This re-org enabled oversight and a more holistic view across my entire team, including TA. Anything that we needed to move forward, whether it was collateral or marketing, regardless of TA, TE, or beyond, Lisa and Vicky helped. More importantly, this more global view ensured that our messaging was consistent across the board—and reflected my overall perspective. I told them: "*Get different specialists from different departments talking to each other!*" Collaborating across disciplines always produces more powerful, better-informed business units.

Avery Calman (Content Development Program Manager, Talent Enablement) was the keeper of our graphics. Elise Graziano (Sr. Director of Global Talent Acquisition) managed a team of 130—made up of programs, people, recruiters, sources, coordinators, you name it, including a DI&B team. A truly global operation. TA was somewhat Thrive adjacent. Its transformation during Year Two was in the areas of AI recruiting tools and building a new recruitment process. As Elise herself put it, "*We needed to evolve.*" Christine Huntley (Manager of Talent Enablement Programs) joined our TE team in Year Two, championing Mosaic—managing the system and rolling it out across the globe. Michelle Mann (Senior Director, Philanthropy and Employee Engagement) was responsible for volunteer work and social impact. She spearheaded NetApp Data Explorers. Aman Musfar, Director, Strategic HR Programs, worked for five years with Debra and me at Equinix and came over with us to NetApp. Her role that first year was critical, supporting me as we launched these transformations.

Marketing and Branding

At prior companies, marketing didn't want anything to do with the stuff I was working on. They considered it a distraction. I had gone back to these various marketing departments each time to say, "*I need to build out a talent brand in the outside market. It's more than just a product brand, it's a talent brand. Why would people wanna work here?*" It was my belief that their "lack of time" was quite shortsighted. Fortunately for us, at NetApp, we had the very dynamic Emily Miller, VP of Brand Experience. She was the first person outside of our team to help. Later, she kindly offered these remarks, "*If we're not helping HR get their brand right? Then we're missing part of our remit. I felt like Larry, with his rich expertise coming from HR, and me from marketing? We're two sides of the same coin. If I can make him successful, then MY larger vision is gonna be more achievable.*" That's getting the right person on the bus. That's a yes mindset. She and her team helped us come up with the term Thrive and then its tagline (People Powered, Data Driven), and provided the spit 'n' polish design expertise our makeshift Wheel needed to really shine, go wide, and endure as as working template for transformation.

The Transformation Engine

Again, my formal title at NetApp was VP of Global Talent, which meant I was responsible for the talent strategy in various functions within HR—both talent acquisition and (what's traditionally called) talent development, which includes performance management and learning development. I was also asked to oversee NetApp Serves, the philanthropic arm of the business, which focused on volunteering and matching programs. Two of my direct reports were EM and Elise. That first year, Vicky and Lisa reported to me, and Avery reported to EM. Aman was my de facto chief of staff, Emily Miller was our partner in marketing and branding, and Christine joined the team in Year Two to launch Mosaic.

Of my core group (EM, Lisa, Vicky, and Avery), only Vicky had done transformation before. Some were already part of HR, but not all. And having an HR background doesn't necessarily make you good at transformation—those who brought expertise from other fields were powerful additional assets. Whether in HR or beyond, they'd all been witness to and had survived the sweeping changes across NetApp over the last few years; now, they were about to help drive the next big company transformation.

I'd gotten lucky—the right talent magnetized to the plan. My core, ragtag group of rebels, with their decades of collective corporate wisdom, built a common change function underneath me. This internal group was the engine for implementing all the change that transformed NetApp in the months and years immediately following our initial summit. This was indeed a small team with a lot of work ahead of them. A lot of communication and change was needed to get off the ground. My first steps were to get them inspired by my story and willing to help me tell the change and build the enablement tools. Then, it was me going to the CEO staff saying, *"Here's what we're doing, why we're doing it, and where I need the funding."* That was a lot of Year One.

Landing Every Plane

The HR team talked about how, before we showed up, they couldn't get anything landed. So, I talked about this being the Year of Execution for my team. Period. No matter what, we were gonna land those planes this year. Together, we jump-started an HR transformation. In Year One (our Year of Execution as we referred to it internally), we vowed to get every plane landed. How did I pull it off? By using those three keys to transformation: I identified the big picture ask (*vision*), built the *team*, and pulled the trigger on GO (*speed*).

This wasn't all planned out to the letter. I would much rather get a small team in a room, work on the vision, get them super-motivated, and then let them help get it out to the rest of the organization every time. If I had twenty people, I probably couldn't have gone as fast. Did we sacrifice productivity for speed? Maybe. Could we have accomplished more? Perhaps, but not at the rate at which we were able to claim our early wins anchored off the momentum we'd started. Avery said it well when we talked about how such a small team was able to tackle such a bold vision: "*Trust. I liked what we were doing. We were (I mean, we kind of still are) a skeleton team. Vicky, Elaine-Marie, myself, Kristine, Lisa... Initially, there were only a few of us. I had trust in all of them, and they did in me.*"

11 · The Best Possible Environment

For many who get involved in Talent Development, they often approach their role with the mindset of, "*I am developing employees.*" They provide training, instruction, or new tools for skill-based aspects of their company's tasks. And many see this as the totality of their job. Developing others. What if you didn't just develop but also empowered? Enabled? To build a team responsible for both an HR and a cultural transformation across a global corporation, the team itself would need to be transformative, right? If your job is to develop, that's what you do. And even that's hit-and-miss. If your job is to create the best possible environment for people to work together, to grow and get faster? If you see THAT as your role? That's an entirely different muscle. And an *enterprise-wide mindset.*

It requires a change of mind about what a role such as this entails. That's the kind of mindset and leadership I was aiming for with this team. I tried to be collaborative and empowering, encouraging everyone to contribute their ideas. I know I challenged everyone, but my idea of success was for them to walk away saying, "*This is the best work of my career.*" Because this was going to be *ours*, not mine. And as I often told them (and myself), the second you start curbing people's growth for your own benefit is the second that you start failing as a leader. I loved watching them thrive—*and* produce such well-received and transformative work on behalf of the business.

Talent Enablement

Changing the traditional title of Talent Development to Talent Enablement was no mere formality. For me, this was a watershed moment. Yes, I'd merged TA and TE to build a more holistic framework for talent management and the *complete employee journey*, but this idea, this name change, remains bigger than even that. It's part of the full ecosystem, the Golden Thread, that my team and I eventually built—providing employees with *ablement* (as I had done for my team), meaning *allowing you to do for yourself*. And providing leaders and managers with the tools and accountability they needed to succeed.

It meant getting away from development. I'm not training you. I'm *enabling* you. This isn't about managing you, it's about supporting the talent and the company so they both can grow. HR should not exist just to chase for paperwork ("*You didn't do this, this, or this!*") or push mandatory training. At its best, HR doesn't act as an enforcer at all. Ideally, it should function like all the other business units—each designed to help the company succeed. Dictating rules and collecting paperwork are not beneficial. I'm not a cop, where the atmosphere changes when I walk into a room. I never wanted to be like that. I drop F-bombs all the time as proof I'm not the HR overlord many may have come to expect.

Part of this is personal for me. I want to change the way HR is viewed inside any company. Not for my ego's sake but because current HR practices were born and shaped out of a time that no longer fits for any of us. That includes those in the field and certainly those affected by it. The era of widgets and early industrialization has been replaced with knowledge workers whose contributions are no longer easily quantified. Ratings and rankings, 9-boxes, old school performance management practices no longer work well, presuming they ever did.

I'm also not here to manage your talent. People know what Talent Development used to look like. "*Give us some trainings; set up our focal review.*" This book is about the future of TD—and for me and my team, that meant bringing the best tools, thinking, and platforms to the forefront to enable the company's talent. It is on this horizon that everyone's eyes should be transfixed. Getting leadership to embrace these new ways of doing things, and this new mindset, proved to be one of the biggest challenges my team faced. It required strategy, patience, and singular focus. But we got it done. Here's how.

Going from Zero to One - Fast

*G*oing from zero to one is the hardest part. I said this early and often during our planning sessions. "*Maybe it's not even zero to one. It's probably zero to sixty,*" shared Lisa. "*The pace at which it happened was so fast.*" Launching from nothing can be challenging. It's why a blank page can be harder than editing, why invention is prized over revision, and why startups need an influx of cash to kickstart the first phase of their business.

12 · In the Foxhole

At this point, I knew I had the right people in place and that they were ready—they'd know how to puzzle their way through any challenges that came our way. My job was just to give them the freedom to do exactly that. When we got to the point where they started coming back to me saying, "*Okay. Here's what I think we should do,*" I loved it! It took a few weeks, but then the engine started really humming.

At some point, Aman was asked if a transformation had happened at NetApp, to which he responded, "*Oh, yeah. Especially that first year, I can't even tell you. It was insane. Our working sessions? I remember…in the corner, we would just sit there until really late at night, making sure that we were getting everything done. In some ways, I feel like that first year we operated like a startup team versus a midsize company team, which wouldn't usually operate that way.*" This is Silicon Valley, after all. It might be fair to say that its work ethic influenced us a bit—to work hard but also to believe we were capable of implementing this much change. She continued, "*Late nights, all hands on deck, that type of thing. All working on things that, even if they weren't necessarily in our area of purview, we were all still in it, just making sure that we could get to that end goal.*" We joked, through that first year of heavy implementation, that we did everything together, including eating breakfast, lunch, and dinner as a group! "*We've spent so many hours and days working together on this,"* reflected EM, *"but it's been inspirational and energizing at the same time as it's been tiring."*

The TE team had quite a year implementing the Thrive Ecosystem. In those dark days of change, when you're grinding away, and I'm about to go into the CEO staff meeting to ask for more money, you get a bit of a foxhole mentality built up. I think that made them stick together. These guys really supported each other, which made me super proud.

I knew I'd hit critical mass when I'd go into a meeting being run by one of my direct reports and hear them use the language from one of our development sessions. They were starting to "spread the message," if you will. I recall noticing this once while sitting in a meeting with Aman. I turned to her, and we were both smiling. I said, *"I don't even have to say anything anymore."* Because I'd hit pay dirt! Nothing makes me happier! I'd finally gotten my message and vision across to the rest of the team. This was what I was after. And I still believe, in my heart, that the biggest reason all of this has carried on is because my team believed in the vision too. *"It was very clear that Elaine-Marie and Larry,"* Lisa generously shared, *"were very simpatico. And I was on board with that too, even as a comms person. That was an interesting first conversation with him."* And EM added, *"I think there's something super powerful about truly believing in a leader's vision. And I truly believed in his vision right from day one. It made such perfect sense."*

13 ◆ Developing Thrive

The Thrive Ecosystem we created was about integrating enablement, democratization, and making 95 percent of the workforce better (vs. focusing on poor performers). Ours was a more holistic, human-centric approach. And tech-enabled. From the very beginning of introducing Thrive, it was ALL about re-humanizing the relationship between the manager and the employee. This, in my belief, is the most central relationship in any corporate enterprise. It's not just about managers, it's also about the organization as a whole. The initial Thrive was for everyone. Our competitive invitation became, *"Hey, come here, and you can build your career. We have the best survey tools in the world, put in your hands so you can Thrive and grow at NetApp.*" This is how we looked at talent and our talent ecosystem going forward. A move that required disassembling what came before and framing the future we were going to build so everyone could be part of the multi-year journey about to unfold.

Building the Internal Brand

I'm a big believer in internal branding and the power of a successfully executed brand strategy. Why brand Thrive? Think about it. NetApp was one of many companies that had moved into this new business model of cloud-based storage solutions. We were in what remains the most competitive talent war *ever*. What edge could a smaller player (relative to the big three hyper-scalers) bring? Among other strategies, we needed to build a narrative and tell our story.

Narrative, a Story

Lisa was responsible for helping build the narratives. Coming out of that offsite, Lisa took the lead in asking the most crucial questions: "*What is the messaging, and how will we get it out? How do we tell the story to different audiences, engaging them beyond a PowerPoint?*" These were the right, next questions. Yes, getting rid of ratings and rankings was the original headline (more on that later), but taking away something is not equal to what you put back in. I could have gotten rid of anything I wanted. Lots of companies do. But then what? You can't leave a vacuum, and posters on the wall aren't going to cut it. The key is what you refill that new void with: enablement and story. Thrive was our story.

Lisa brought her expertise in communications to assert one driving idea: We need to build a compelling story to grab attention and focus people. She pulled together our first messaging and positioning sessions and what eventually became Thrive and the Wheel. From these sessions, which included a positioning exercise, she compiled our *message house* (a PR term) of core positioning statements. This included how the four quadrants fit together—with messaging for each quadrant. This is how Thrive began.

Naming Process

Coming up with the name Thrive was a whole process, and it happened during one of our early brainstorming sessions as we were sitting around the collaboration space in the Sunnyvale office. We knew our name had to reflect all our core ideas: enablement, democratization, strengthening the employee-manager relationship, and leading with authenticity, mental fitness, talent mobility, and more internal hiring. And we knew growth mindset would be a key pillar.

Off to Marketing

At some point, I reached out to Emily, head of marketing, for help. "*I need to build out an internal talent brand. Can you help us with visual identity and naming?*" I asked—and could not have been more thrilled with her response. It grew into a terrific partnership. She and her team helped me come up with all the components of our internal branding, with Lisa functioning as chief liaison and keeper of our plans throughout. "*In working with them on Thrive as a partner,*" reflected Emily, "*HR was one of our best clients.*" Marketing upgraded our existing narratives across the board. Together, we narrowed the proposed titles down to the couple that resonated most. Ultimately, they came up with Thrive.

Ecosystem, a.k.a. Golden Thread

We then also worked with marketing to develop the log line. We wanted to incorporate the concept of the Golden Thread, so we landed on *ecosystem*—thinking of it as a more business-like term and stand-in for this idea of an integrated, interdependent, cohesive, circular whole. Our round table. All this titling was co-developed with the Wheel—the full title of which became the Thrive Ecosystem for High-Performing Teams. Soon people just called the whole wheel Thrive. (During the pandemic, it became *Thrive Everywhere*.) In addition to designing the first (more polished) graphic version of the Wheel, they created a little logo for us and a tagline. The company tagline at the time, Data Driven, was changed to reflect the idea that our core driver was all about the people, and thus, the new and improved: People Powered, Data Driven. This became the formal definition of Thrive. People Powered, Data Driven. *"Our new branding was huge,"* comments Aman. *"Because now everything in HR is branded with Thrive—even outside of Larry's space. It really stuck."*

A Consistent Narrative

During my first All Hands meeting that August, I made a point of crediting and thanking Emily and her team from the stage for their game-changing contributions. By then, we'd begun to build a consistent narrative. I now had my talking points and had planted the seeds of what was to come. It was clear that internal branding would be central to our success, so we continued harnessing and sharpening our story and messaging throughout those spring/early summer months. In conjunction with the slides, a few bits of my talk that day included:

> *So, with Thrive…we have a chance to build a high performance environment, a culture in which everyone will be able to develop into a top performer. Thrive is people-powered and data-driven.*
>
> *I want to give you a couple of examples of what you can expect to get as an employee around the world. Alignment between pay and performance, professional development, and career growth, where… you can be agile, and go in different directions and make different decisions throughout the year. There's not one big grade at the end of the year. This is the most powerful moment at NetApp for you to start your*

growth path. And it starts tomorrow, August 16th. Thrive…is how we look at talent and our talent ecosystem going forward. People-powered. You are now democratized. You have all the data. You can get better NOW. And data driven.

SECTION 5

Thrive: The Core Strategies

Thrive began as an idea, and at NetApp it was now materializing. I can't tell you how exciting this was for me to realize. Yes, it was a milestone for me professionally, but as it began to come to life for everyone, and grow, that was a thrill to be a part of.

14 · The Wheel

The concept for Thrive may have begun at that first offsite, but the Wheel took its basic shape well before the Thrive name was finalized. (See page 22 for image.) I came in with this vision of what I wanted to accomplish. I knew we were aspiring to build an organization for the future, which included a new approach to hiring and cultivating talent. I envisioned a new talent ecosystem using cutting-edge technology, tools, and programs to activate powerful employee experiences throughout the employee cycle. All while embracing the themes of growth mindset and inclusive leadership. I framed these ideas using four distinct areas of focus. I was so excited to take this on as it seemed the perfect culmination of my work up to that point. The opportunity to implement bigger, better versions of all my previous change efforts. It might be fair to say I was doing bigger but similar versions of the same concepts at NetApp, plus a lot of new initiatives—all built around a more progressive take on talent and growth. I knew what I wanted to do and where I wanted us to go as a company, together.

And that was what EM and I brainstormed about at the whiteboard in my Sunnyvale office conference room. It was early days. In erasable black ink marker, I laid out the four quadrants of my vision for Thrive. First, the re-humanizing of the manager-employee relationship and connection, centering around the Quarterly Conversation. Second, the manager-to-team relationship and building team effectiveness and high performance through the Pulse results. The third was based on a planned Breakthrough Leadership Program and a NetApp business school. Part of the fourth, which we focused on in Year Two, was the Internal Marketplace and implementing the Mosaic tool.

Quadrant	Goal
1st	Strengthen manager-employee relationships with the QCs
2nd	Strengthen manager-to-team relationships with Pulse Surveys
3rd	Build up an Enterprise-Wide Mindset
4th	Build the Organization for the Future

I sketched the first iteration of the Wheel on the board based on these ideas. Since I'm no graphic artist, it had a super-rough, back-of-the-napkin look. At this point, *Activate* wasn't included. That came later. The Wheel had only a few words and core initiatives, fleshed out and refined over the next couple of years. Our team made some passes at better design; then, finally, we handed it off to the creative team. It got much better after that! Avery reflected on our process, *"I can picture the first Wheel. It was just a circle in a PowerPoint. It's pretty cool because it's just the evolution that we were all going through."* Year One was about leaving old HR behind and installing a growth mindset. Carol Dweck's ideas were at the center of the Thrive Wheel. That original Year One Wheel was the core, basic transformation.

This visual of the whole Thrive Ecosystem became a key tool during our many fundraising campaigns and staff orientations that followed. I went on the road with it, basically sharing it with executives and their teams and anywhere I was invited, taking advantage of that powerful, handy slide to draw upon and continually refer people back to. It synthesized everything we were doing and had in the works.

First Quadrant: Activate Yourself

This first quadrant is about all things related to the individual employee. This is about *Activating Yourself*. About humanizing the relationship between the employee and his manager and the company at large. By removing ratings and rankings, 9-boxes, long development plans, and implementing QCs, we look to enhance the employee-manager relationship (details on each later). With Thrive Rewards and regular performance feedback, we offer fresh ways to differentiate performance. In Year Two, we added BetterUp Coaching and opportunities for employees to receive one-on-one feedback to assist in their professional growth. As BetterUp likes to say, "Precision Development at Scale." A summary of some of our key points for the quadrant include:

- Regular Performance Feedback
- Better Quality QCs
- More Meaningful Performance and Rewards Differentiation
- AI-driven talent mobility tools and new career architecture with Fuel50
- Elimination of ratings and all forms and tools that get in the way of employee-manager authenticity

When asked how this pivot was good for the company, EM kindly replied: "*We were addressing things for the masses that we just had never done before. We hadn't had the bandwidth…[and] it wasn't top of mind. This approach is broader. The work that we're doing touches ALL employees in the company, not just a particular segment. And I think it was missing. People have been hungry for it. The response that we've had has been tremendous, and for the most part, through the past two-and-a-half years, it's been a pull from the organization rather than a push from us. Which has been nice.*"

This was a sea change in how employees saw their voice and strength in advocating not only for themselves but also for their teams. They now had a very clear venue and agency to talk about where and how they wanted to direct their careers. They could sit down with their teams and work on improvements. That was when people started understanding the power of democratization in leadership. And managers had a burden lifted as well. Prior to this change, managers did not have the tools to help their employees plan out their careers in solid, tech- and enablement-backed ways. Once the responsibility for Pulse Survey results was in communal hands (see the

Thrive Pulse Survey section), it sped up decision-making and planning on how to improve as a team. This is what active leadership development looks like.

We were and still are passionate advocates of and for a positive employee experience. You likely know of all the research out there that shows how when employees are engaged, feel supported, and believe future opportunity exists for them, it translates into better company performance overall. So, NetApp directly benefited from these employee enhancements—and still does.

Second Quadrant: Activate the Team

The second quarter was about becoming better managers and developing better teams. Becoming high-performing teams through employee listening and engagement. Employee listening means moving from no data to twice-yearly Pulse Surveys with AI-driven insights. Employee engagement means a shift from corporate-level to relevant, team-specific feedback and the replacement of cumbersome action plans with personalized, high-impact recommendations—teams driving improvements together.

- Thrive Pulse Survey—continuous team improvement with Pulse
  ▷ Real-time team feedback access by managers
  ▷ AI-driven- and team-discussed recommendations
  ▷ Action planning
- BetterUp Coaching for Managers
- Thrive Talent (Enablement)

Again, we wanted to break every traditional HR process. Just rip it out and focus on our strategy. This was the first moment when we shifted people's mindsets, telling them, "*Forget about process and filling out forms and focus on you and your team.*" The goal was to show how a combination of surveys, coaching, and enablement would allow teams to multiply their talent and potential.

Third Quadrant: Activate the Enterprise

The third quarter was about cultivating an enterprise-wide mindset, which included fostering an *owner's mindset* across the organization. When I arrived, the goal of building an enterprise mindset was already a consistent theme. In the face of this transformational shift from a functionally structured to a business unit-based company, CEO staff were asking, *"How do we get our leaders, in particular, thinking with an enterprise hat?"* They realized that they were going to have to operate and pull on resources from other parts of the business more than was ever needed under the previous structure. So, the aspiration for an enterprise-wide mindset was a key component of the Wheel from the get-go.

- Future Proof NetApp: Driving Results through Enterprise-Wide Thinking
- Cultivate an Enterprise vs. Functional Mindset
- Understand NetApp's Business Inside and Out: Act like an owner; optimize for the enterprise
- Create the NetApp Business School: Building leadership at all levels
- Breakthrough Leadership Program (teaching team collaboration)
- Add Earnings Calls
- Silo-Bust Across the Enterprise: Tools to encourage cross-functional collaboration
- Silo-Buster In-a-Box/Dash (improve collaboration to optimize the enterprise)
- Hackathons and Process Busters
- Business Owner Mindset Activities
- Thrive Talent Career Week
- Mosaic Implementation and Enablement

Fourth Quadrant: Activate the Future

The fourth quarter was about *Building the Organization of the Future* and is largely still aspirational. The part of the fourth that we DID focus on was the Internal Marketplace and implementing the Mosaic tool, which helped us zero in on some important questions, namely: *How do we build AI-enabled career paths and help enable people to look at the skills that are needed, aligned to roles that they aspire to in the future?*

- Internal Marketplace/Mosaic
- Thrive Talent (Talent Acquisition): Global Hiring Process
- Eightfold and HireVue Implementation
- Hire and Develop Talent for the Business Today and for the Future
- Create High-Performance Culture
- Leaders and Teams Hire Strategically for the Business
- Equip Leaders and Teams to Hire Strategically for the Business
- Plan Workforce for the Three-Year Horizon
- Establish High-Performance Teams as the Foundation for NetApp's Talent
- Create an Enterprise-Wide, Strategic Approach to Hiring and Develop with the Future in Mind
- Provide a Global Career Framework Through New Organization Architecture

I had a three-year plan, but in Year One, my focus was the masses. We kept our goals achievable and were after some early wins. Our goal was to implement the top half of the Wheel (only), addressing the singular employee (1st quadrant) and the team (2nd). Raising the accountability of employees and managers, strengthening team relationships, and building high-performing teams. The bottom of the Wheel was still just a promise; the only thing we began planning in the 3rd and 4th quadrants was how to implement new HR technology.

Nonetheless, I shared the whole plan with the entire company, though many people in my shoes wouldn't have opened the kimono that much. I said, *"Here's my Golden Thread! But I'm only gonna spin the first two."* I was intentionally very transparent with leadership and employees, offering the whole story so we could grow this together. Remember: You can't pilot transformation. You've got to be all in. Sharing the full, multi-year strategy was a piece of that thinking. A systemic change was coming across the enterprise. By telling everyone *"This is coming,"* I made them part of the story too. From the stage, I continued, *"I want to tell you my entire vision, so you know what it is, and this doesn't look like just a bunch of programs. For now, those top two quadrants are all I care about."* Based on the full Golden Thread story, the Thrive Wheel became a known plan for the future. I figured, if everyone got that, they could see it for the wholesale transformation it actually was intended to be.

Many were surprised and asked, *"You're not doing any leadership development this year?"* "Nope," I answered. *"That's your development. Everyone, do these two things. We'll do a bunch of enablement to help, but with Quarterly Conversations and the survey, you have everything you need to start a high-performing team."* BetterUp coaching was launched right after, along with Thrive Rewards. Mosaic (what we named the Fuel50 platform) came a year later. In Year Two, I added Activate. Doing so made everything clearer for the organization. Activate Yourself, Activate the Team, Activate the Enterprise, and then Activate the Future—a plan more succinct and much more tangible for people to follow, but again, during Year One, I only delivered two quadrants, later named Activate Yourself and Activate the Team, along with a lot of enablement assets produced by Avery, Lisa, and Vicky.

On the most basic level, we wanted to see the Wheel move from theory to full-blown execution. It never changed at its core, but the Wheel did evolve—exponentially—through successive iterations over the coming eighteen months and beyond. Its key philosophies and central ideas have remained intact. And the messaging, thanks to Lisa Melsted, has remained consistent as well. Transformations can fail for many reasons, but a central one is constantly changing the message instead of *building* on that messaging over the years, as NetApp has done.

A huge part of this first-year success had to do with all the enablement assets we launched. A Quarterly Conversation trifold, videos of me and George, office hours, and the rest. The value in this mass enablement step cannot be overstated. It is the engine that drives transformation, the difference between launching and languishing or launching and reaching the stratosphere. This step alone allowed us to hit max velocity, speed, direction, and enterprise-wide digestion and usage of the tools and mindsets.

15 • The Employee-Manager Relationship

Many research reports over the years link a sense of fulfillment to engagement and retention. A 2023 global culture study[5] from the O.C. Tanner Institute reports that *"personal fulfillment had the most decisive impact on an employee's choice to stay in their job, do great work, and define their organization as a great place to work."* Lack of fulfillment means employees actively look for a different job—or leave an organization in one year or less—nearly four times more frequently. Those are powerful statistics. Not feeling valued drives them to look elsewhere or ultimately leave. It's crazy.

We Gave Up on the Manager

It's been my belief for many years that the employee and the manager, that working relationship, is *the* most important connection in the entire company. I've heard it said countless times, that organizations had given up on the manager—which leaves little room or hope for a productive, fruitful manager-employee relationship. It didn't start out this way, but there was a slow erosion in the system over time. A trend I believe the time has come to correct. From the very beginning of introducing the Thrive Ecosystem, it was ALL about building and re-humanizing the relationship between the manager and the employee. The simple fact is, a more functional working relationship is better for the employee and the manager; ultimately, though, the biggest benefactor is the company. EM said it well: *"I was often frustrated that some had quite a negative view of our manager's capabilities. 'Oh, they can't do this. They don't know how to do that. They're not ready.' Really downplaying their level of maturity. I just found it frustrating that they were always brushed aside as in 'Oh, they don't know how to manage. They're just not capable.' In my experience, that was simply not the case."*

Remove Scaffolding, Artifice, Monitoring

This all begged the question: Why doesn't the average worker trust managers? And why do companies make it so difficult for employees and managers to talk to each other? In my history, it's generally been felt that managers couldn't be trusted with actually managing other people. *"Let 'em do their jobs and hold their meetings, but they can't do anything around people. I don't trust them, and you know, they're just not up for it."* It was a big problem, definitely. I had to ask myself, *What was the solve?* The problem is clearly multi-faceted. For one thing, companies have built scaffolding designed to buttress the manager and their duties—performance ratings, 9-boxes, mandatory training, lengthy forms, leadership competencies, and so on—all artificial devices to stand them up. And the paperwork has mushroomed over the decades. Multi-page forms, boxes to check...it can feel endless. I recall, for example, writing up ten-page development plans for every one of my employees and never looking at them again for the rest of the year! How can that be helpful?

And then there's legal, which de-risks a lot of stuff. If you're a middle-level manager, you're crushed, pulled in a hundred directions at once. What's more, we train managers to expect heavy oversight. The more a business surrounds people with scaffolding, without expecting or requiring (or allowing) accountability, the lower you make the bar for managers. Not all, but most will follow you down. *"Hey, if you're going to do it for me..."* And even the best managers can only take on as much responsibility as they're permitted to. As you build that scaffolding, you lower the accountability of the employee-manager relationship as well. *"I'll just do that HR stuff that they make me do, and now I'm doing leadership."* In other words, it's just a whole lot of managing managers. And yet, they're managers! They're supposed to know how to manage, right? This is where the problem begins.

What's the Impact? HR Police

In building this type of model, intentionally or not, we turned HR into babysitters. The HR police. I've seen it everywhere throughout my career. The HR I've known monitors, reports, tracks, and archives. I used to have twenty-five direct reports. Just think of how many pages upon pages of things I had to write! (Perhaps you've done a few of these yourself.) Then they'd be collected, and someone would come by and say, "*You've only turned in 80 percent of yours.*" Ugh. So, the question then becomes, where does the buck stop? Who is ultimately accountable? HR? The managers? The employees?

Catch the Underperformer

These systems—and mindsets—got their start among the leading companies of decades past, where employees were treated more like resources than humans. Beginning with those early factory floors, the department of human resources was referred to as *personnel*. Regulating where people needed to be and when. A common old-school personnel tagline was "*Making sure you stay compliant.*" That was a lot of what HR was then. Compliance. Legal. On the factory line, where work was either done by hand or with a machine, one could easily measure productivity. The world has radically transformed since those early days. Work duties and roles have vastly diversified and evolved while our performance management systems somehow remained stuck in the past. The current world workplace is packed with knowledge workers and life-changing technological advances. We've put people on the moon and are on the threshold of an AGI-enhanced generation. And yet, these systems within HR have changed very little over the decades. Many companies use a working model of performance management today that is a recognizable descendant of these old, unit-based measures of productivity.

These legacy systems ensure not only that all employees are compliant but also that HR can legally terminate low performers—at all levels of the organization. We've built HR to manage managers but also to protect against that minuscule fraction of troublesome underperformers. (The max is 5 percent but usually much less!) And this mindset has been generalized across the entire population. Are there leaders who get it wrong? Absolutely. There are also some who did (and do) really stupid things. We can all point to anecdotal or specific situations in which managers have made really bad decisions. But because of a few bad apples—and louder voices—we've built a whole system to protect the company from the underperformer who might sue you. The whole system!

While well-intended, many companies throughout the decades have made this relationship between the employee and manager even more difficult. When I worked at Citibank, managers were required to follow a three-step process. If you were not performing (X number of calls, X number of minutes), you'd get a verbal. Then you'd get a formal written warning from the manager that basically said, "*You're falling behind.*" Then you'd get a final warning. Can you imagine functioning under the weight of this? Trying to stay motivated under such a system? How invested would you be in your work or the company in general? It was horrible. And the poor managers at the time had to write these things up. (I know because I was one of them.) HR's job was to look at 'em. And if you talked to that person about their citations, they'd more than likely become mad and distracted. "*Now I'm in trouble and can't focus on my job.*" During those Citibank days, I often thought, *This is brutal.*

Accountability Needs to Go Up

Managers of today are filling out more forms and becoming better at paperwork as opposed to improving how they talk to their people. AND it's created a wedge, fueling FUD between the employees and managers and eroding trust. And little wonder. If I'm using all this artifice to monitor and manage you, I'm really just making it that much harder to build the kind of rapport necessary to cultivate a high-performing team. The common mentality among current workers: "*If I don't feel connected to my boss, I may look at a job, but if I feel I'm not being cared for, I will apply for one.*" Losing talent is undesirable and expensive.

Focus on the Performer

I don't want my managers to be data analysts or form-filler-outers. Accountability between managers and employees needs to go up. Which means creating a system that provides for that. I want them to have responsibility and accountability. That was where my epiphany came in. I decided that we needed to flip the whole system on its head, to rip the current system out, burn it to the ground, and start over. So, I said to leadership, "*We need to focus on the performers, not the underperformers. We need to put all our efforts into the 95 percent. On the democratization of growth. And you know, we'll deal with the 5 percent.*" I then told my team, "*I'm done with all that. Let's rip it all out. And if there's 5 percent who are underperforming, give them three months or write them a check.*" (Anecdotally, the percentage of people on average who underperform at a company to the degree that you're gonna to fire them? It's always such a tiny fraction. And a lot of times, if they know they're underperforming, they ultimately leave on their own.) We wanted anything that slowed down the growth of that relationship removed and replaced with actionable, forward-thinking enablement concepts. Let's trust humans to be humans.

Unleash Talent

During my discussion with leadership, I continued with, "*I don't wanna design a program for the bottom 10 percent. That's not the focus of a talent organization. I want to design a program for the top 90 percent.*" After tearing it all down, you put in enablement, incorporating accountability for the manager and employee together, where the focus is on good performances and embracing best practices. And where do you suppose that begins? When

HR moves away from being the police, that's where. It's a tectonic shift. A shift in mindset and in responsibilities, from HR to the managers and back on to the business. Let HR step aside so the business can own it. I know, it's a different role than we've taken in the past. HR isn't here to control; we're here to enable. We'll consult, but we don't mandate. We offer opportunities, not forms to fill out. We'll provide solutions, not push people into boxes. Instead of managing humans as resources, we'll give staff at every level the development they need and aspire to engage with. To unleash talent and focus on helping everyone understand what a growth environment is, what a growth mindset is, and how their future is intertwined with the future of the company. And as HR, our new reason for being is in the form of another business unit of the company, to facilitate the emergence of an ecosystem of high-performing teams. To focus on performers, not underperformers. THAT'S the ultimate HR transformation.

And then my big push to managers came: *"I'll give you everything I can to provide you with the tools, the mindset, and the ability to be successful. I'm here to enable you."* One key strategy: Give them real-time data (via survey results) they can then apply to their specific circumstances, then let them be the people who design the rules and give directions to their people. Let them know it's theirs to own and then trust them to make the right decisions. Accountability. Responsibility. *"I would sit in these leadership programs,"* shares EM, *"and my experience of them was…it wasn't so much that they weren't capable of making decisions, it was that the company didn't have a clear decision-making framework. Nor was it clear who was the ultimate owner or held accountable for a decision. They weren't empowered, and it wasn't clear. So, I think there were a lot of instances where organizational governance structure (or lack thereof) was read as a lack of capability on the leader's part. And I never thought that was the case."*

Clearly, we needed to be building managers for the twenty-first century, not last century.

16 • Ratings and Rankings

"*Woohoo!!!*" Yelling and cheers could be heard from every corner of the room. It was August 19, 2019, the NetApp quarterly All Hands meeting (eight months before COVID hit) where I gave my first all-company presentation. I was the first non-C-Suite staffer to ever speak at one of these. Thousands of employees around the globe watched our much-anticipated launch of Thrive via livestream. As I watched this playback a couple of years later, I was reminded of how excited the staff was to hear our plans to rip out the system of performance ratings. People were psyched. Here's part of my presentation from that day:

> *We don't trust the managers all the time, so, we have a lot of FUD between the managers and the employees. Because we just don't trust that they can do it. So, you have to rate people. You have to rank them, fill out long forms, and make sure that the employee knows that they get a grade at the end of the year. You know what that does to people? It makes them not want to come to work. But because so many companies do it, there's nowhere else to go. So, we are changing that. It's true. Everybody sucks. But not us. We are about to change. We are ripping out ratings, rankings, forms, anything that gets away in that relationship.*" [Crowd cheers.] "*So, starting today, you don't have to worry about that bad day at the end of the year, when you get a grade. Starting today, you are in growth mode together. And I'm gonna show you how that works.*

I'd been talking to everyone for the preceding months, so I wasn't entirely surprised by their reaction. I knew that many felt bogged down by the forms, ratings, and forced distributions. Many a manager had described it as "*painful,*" and "*frustrating.*" I used my from-to technique to pitch our solve. I identified the current situation, let them know what we were going to do about it, and then painted a picture of what it was going to be replaced with. From, To. Before, After. Antiquated, Growth-Oriented. Hard, Way Easier.

Getting rid of ratings and rankings should be the headline. But what you fill the space with instead is the story, right? Thrive is that story. At NetApp, we took out ratings and rankings, 9-boxes, and loooong development plans. And I said, "*Yes, we can. If you make it easy, they'll do it.*" Since that day, we've worked to rip out everything standing in the way of the manager and the employee and replace it with an idea of "*How do we grow together?*" More specifically, my goals for transforming process management involved a more human-centered approach:

EVOLVING PERFORMANCE MANAGEMENT

FROM	TO
Process-oriented	People-oriented
Forms, ratings, and distributions	Relationships, connections, conversations
Numerical assessment	Qualitative and Quantitative Assessment
Feel like you're being graded	Feel like you're being challenged
Directive-driven	Supportive
Manager-driven	Joint accountability
Backward view	Forward-looking
Fixed. No opportunity to change something	Opportunity to grow
No reflection of the employee experience	It's all about the employee experience

Let's back up a minute and be specific about the performance management systems we had in place at NetApp. I recently asked OpenAI's Chat GPT-4, "*What are Ratings and Rankings?*" and it gave a decent answer so I decided to lift an excerpt from that response and share it with you here.

It also demonstrates how ubiquitous and globally standardized these old-school methods truly are: *In human resources (HR), ratings and rankings are useful tools for HR managers to evaluate the performance and potential of employees within an organization. Performance ratings are typically used to measure how well an employee is performing their job duties and responsibilities, while potential ratings assess an employee's ability to grow and take on additional responsibilities in the future.*

Performance ratings can be based on a variety of criteria such as job knowledge, productivity, quality of work, teamwork, communication, and customer service. Employees may be rated on a numerical scale, such as 1 to 5 or 1 to 10, or they may be given a letter grade. These ratings can be used to identify areas where an employee needs improvement, as well as to determine rewards, promotions, or disciplinary actions.

In some organizations, performance ratings are used to create a ranking system, where employees are compared to one another and ranked from highest to lowest performance. This can be used to identify high-performing employees who may be eligible for promotion or other opportunities, as well as to identify underperforming employees who may need additional training or support.

NetApp generally followed the structure described above, along with the preceding *From* column of process management. They would do their reviews once a year. What this would result in, basically, is that unless you were a really amazing or horrible worker, you didn't get the right feedback for 364 days of the year. Then, on that last day, they'd give you your score. What they're doing behind the scenes is writing this long development plan. They're measuring you against competencies that probably don't match up to your job—and these competencies are supposed to go to every employee. And then you get to the end, the day of your evaluation, and they tell you, "*You're a 3.*" To which you'd likely respond in shock, "*What? Why didn't you tell me something earlier?*"

You're a Four!

Like much of corporate America, NetApp used ratings and 9-boxes. For ratings, let's say five is the highest some would do. They would say: "*This person does excellent work and hits their productivity goals.*" So, you get a five. And then another would get a four, then another a three. Across a company of twelve thousand employees, a conglomerate of vastly different roles and levels of experience, what nuances can be found on this kind of five-point scale? What's the difference between a five and a four, really?

Remember, performance management started with the early twentieth-century widget worker. If you finished fifty widgets in a day and another on the line only did forty, you'd make more money. But the vast distinctions in how people work today are so complicated, a simple rating no longer cuts it. I mean, think about it. The very concept seems embarrassing. Imagine, at a time when your productivity is based on the major current complexities of delivering things, a process completely different from the person sitting next to you, who, in turn, is working within a system different from the person next to them. The intricacies of your job can't be boiled down to "*I gave you a four.*" Despite this, there are still companies that do shadow ratings. Because some people feel the need to give and/or receive that number, offering the argument: "*It's the way it's always been done. It's not meaningful without it.*"

But for most, based on all I've seen throughout my career, it's one of the most universally disliked events in the calendar year. (So why in the world do we still do it?!) Just think, you have a VP who runs a complex division and manages dozens of people, and to evaluate him based on an arcane numbering system and tell him, "*You're a 4!*"? What does that do for the company or the VP? And then to have to turn around and give another a 3? What kind of feedback is that? How does that make the worker better? It's just so silly. What makes it worse is the majority of people are rated as 3s. To management, that means you're doing your job; maybe you're even great at it. But to the recipients, three means a C, not an A. And if you're getting a C? That's not a grade that makes people happy, especially when they're meeting all your expectations and doing great work. Let's say this person doesn't leave but decides to stay with the company. Guess how motivated and excited they're going to be working there now?

Broken Trust

Worse still, this ratings system produces the most dehumanizing kind of relationship you can possibly have in the workplace, where a manager can hide behind a number and say, "I *would have given you a higher score, but they told me I couldn't.*" Right there, you have broken trust, immediately. And since everyone uses ratings, there's no reason to leave because, "*Well, they do it over there too.*" This is the way corporations work. This system isn't necessarily kind to managers either—forcing them to label their employees and reduce them to a number. Confining people to a single digit—and once a year? Beyond how inappropriate it is for today's type of work processes, it's just downright inhumane (and, arguably, counterproductive). That's a big reason why our goal—mine and my team's—was to rip out everything that got in the way of the manager and the employee (including—and especially—this) and replace it with an idea of *How do we grow together?*

Nine-Box Grids

McKinsey created the 9-box grid in 1970. Since then, HR institutions have embraced it as the penultimate matrix from which to work—and that includes the talent management process. Today, it's still one of the most widely used tools for worker evaluation. Each box has specific titling. "High potential," "Great performer," "Needs this." And so on. Managers go into a room and try to put their people in these boxes (another inhumane process). While in this room, managers would be forced into a battle-mode mindset, thinking, *I have to fight for this. Now I have to fight to get my guy in this box because only a certain percentage get in.* They would argue with each other, "*My guys should be in this box. My guys, they...*" And then they'd worry about this box for the entire DAY.

Here's the worst part of the process: At the end of that day, that box doesn't even matter. Why? Because the company has only a set amount of money to work with, and you want to give more to some and less to others. So, what have you taught managers to do? Use artificial numbers and fight over a box when they could have used that time to talk with their employee about their growth. So wasteful—and this has been going on for decades! And then what happens with that 9-box? Nothing! What eventually happens is that your people start to manufacture ratings, right? If the manager puts this worker in *this* box, then we're gonna build out *this* training program—all based on a forced system that does not take all the nuance of an employee's performance and growth aspirations fully into account. A forced system that may, or may not, represent any given employee's real strengths or needs. Or the company's either.

We Need to Catch Up

When automation began to spread across our production processes, it created what should have been a perfect time to pause and say, *"Okay, so machines are now doing what humans used to do. Humans are now in new jobs, with more complex roles where performance isn't necessarily delivered in discreet units. How are we going to assess performance now?"* Maybe some asked, but that question did not get answered. No transformation went on there. We left people in the same old, same old. Up until I got to Equinix, HR still treated workers as a number (this problem is still ongoing in many companies, as many of us know). At the end of the year, it would be as though Uncle Sam were pointing right at each worker, yelling, *"You! You're a number."*

Technology has advanced a thousandfold, yet our people practices have not evolved at anywhere near the same clip. We would never use antiquated tech today on any front, so why are we still applying such an outdated, outmoded philosophy and approach? All it tells our people is *Not only did we give up on the manager, we also gave up on evolving and modernizing our people practices.* Leadership had to have said at some point, *"Forget that.*

Focus on the technology. People will figure it out on their own." I'm here to say, I don't believe that. We need to catch up.

This starts with decoupling the performance assessment part of the process from the discussion about money. With separating the discussion about your goals and how you're doing on the work front from the conversation about your compensation. We need to get to the point that instead of waiting until that one day at year's end to learn your fate from your manager, you have ongoing conversations in which the subject is exclusively on growth.

Neuroscience and Statistics

There are a lot of good reasons to *not* combine discussions about performance with giving an annual rating. The main one is based on what we now know about neuroscience and what new scientific research has taught us about how humans commonly respond to feedback. According to research from the Neuroleadership Institute, the very act of giving employees a rating jolts them into a 'fight or flight scenario' that makes them feel disregarded and undermined. In an article by David Rock (co-founder of the institute) and colleagues, they further conclude, "*The employee may not say anything overtly, but he or she feels disregarded and undermined—and thus intensely inclined to ignore feedback, push back against stretch goals, and reject the example of positive role models.*"[6] That means when employees sit down with their manager, they're either gonna want to run out the door or punch them in the face.

In fact, long before this annual meeting begins, workers tend to ramp up to protect themselves. "*People were so obsessed with the rankings,*" shares Emily about her management experience. "*It was such a stressful experience for them.*" Studies also show that even using the words *feedback* or *annual review* can trigger a fight-or-flight response. EM recalls planning last year's review process, which she was responsible for leading at NetApp. "*I was looking through our performance management website and recall saying, 'OMG, this is awful.' I remember writing this and boring myself! It was such a drudgery...and I hated having one! And yet here I am saying, 'You have to have a performance review.' It was the most awful thing to experience."* Does this seem like the best time to discuss career development with a worker? This old-school thinking needs to go.

The study also shows ratings *"often blindside employees, directly affecting their performance. Many expect a higher rating than they receive, leading to a steep drop in engagement. About half of all workers are surprised at their rating, and 90% of those workers are unhappy, leading to a 23% drop in engagement."*[7] So, when employees come to their annual, twenty-minute-ish performance management meeting, if they don't get what they wanted, everything else the manager says goes out the window. Their brains shut off.

For those who are negatively surprised, what do you suppose happens in the aftermath? Attrition numbers spike. The company loses talent. NetApp was seeing this every year. This steady trend wasn't just happening at NetApp but with other companies following the same model. Then there's the investment to find and train replacements, and the cycle continues, with real business consequences.

Should HR just accept this as the norm? It doesn't need to remain a given, especially in light of new data from neuroscientists. For the most part, departures are not for compensation but for career development. That's something you can tackle early if your managers are freed up from mandatory paperwork so they can focus on learning more about what their employees actually want. Instead of writing reviews and development plans no one ever looks at again, managers should focus on their working relationship with their employees. With my staff, I always tried to make sure we were on the same page. The last thing I wanted was for them to be surprised at their score. So, I said to NetApp leadership, *"Well, why can't we just do that? Just let people know where they stand?"* I continued, *"Employees should be talking all the time about how your performance is going and how their growth is going."* That was why the Quarterly Conversation became so important. And why NetApp began eliminating annual performance reviews as many companies (such as Adobe, Cargill, ConAgra, Gap, Intel, Juniper Networks, Medtronic, Sears, and Microsoft) have begun to do.[8]

Improve, Polish, Level Up

When I was working as the head of HR at Glu Mobile (a mobile gaming company in San Francisco), I took my first stab at removing ratings and rankings. With the help of my HR partner Stephanie Greenberg (Glu Mobile's HR manager), I was able, for the first time, to move an organization away from numbers and (at least) into categories.

One of their studios was in Moscow (getting to go to Moscow was, in itself, amazing). There, I first had this idea, one I had been pondering in one form or another for the entirety of my career. How to be able to say, "*Okay, I'm not going to give you a ranking like a 1, 2, 3, 4, or 5. That's so judgmental. And so difficult to absorb. What does it mean, anyway, if I give you a rating of a five versus a four or three?*" I had long wanted to find another way to give people feedback without giving them a number.

Part of the game development process at Glu Mobile was to pull someone in who wasn't designing the game, maybe someone from finance, for example, to come sit in a room with all the creators and have them play while the developers watched, allowing them to analyze the choices that person made. If he got stuck, they worked to figure out why. It was so freakin' cool. And so much fun. It inspired me to consider using game terminology to bucket people rather than the traditional ratings system. It wasn't eliminating a ratings system entirely, but it was a step in the right direction and more development focused.

The categories represent the three stages of how a game is developed. As developers build out games, they go through three phases: Improve, Polish, and Level Up. Improve means being in the first phase of building. It represents a kind of *new-to-job* mode, or *lower bucket and need to develop*, and would be comparable to a 2 or 3 out of 5 based on the old ratings systems a company would use. The second stage, Polish, means the game is in *need-to-polish-in-some-areas* mode, as in, "*All right, we have the bare bones here, but now we need to make this character polished and ready to go.*" In HR speak (based on the old system), that might translate to a 3 or 4. For game developers, stage three, Level Up, means playing the game and evaluating its potential. In HR, Level Up then meant, "*Yeah, you may get promoted,*" or "*You're on a path to being amazing.*"

I felt that kind of system would take the sting out of ranking people. I wanted it to feel like it was just a moment in time that you would continue to grow from rather than an admonition. If I were to give an employee a 2, they'd likely think, *Oh, my God, I suck.* Because it's so finite, right? That person's whole year would be a 2. But if I were to say instead, "*You're in an Improve phase,*" it would just mean they need to get better—and they will. I could frame it in the perspective that, if this were a game, it would still have the potential of being a big, best-selling hit. So, it's just a point in time for the worker. Transitional. If you get an Improve or a Polish, it's just a momentary state—instead of having people feel like they're in a finite "*you suck*" point in their careers.

The point I wanted to get across is that everything goes through such stages. Even our #1 hit game at the company went through the same three phases. Even if you are in the lowest category, it is only temporary, and there is an obvious path to the next stage. Looking back, I had set into motion a growth mindset even before I started using that term. Instead of the finality of "*You are a 3 out of 5,*" this was more of a "*How do we get from this stage to the next stage, together?*" It offered a more humanistic way to think of performance and growth. Yes, the evaluation would still include a conversation about the past year AND a discussion about ways to get to the next stage in common terms, but without the kind of heavy-duty development plan that people spend two hours writing and zero hours ever discussing again. Even back when I worked at Citibank in the late eighties/early nineties as a brand-new young recruiter, and then in leadership development, I was already trying to figure out ways to at least SHRINK this system. "*Hey, how about we have a ONE-page development plan?*" I recall suggesting. Just anything, anything, anything! To streamline the process. But at Glu, this was my first foray into HR transformation before I even thought of it in those terms.

This was my first shot at trying to get people's minds around getting away from numbers and 9-boxes. My time at Glu was building me up to say, *"I'm gonna try this and really make it happen,"* once I got to Equinix. Years later, I asked one of my former Glu team members, *"Do you remember these?"* And she told me, *"Yeah, they still use them!"* It's nice to know the system stuck.

17 • Thrive Rewards

The first question that goes through everyone's mind when you say, *"No more ratings and rankings,"* is *Pandemonium! How will we know what to pay workers?* After all the things that we pulled off the table—ratings, 9-boxes, annual performance reviews—people wondered, *"How will the company handle compensation if we leave that all behind?"* One of the biggest challenges with this kind of transformation is helping people understand how worker pay will be handled at the end of the year. Pay was reliant on that numbering system. A number meant a certain amount of dollars. And the ratings and rankings were so tied to Total Rewards and end-of-year performance reviews that it was hard to imagine how performance could be rewarded without it. When we hired a new HR leader (not long after instituting this change at NetApp), she even asked, *"Hey, where's the 9-boxes?"* because everyone in our industry had just become so used to it.

That was why this removal of ratings and rankings represented true transformation, not just change. Yet there remained that big question: *How, then, were we going to differentiate people?* Our answer: Thrive Rewards. It would be an annual event, incorporated as part of the Thrive Ecosystem and the transformed approach to the employee experience.

Still Pay-for-Performance

NetApp has been and remains a pay-for-performance company. And yet, we still wanted that differentiation. Every company has a total rewards philosophy since they require some system in place for compensation. Whether you are using ratings or not, companies always have a finite rewards budget. The key, for us, was to figure out how to distribute that budget without a ranking. That was where the six questions came in (see below). At our August 2019 launch, I provided reassurances. *"We still have a total rewards philosophy. We believe in differentiation and still believe that the highest performers should get most of the pay. NetApp does believe that. That's a public statement. Most companies think that. Maybe not in Switzerland, but we do. And we think we can still achieve that without using numbers and putting people in boxes."*

Detractors remained. I heard such retorts as, *"The only way you can pay people is if you have all of these levers,"* but it's simply not true. You can still fulfill your total rewards philosophy without all those old things we ripped out. I continued, *"We guarantee pay-for-performance, and there's still an evaluation. It's just gonna be a much shorter process and a much easier way."*

We Believe in the Manager

To recap, NetApp would no longer have an annual performance review. In its place would be Thrive Rewards at the end of the year. As mentioned, in the old days, HR measured performance by coming up with competencies, or what we thought people should be measured against. When it was widgets, or for someone running a data center, rating productivity was easy. Nowadays, everything is a lot more nuanced. An engineer shouldn't be measured the same as someone in accounting, right? (The sales guys are easy—did you hit your quota, yes or no?) But for many departments (engineering, accounting, HR, marketing, sales enablement, IT) the statement, *"This is a structure of how you measure your people, and these are the competencies to measure them against,"* no longer holds true because they're so different. As the CHRO, how can I know how to measure my workers' performance? Well, I don't, but I don't need to, because there is one group of leaders within each company that does. The managers.

Historically, you'd tell a manager: *"Your budget is one hundred dollars."* Looking at potential salary increases, for example, those who were rated 4 and 5? The manager would be told: *"Give them most of the salary. You need to spend sixty of your dollars on that."* For those who are in the 3s?

"*Spend $30.*" Anyone with less would get $10. So managers were handed specific guidelines for percentage increases based on that year's ratings. The belief was that if we let the managers decide, they wouldn't do it right. They wouldn't go through with the difficult conversation. Understandable—they had to deliver the news, yet had little control over what that news was going to be. Thus making the old number-based system demoralizing for everyone involved.

I've also sought ways to simplify HR processes. In my mind, it's never *not* a good idea to try. This book title says it all—this idea that talent management doesn't have to be complex or cumbersome. So it got me thinking and it hit me—this idea that you *can* simplify TM with *transparency* (meaning having honest conversations, especially around promotions) and *accountability*. Giving managers room to run their own show and talent. And surround them with easy-to-use enablement tools to help them do just that. Those two ideas came together and ultimately became part of Thrive.

Next, what we said to the managers was "*This is your team. And we trust that you know how to manage it.*" This gave managers agency to make decisions about equity, bonus, salary, and base. They were handed that responsibility—and the accountability that went along with it. They could have those conversations with workers while having more flexibility in how to differentiate rewards—and celebrate employee contributions toward meeting NetApp's goals. They still had a budget to apply those rewards against, but what we told them was "*Here's your budget. You can use the tools we offer, but either way, we trust you to make the right decisions.*" Some people worried that by going to Thrive and getting rid of numbers, we'd changed NetApp's total reward philosophy. We did not.

Assessment Tools: Scattergram

We still wanted to differentiate and give the better performers higher money but believed that it could be done in a much easier way than, say, the 9-boxes, for example. No matter how HR was getting there, they were still doing the same basic math, right? Managers spent hours in a room calculating numbers, when, in the end, it didn't really matter what box an employee was put in.

We gave managers tools to talk about productivity in a much calmer, easier, and faster way. One such tool was the Scattergram, an in-house tool EM and I built to help managers in their promotion and compensation decisions at the end of the year. Tailored specifically for NetApp, the Scattergram is an optional enabling tool that asks some critical questions of managers to help them make those decisions and calibrate who they're going to give more money to. They were free to use it—or not. Like the ongoing QCs, the Scattergram gave managers a fresh method for differentiating their employees. The questions, six in total, are about each of the company's employees. Other companies may ask similar questions about other performance indicators, but we wanted to keep it simple and in line with what the Thrive Ecosystem for High-Performing Teams was all about.

How It Works

Specifically, the six questions relate to performance, impact, and growth. Each manager selects options from a four-point scale ("Almost," "Always," "Sometimes," "Never"). The main gist of this exercise is to determine two key things for each worker: *Is that person hitting their goals?* And *Is that person a good teammate?* The six questions are:

1. Is this person doing the things that we expect them to do? Or even exceeding those?
2. Does this person consistently seize opportunities to make an impact?
3. Is this person a good teammate?
4. Is this person a good cross-collaborating teammate?
5. Can we see this person grow into a new job?
6. Can this person have a great future here?

The first two questions center on impact. The next two relate to working with others. Others, in this context, could be anything, depending on the job. In HR, we need to work not just across the HR division but across the entire business. In engineering, they just work with the engineering team, for example. The last two questions relate to long-term career growth and agility, especially around stock. Since stock is a longer-term vesting reward, it's what we wanted to grant to high achievers with a bright future. The last two questions were designed to help managers think about using stock grants in a more thoughtful way.

Here's how it works: The answers get plotted, and then the Scattergram output provides recommendations based off of how the questions get answered. If the answers fall in the upper right (almost always), a base recommendation is to give them 100 to 110 percent of their bonus. As we move toward the bottom left, the recommendations decrease. Now, no two employees' results would necessarily turn out the same, even if their plots showed up the same way. At NetApp, for example, managers were given the flexibility to differentiate as they saw fit, as long as they stayed within their given budget. Let's say a manager received a bucket of ten thousand dollars. If, after reviewing the Scattergram, the manager decided to give one of those two people four thousand, the other six's compensation was their call. In the end, the results are the same as a 9-box; the process is done without having to demoralize anybody.

No More Than a Tweet

If a manager wants to add a comment on top of those questions? The new system only allows them 180 characters—the length of a tweet! We didn't want a diatribe. Why? Because the manager should have been talking to their people all year long in their QCs. We were no longer hitting people over the head, like the old days, with the twenty-page manuscript once a year and pissing everybody off. And no one could hide behind a rating anymore or try to solve the year's problems in one meeting.

Interestingly, we had better differentiation after taking the numbers away than we got before. (I believe it's because we made people think!) This is when transformation gets really exciting. To actually see managers' behaviors change during an event that they have been participating in their entire careers? Pretty interesting, and here's why: The new Thrive Rewards process gave managers more flexibility to respond and evaluate each person's performance *individually*—enabling them to recognize and reward outstanding performers (for example).

By eliminating the strict rating and ranking system, managers gained more freedom to consider a broader range of factors; they could now apply their own subjective conclusions about their people. Plus, by being able to consider more factors, their resulting assessments had more nuance, meaning pay could have greater differentiation as well. This shift also provided greater discretion toward rewarding exceptional performers based on what they'd seen, heard, and generally observed about them throughout the year. Managers were given the opportunity to answer specific performance-related questions and consider factors such as achieved results and collaboration—further contributing to greater differentiation in pay for employees who consistently delivered exceptional results. The idea was to give managers a chance to focus more on *results* than compliance to a process. And the thinking was to create an atmosphere of fairness and transparency in the hopes of getting everyone more engaged—to inspire even greater motivation and higher morale.

18 · Quarterly Conversations

The True North of Engagement

We've already established that the employee-manager relationship is the most important in any company. If the aim is to build high-performing teams, why wouldn't leadership do everything possible to enhance, improve, and strengthen these connections? In and of themselves, Quarterly Conversations are not necessarily new. As a concept, it's been known in the industry for some time. We certainly didn't invent them at Equinix, or NetApp. But these conversations alone will not necessarily achieve the enduring, positive business goals any company might be after. It's not a huge hurdle to implement a one-off. It's another thing entirely to build a strategy for upending the existing culture and have these progressive changes stick.

The central question we were always looking to answer: *How do I make it easier for managers and employees to talk about the future and their growth?* I'm big on removing as much noise as possible between the manager and employee. I told my team, *"We're gonna enable the manager and the employee to have better conversations."* Many in our field are now beginning to embrace this.

A central piece of Activate Yourself in the Thrive Wheel, Quarterly Conversations are the True North of Engagement. Our surveys have shown that when employees have QCs, they are more engaged and focused on the future as a result. It's got to be open dialogue. The goals must be achievable. With these guidelines in mind, we want managers to go in, talk to their people, and be familiar with—and able to respond to—their real concerns, opportunities, and challenges.

I mentioned all this to my friend Andy Storch, a career development expert and author of the book, *Own Your Career, Own Your Life,* during one of our multiple conversations on the *Talent Development Think Tank* podcast he hosts. He immediately got excited and agreed that this was a huge, much-needed shift, telling me, *"As I've been having conversations with talent leaders around the country...I find that is the most critical component—conversations that managers are having with their employees. Culture is defined by that engagement, per the old adage that 'People join a company and leave a manager.' And I am finding more and more, as times change, people care more and more about career development, career direction, where are they going. If they're not getting that guidance from their manager, eventually, they're gonna go somewhere else, right?"* *"Absolutely,"* I replied. If you're forcing your manager to get into these really difficult conversations that are out of their control as opposed to giving them tools to talk about someone's future and alignment and engagement? It just changes the whole dynamic. We've got to get away from these mandatory policies, from forcing people to do things that don't make sense, and make it easier for them to want to lean into these kinds of conversations.

What Is a Quarterly Conversation?

What does a Quarterly Conversation look like? What are the goals, and who drives it? These conversations are not about checking a box on how hard the employees work. QCs are different than, say, in-the-moment feedback such as, "*Great presentation!*" or "*I liked what you did there, but…*" What EM and I were introducing was more purposeful and future based. More than just a "good job" or a regular one-on-one, this critical part of the first quarter of the Wheel was about strengthening and re-humanizing the manager-employee relationship long term. QCs, by definition, are about the move from annual performance reviews to these time outs, during which the two get together and discuss the employee's future: performance, impact, and growth. QCs mean that four times a year, managers ask them about their growth opportunities, career aspirations, and more.

QCs have plenty of benefits. Growth and potential are no longer correlated with the day you talk with the worker about money, which was the only time compensation issues were addressed in the past. There were no separate conversations about it. That's why QCs became such a central part of the Thrive transformation. Now? No more surprises. Full transparency—you know how you're going to be evaluated at the end of the year. If managers can check in regularly and ask: *Are you on track for your goals?* Everyone can be genuinely accountable for moving forward. Employees who can discuss their performance and potential year-round will always know where they stand—and respond and pivot faster for their own betterment as well as that of their team and the company.

Usually Backward-Looking

Managers and their direct reports typically meet one-on-one, sometimes weekly or bi-weekly. That's usually the time when the actual work is discussed. We did not change that. To the managers, we said, "*Incorporate the Quarterly Conversation into your regular one-on-one meeting schedule. It should replace just one of the one-on-one meetings that you have. Use ONE of those meetings each quarter for a QC about performance, impact, and growth."* One-on-one meetings (as was the case with end-of-year performance reviews) are normally backward-looking, comparing past work performances against your day-to-day goals. So, we told the managers, *"Stop and think about what gets discussed. At least 51 percent of these QCs should be about the future."*

Avery describes his perspective on the difference between a QC and a typical one-on-one. *"Usually, when you go into meetings with your boss, it's 'Okay, I'm doing this task, this task, this task, this task.' But QCs are meant to go deeper. [I think of it like] an iceberg. You don't even see the majority of the work and the support because it's underneath. And that's what QCs attempt to do. Don't look at the stuff in front. Let's talk about your career and what's underneath."*

Be a 21st Century Manager

This approach does put a bit more pressure on the manager in some ways while lightening their load in others. No more ten-page development plans to work up, but the manager does instead need to explain their assessments of their employees' work—in face-to-face meetings and at the end of the year. That means they need to understand their employees and what motivates them. It's not just a number anymore. We know why people leave companies. Largely, it's not about compensation but career development. They want a path forward, whatever forward means for them. Every person is different and motivated by different things. Some want recognition; better projects; more money, responsibility, or flexibility; giving someone a number is easy, right? Now, managers must really understand the person and what's important to them. So, our pitch for the managers was *"You need to be a manager of the twenty-first century."*

Good managers have probably already been doing this. There are great leaders, and no matter what I brought in for them to work with, they would have done great with it. There are and always will be those who are naturally good at managing others. But the idea with these new structures, and this kind of enablement, is that whether you're a stand out leader or a first-time manager, the system naturally provides the kind of pathways you require to support your employees. Take Talent Reviews, for example. We no longer 9-box it. Instead, we started this new program at the top of the house (first at Equinix, then at NetApp), where CEO staff, twice a year, reviewed the SVP population against criteria similar to the six questions mentioned above (depending on where the business was heading). Actual dialogues about each SVP against a simple criteria where the outcome was focused on transparency, feedback, and growth—not checking boxes or completing forms. The thinking was, in order to know and develop their people more, and be truly accountable for and about them, they were asked to discuss their direct reports in front of their colleagues and superiors. We began with the CEO staff talking about SVPs, then SVPs talking about their VPs. These later evolved into extended executive offsites (see Part 4, Section 2). Later, we continued to have talent reviews at the next levels below SVP. One of the moments I knew talent reviews were working was after the first one I conducted with the CEO staff at Equinix. One of the execs said to me, "*I used to go into these calibrations ready for a fight. Now, I go in talking about my people. What a difference.*" In my mind, that was a Bing! Home run moment.

During a Year One All Hands, I brought two long-term NetApp staffers up on stage to discuss their experience with Quarterly Conversations, good and bad. One was Anna Schlegel, Vice President, Globalization, Information Engineering, Product Portfolio Solutions, and WIT Chair. The other was Regina Evans, Engineering Program Manager. Examples of both types of conversations follows.

GOOD CONVERSATIONS

LARRY: My first question is for Regina. We talked about Quarterly Conversations and this idea that if you're having [one], you could really think about your future. You can really take the time out. It's not a one-on-one. It's more about you and your manager. Tell me about a time when you've had a great conversation about your future.

REGINA: One of my memorable ones is where my manager was so candid with me about what steps I should take in order to improve and go and do better. He encouraged me to be strategic, to be genuine, and build relationships across the businesses and to stretch myself beyond my comfort zone and to continue to make an impact on what we're doing in our bottom line. So this made me empowered. It made me be creative about how I was going to own and go forward and continue to pursue new opportunities and grow.

LARRY: Great. Thank you. That's a great example. Anna?

ANNA: So, I run a few teams in the company, and the one-on-ones tend, sometimes, to be firefighting or HR situations, new projects, new products, new ideas. I really enjoyed it when my manager actually took the time just to talk about my teams, my career....And because we are working so fast and so hard, when we decided to stop and have that conversation, it was very special...[and] I feel that I'm connecting with my manager. Then I can pass that down to my teams, and it's that domino effect and that beautiful rowing team. I've been a volleyball player for many years. You have one position to play and everybody's counting on everybody. So, if I had that conversation with my manager (my manager's almost like the captain), I know my position. Then I can explain this further to my team. I felt that I mattered, you know? All of a sudden, this person is interested in what I'm saying. And maybe I'm a little bit off? And the manager I'm thinking of used to set me very straight, like, *"It's this way."* Right? So then I can go and reposition things to my own team. I feel that I'm better aligned. And my compass is much clearer.

    I made it a point...to [always] come prepared. I have people that come to my meetings who say, *"Let's talk about my career,"* and they don't say anything. Or people that I mentor. I say, *"Come prepared. Really think about it. It's your time. Why do you wanna come here? Why do you wanna show up here and work ten, twelve hours a day?"* But you know, *Why do we come here for so many years? Why do we care so much?* You need to know that it's actually pointing in the right direction.

LARRY: So, instant alignment, right? And second, it IS the employee's Quarterly Conversation, not the manager's, right? Bring your growth plan and impact and how you're doing against your goals and get alignment.

BAD CONVERSATIONS

LARRY: So, I'll stick with you again, Anna. Tell us a bad conversation.

ANNA: When it didn't happen.

LARRY: It didn't happen?

ANNA: Right. So, the close of the year comes down to this one meeting that you're like, "Oh, my God. Oh, I'm gonna be rated?" And the conversation didn't even happen.

LARRY: That's fascinating. I don't even know how to respond to that.

ANNA: Did I do okay? Did I do bad? Do I matter? Is my team still here? I did get a letter with my rating, which was a good rating, but I didn't understand. Why wasn't I worth sitting down with? And in your head [you're thinking], "Should I leave the company? Should I...?" Right? And so, you can then explain to your team, you know, "I'm doing pretty well." So, we're doing pretty well because I'm just one person in that team. So, I want to go back and show that I did well and that we're focusing in the right direction. If you don't have these conversations, you're sort of working, working, working, but your compass may be off.

LARRY: So Regina, what was your worst conversation?

REGINA: So for me, I had an experience where I received and met expectations and it was not because I did average work. It was a recent promotion. And so it kind of translated into "you met expectations." This left me feeling kind of unappreciated. I was thinking that no matter what I do, I can't get to the next level in my career because I'm constantly being told to do more. And yet my performance rating doesn't reflect the amount of work effort that I put into what I was doing.

LARRY: They force you into a box because that's all they can do.

REGINA: Exactly.

LARRY: Okay, good. Thank you.

Enablement Tools

If we're saying to everyone, "*You should be doing these Quarterly Conversations on growth,*" of course, we'll provide tools to do that. In terms of leadership development and training, my philosophy is to tailor to your specific work environment. You should be teaching people what to do to be successful in *this* company at *this* time. We created a lot of enablement around this approach and told both managers and employees, "*Use the tools provided in order to have successful Quarterly Conversations.*" So, we provided a bunch of company-specific experiences and tools to support everyone who had them. Then, everyone is doing them the same way. We show videos, provide workshops, brochures, instructional materials, check-ins—especially at the beginning of the process but also ongoing.

One asset Avery produced was quite well received, something we (internally) called the *trifold*. The trifold brochure is a guide to Quarterly Conversations. There's a version for managers and another for employees. It includes several starter questions to think about for that conversation under the topics of the six questions related to Impact, Teamwork, and Growth. It also shows how to structure one from both perspectives. Both the manager and the employee can access these questions anytime—for contemplating and preparing in advance.

The manager doesn't necessarily drive these meetings—both the employee and the manager are responsible for them. They are for and about the employee, but, as you'd expect, both are accountable for being productive and successful. To the employees, we said, "*You're taking time out to talk about your productivity and impact and growth. Don't treat it like a normal one-on-one. It's a workbench day where you're 'sharpening the saw,' as the* 7 Habits of Highly Effective People *call it. So, stop. Take time out. Take a breath. That project will be picked up later. Really focus on your relationship and the future of it.*"

Yes, I Had a Quarterly Conversation!

The response from most was "*Oh, okay. That makes sense.*" But Aman describes how it was challenging for some, at least at first. "*Initially, it was hard,*" says Aman, "*because everyone's like, 'What does that mean? How do you do that? Why isn't it once a year? We're doing it four times a year? How does that make a difference?'*" She mentioned that technical folks, in particular, were reacting with comments such as, "*I wanna write something down,*" but they didn't get to write any of it down. So, again, it was change. We did a lot as a team to continuously provide the necessary change management. And NetApp continues to do this—there's always something on the calendar on *How you have a Quarterly Conversation*—especially for those new to the company. Everyone needs to know how to have them. Overall, the team did a great job of providing people with resources, tools, and information needed to get them acquainted with the process.

Not long after I'd introduced QCs, I told the CEO staff, "*Okay, everyone. Expect this number to go down,*" because I didn't think they really knew what Quarterly Conversations were. And because of the ongoing business transformation, NetApp was already—not surprisingly—having an engagement problem (which I didn't think could be fixed overnight). My theory was that QCs were a true north of engagement. That if managers had regular conversations with employees, talking about their contribution, impact, career, and growth, employee engagement would be higher. But our numbers never went down. One of the questions we asked in the very first Pulse Survey was: *Have you had a Quarterly Conversation in the past four months?* Shockingly, 82 percent of people said yes. And it has remained at about 82 percent. I'd have been happy with 75—three-quarters of the company doing a change thing. So, one of the biggest shocks for me is that the number has stayed so high. It's a testament to Vicky and Elaine-Marie for driving it.

19 · Thrive Pulse Surveys

When I first joined NetApp, one of the things I heard a lot was that attendance for Global All Hands was low and continuing to drop. When people become disengaged, they also get frustrated. This kind of mood doesn't exactly inspire high performance—in fact, it usually leads to people quitting. Especially in a tough market. So, I went to the CEO staff and said, "*You have an engagement problem. People are not coming to the All Hands. They're not connecting with the vision and the story of the company, and we need to find out why.*" Surveys are the most reliable way to achieve that. Without surveys, management has no way of knowing what people want, what their needs are, or what's going on with them. Were the current employees even happy to be at NetApp? The most recent NetApp engagement survey had been conducted five years before, which led me to ask, *"If we're not listening to the employees, and they're not engaged, how can they be involved in the cultural transformation?"*

We're Flying Blind

I had no idea what the employees wanted except anecdotally. And when all you're listening to is anecdotal, the louder people usually dictate what's considered real and what's not. Or you see a scenario like this: The company has an All Hands meeting, followed by a survey in which a few people answer, and that becomes the "Voice of the Employee." Thus, all the talent strategies would be crafted based on this anecdotal, minority feedback. In the old days, surveys were very data heavy, time consuming, and slow. And then corporate would come down the mountain to report, *"We looked at all the survey data and...here's the program we're giving to you. It solves all your problems!"* This coming from a small group of high-level leaders who, again, were working from that anecdotal information and/or old files.

Without fresh, AI-enabled data from employees, these fragmented, legacy ideas became the data that decisions were based upon. And the more influence you had over the CEO staff? The more your opinions guided decisions. I continued with the staff, *"If you have been here for fifteen years, and you've been successful, and you're viewed as a leader? You're talking to CEO staff and influencing them on what the employees are thinking. Which is probably through your prism. So, you are informing the talent strategy, and if you've been here that long? More than likely, that talent strategy does not include change."*

Now, there are some leaders who will tell you, *"No, this is what our employees want, and this is what they need."* And some may be spot on. Even so, you're not really providing solutions to anyone's problems because every single team has a different issue that they're dealing with. To expect corporate to solve them all and/or each individual one is impossible. In this first year, Year One, which we also called the Year of Execution, we were looking for solutions that would fit the individual. Each employee. I wanted to get a survey in right away because all we had to draw from was anecdotal. Beyond that, I wanted to hear directly from THEM, the employees themselves—and luckily for all of us, AI is making this more possible today. And those people who are influencing CEO staff? It mutes them—or, at least, brings more voices to the table. As you might imagine, not everyone was a fan of this idea because now, we'd really be listening to employees in real-time as opposed to a chosen few with an outsized influence on what staff at large might be thinking and feeling.

After conferring with Debra, I wrote an email to the CEO: "*George, we are all flying blind. We have no idea if our employees are engaged or what they wanna do with their careers. We really don't know anything. And if we can't start getting a better understanding of how talent works in this company? We're gonna lose. AND you're listening to people who are guiding your people decisions who are not listening to the employees. For $19 per employee, you could know for certain whether you have an engagement problem or not!*" Since I was in the midst of a lot of mandated cost-cutting for my department, I was not optimistic regarding how my message would be received. But his response, "*Okay. Great point,*" was a nice surprise. So, I continued,

> *I can't build a comprehensive talent strategy if I don't know what our employees want. I can build off-the-shelf, one-size-fits-all things like every other company does, but it will be very difficult to implement any kind of lasting transformation. If we don't have the voice of the employee, my job's gonna be a lot more of a guessing game—and if we can't engage them in the change, they won't be able to be part of the company story.*

He Said Yes!

My first (ever) Pulse Surveys were actually implemented pre-NetApp, back when I worked at Equinix. While Equinix was more of a sales culture, NetApp was and still is all about the data. You couldn't just sell to them. You had to prove it. So, I said to George,

We can invest in any people strategies you think best, but aren't we a data company? We're trying to be a data-centric company for our customers. We need to be a data-center company for our employees and try a more data-driven approach. An artificial intelligence Pulse Survey will tell us more accurately how the company is feeling and what everyone is thinking. With AI, you don't have to be a data scientist. It does all the work for you. And if we're going to reach our goal of high-performing teams, we need to have the real data.

Then I got down to it. "*I need $300,000 to get a Glint survey.*" George's response was: "*Yep! Makes sense.*" Just like that. To be in a data company and be able to show data? It was a language NetApp leadership readily understood. And so, they told me, "*Okay, yeah, go do it.*" And that was how we got funding for our Year One Glint survey (internally referred to as the Thrive Pulse Survey). That green light changed everything. It was the crowbar that opened my door and the first AI we brought to NetApp, but that was also just the beginning. Like these surveys, "*All the tech investments that followed were driven out of the cases that we built around them,*" EM recounts. "*And they were really great investments. They were very needed because the HR technology was outdated.*"

On September 17, 2019, fresh off our late-August launch of Thrive, we ran our first bi-annual, internal employee Thrive Pulse Survey. The survey results, from this and all those that followed, the Voice of the Employee, drove our talent strategy and, later, our Thrive Everywhere decisions. In retrospect, it's hard to imagine being successful with our plans without having had this essential input.

What Is a Pulse Survey?

As its name suggests, Pulse Surveys are brief, regular sets of questions asked of employees (anonymously), designed to be carried out at regular intervals to gain employees' views on subjects such as engagement, alignment to the company goals, communication, or whatever you feel is most important to hear about from them. Surveys alone are pretty common in corporate life. Everyone in the industry uses Pulse Surveys. It's *how* that data is used that can differentiate you. Our objectives were more targeted than what's typically available. Big picture, we wanted our Thrive Pulse Surveys to bring the shift from corporate-level to relevant, *team-specific* feedback and replace cumbersome action plans with personalized, high-impact recommendations.

Historically, you might ask over one hundred questions per survey or so (in order to cast a wide net), and HR would often be on the hook for the laborious task of processing the responses—a grueling, data-harvesting procedure. HR workers aren't data scientists! Instead of some high-level, in-depth analysis, HR was drowning in too much information. It was a slog by any measure; the best hope was to eke out some bottom-line trends in the end. Results usually arrived after a long lag time (sometimes extending to months or even years)—and the analysis was very much about top-down action planning. Before AI and advanced technology began to do much of the data analysis inside Pulse Surveys, managers were left with the task of analysis.

Companies would also often use the Pulse Survey results to grade the manager. Bad results mean a bad manager? That's simply not true. So many factors go into Pulse results, including company culture, business performance, and bad news in the industry. We wanted to know which internal, external, and manager issues are causing these results. The only way to do that is to ask the right questions and ask for anonymous, authentic answers. Then, it is up to the team and manager to work together to improve their results together. The second a manager thinks they will be judged on the results and not encouraged to see it as a learning and growth opportunity? The purpose of the survey erodes. And bad behavior can creep in. Managers may then try to influence the team to submit more positive, desirable answers instead of truthful ones. Employees start to see the tool as another wedge between them and the manager or team. In the end the survey becomes useless. That's why one of the most important questions on any survey is responses to: "*I believe action will be taken with the results of this survey.*" If employees don't believe that to be true, trust begins to falter.

Alternatively, we believe that employees and managers should work together, with quality data and real-time feedback. This piece of the strategy enhances overall improved performance. It means re-humanizing the manager-employee relationship (the 1st quadrant on the Wheel) while strengthening the manager-to-team relationship (2nd quadrant)—by boosting team effectiveness and high performance through the Pulse results. Given the general pre-tech history with Pulse Surveys, we needed a completely new approach. This next generation of AI-driven surveys provided precisely the opportunity we were looking for. It's a new paradigm for more precisely measuring employee experience (in real time) and taking action—and has become another component of the Golden Thread, capable of removing yet another layer of unwelcome friction from that most essential employee-manager relationship.

Choose Enabling Partnerships

There are many companies out there now providing AI-enabled Pulse Surveys (such as Glint and Perceptyx). No matter who you pick, be sure you've got an *engaged* partner. For the surveys to be effective, they need to be part of your larger strategy—not just off the shelf. (That's true for this and any third-party technologies you might bring in.) The more involved and educated your team is on how these surveys work, the more training and outreach they're able to conduct, the more employees will do them, and the more accurate and applicable the results will be.

You want a hands-on partner. One who will come in and do walk-throughs with your executives or help you put decks together and other assets as you broadcast out to the company. Self-serve is an option but isn't as effective as folding your third-party survey partner into your larger campaign. Anne Fulton of Fuel50, one of the terrific partners we had at NetApp, speaks well to our shared philosophy around what it means to be a good business partner.

We've always believed in having a deep partnership. Across my business, there's multiple touch points into the NetApp business. Wonderful working relationships with support going two ways…. So, I and a number of my other team members have done speaking engagements and education…and also enabled some of the NetApp people to continue to tell their story. So we'll help them power up. So there's a knowledge transfer to be able to support the mindset shift in the business. So it's self-sustaining. Then we don't have to come in and do that workshop for the next twenty years. There's multiple people that are enabled and supported across NetApp to be able to do that now. A true partnership. An enabling partnership.

AI: Seeing the Unseen

AI is exploding now, as is Generative AI, but in 2019, AI-enabled technology solutions were just beginning to arrive. Especially for high-volume data processing. Even then, the survey tools popping up were powerful game changers for us. Now, there are AI and neurolinguistic processing reports that can tell you specifically as a team (for example): *Here's the one thing you need to work on to make your team better.* The benefits of using such tools are obvious. For those of us in the business of talent enablement (as in so many other aspects of work and life), AI-enabled technologies provide a global step change in what's possible for performance and talent management for workforces across the world. And with it comes the opportunity to re-evaluate management philosophies such as the ones we were newly deploying at NetApp.

Our view, then and now, is that technology exists in service of human relationships. It democratizes information, gets you to the human relationship faster, and puts the survey data into everyone's hands. Not just the corporate leadership. Technology aided us in our campaign to democratize and enable. Our current surveys do all the data processing for us, as well as spit out AI-synthesized insights and recommendations. It processes all the comments, formulates results on current sentiments, and can direct you to high-priority actions based on the full spectrum of data. Below are a few of the benefits listed in our pitch deck for the 2019 Pulse Surveys.

PULSE SURVEY STRATEGIC OBJECTIVES

- Create the conditions for high-performing teams
- Provide measurable, data-driven snapshots into employee engagement
- Inform decisions that improve the employee experience
- Drive manager impact and effectiveness
- Enable joint accountability-localized action at the manager and team level
- Focus on growth and development
- Easy: Only twenty-six questions and takes ten minutes
- Inclusive: Available in eight languages

Data In Your Hands!

Specifically, the Pulse Survey results were designed to be much more user-friendly—for everybody. The surveys themselves are short, statistically valid, and focused. You no longer have to pour over all the details. The AI processes the data and delivers it to you. The results? Immediate. And best of all, you can directly disseminate the results to the managers and their teams. We choose to put the Pulse Survey answers in the team's *hands*, not just corporate at the top. True democratization. We told them, "*You have it! There's the data. The AI's handing it to you. Work on it.*" True enablement. As I always say: "*Artificial intelligence speeds you up to the real human connection.*" This process accelerated managers' ability to develop and turn their groups into high-performing teams.

Survey #1: Engaged...or Not?

Our first survey had only twenty-six questions, which focused on engagement. Of those twenty-six, the two key questions were: *Are you happy to come to work? Would you recommend someone to come work here?* Both questions have been scientifically proven to determine whether the employee was engaged. So basically, all the other questions were measured against those two. These tech-based surveys were much shorter than they traditionally were (they take ten minutes max) because, with AI, you don't need a lot of questions to triangulate the results. The AI triangulates for you. (And if it's not a long slog, more employees might even take the time to fill them out!) Yes, the survey was always optional, but employees started to get that we actually planned on DOING something with the results. *"It was something that was exciting to employees,"* shares McKenna. *"I still like participating…because you get to have a voice, in a sense. And the questions are tailored to relevant events at the time."*

We're Not Data Scientists

The survey output includes answers plus comments. Let's say, for example, the AI connects answers to question #17 to the two main questions and is able to tell you what's more impactful and what's not—something we were never able to do in the past. Instead of a (potentially poorly qualified) human, AI does the analyzing. As humans, we'll never fail to draw conclusions, but there's no guarantee those conclusions are going to be useful.

An HR employee might look at the lowest score and say, *"Let's go fix that."* While the AI might instead say, *"Even though it's the lowest score, it may not be the most important. And it may not have the biggest impact on engagement."* In other words, it provided an accurate correlation analysis. Or it might say, *"It's your lowest score, but it's only medium impact to engagement."* Meaning it only *sort of* matters, even though it's the lowest. Then it might also say, *"But this one that's fifth lowest is reporting as having high impact and is dragging down engagement."* So, these low scores may reflect something managers don't like, but at the end of the day, it's not really impacting anything. (For example, a worker might say, *"I don't think we do X well, but I'm happy here."*) Meaning, on the scale of things to address, nothing necessarily needs to be done about "X." So, don't work on it. Work on other things. This is where AI is so impactful. Humans alone wouldn't have the computing power to deliver parallel results.

Every time you do the survey, those impacts are different. And only AI can do that. We, as humans using the old systems, would have to look through THOUSANDS of comments and then try to figure out which is more important. With AI, the survey spits out such results as, "*It may be your lowest, but it doesn't matter to people as much as your fourth lowest. That one really bothers them. And that's the one you should work on,*" Or "*Here's the only ten comments you need to worry about.*" (Oh, my god, *Thank you!*)

In addition to survey question answers, the platform provides for comments as well. It reviews what's been entered (even if in a foreign language), analyzes, and provides synthesized results. If you like word bubbles, it can tell you, "*This is all you need to care about. Don't go read every comment and dismiss them like you used to do.*" (Ha, ha, just kidding.) It would distill down the input from the employees and produce these specifics for you. The biggest issue we uncovered recently, for example, was working nights and weekends. That was the largest "read" we saw across eight thousand employees. So, the AI tries to guide you to what's most relevant for the issues that the majority of the company cares about (right now). The issues that, if addressed, will have the greatest positive impact for both the employees and the company.

Moving Nine Hundred Needles

So, who then gets this AI-derived data, and what gets done with the Pulse Survey results, exactly? The manager-employee relationship is central to this ecosystem we call Thrive. And we want managers to be problem-solving at that *team* level, where this democratization of data enables teams to directly improve their circumstances. The process was done in the spirit of avoiding what had so often happened in the past—you get survey results, the powers-that-be go off and come up with this whole plan that takes six months to execute, and then nothing ever really gets addressed. Plus, instead of the data slog we dealt with old-time surveys, we had one person connected to the survey who worked with the vendor to make sure that all that AI-processed data got distributed out and was presented in a form that distilled what was relevant and reported what the most important scores were. The analysis was done for everyone. And the results were in everybody's hands—the day it was available. So, they got it and could review it together, and then everyone could go to work on it at the same time. I always say, "*You want me as the HR guy trying to move this giant needle for the whole company of Pulse results? Or do I want nine hundred managers moving nine hundred needles that fit them, fit their suit, their clothes, their fingerprints?*"

1-2-3 Go!

One of our key aspirations was to establish methods for divisions, teams, and managers to make progress on their own internal challenges. Each manager would get their own report. HR wouldn't be the manager's data analyst, but neither would the manager. It came predigested by the vendor, already in a form that told them what the most important scores were. Providing this kind of data on a regular schedule was a potent game changer. The data would come in, and we would say, "*Here's your own report. And you'll get your own impacts. Do something. We want you and your team to tackle your problems. It's in your hands.*" But we also didn't want the manager tackling this solo. That would just reinforce yet another divisive employee-manager tension point—and be the opposite of what we were trying to accomplish. Instead, we laid out a game plan, an outline with a timeline and our expectations. We called them *1-2-3 actions.*

Here's the process: Four survey responses go directly to the manager and their team. Every six months, when the results came in, we'd say to them: "*Okay here's four Pulse Survey responses. You and your team work together. Pick one thing to work on, take two actions, and communicate three times—and work on it as a team. We'll see you in six months with the next survey.*" No need to try to boil the ocean anymore, right? Just one, two, three. That's it! Select one Pulse Survey insight, commit to two actions, and communicate progress three times for accountability and team improvement. This immediately creates a better one-on-one relationship with the employee and their manager and a better team relationship. There's an enterprise-wide mindset and development for the future. Data, Alignment, and Action. Accountability—and results. Here's an example of how we partnered with Perceptyx at Equinix to drive easy improvement planning (which I later took to NetApp):

1-2-3 (Global Talent) Action Plan
Our commitment to driving the right behaviors and outcomes.

One Insight
Barriers to execution: Multiple reports, decks, and ad hoc requests are time-consuming and seem redundant.

Two Actions
a. Reduce and consolidate the number, frequency, and repository of reports.
b. Begin each reporting cycle with cherry-picked topic areas and then request the input (so all input gets used).

Three Check-Ins
Target action item three times to check in on the status before the next Pulse Survey.

So then the team has to take action on their chosen insight. Because they've picked it, it makes them all the more invested in the outcome. It becomes their focus until they report that the action's been taken and the task is complete. The issue resolved and the point reinforced (whatever reflects the right outcome). This process of 1-2-3 actions is completely different from anything that's gone on before. "*Other companies will do employee surveys,*" McKenna shares. "*But do they actually sit there and do a deep dive on the results at the team level, like our company does? And then take those results, share them with the employees, and then actually try to take action on whatever came out of it? I don't think there's a lot of companies that do that.*" Perhaps not.

The CEO staff have 1-2-3 actions as well. At NetApp, each CEO staff sat down with their teams. "*One issue that got discussed,*" shares McKenna (in her role working for multiple leaders across HR simultaneously), "*was cross-functional collaboration. There were some areas we were lacking, and the Pulse results showed that we needed to step our game up in this area.*"

Our survey process would get mapped on the calendar so there'd be no surprises. The whole company would know what to expect and when. First, Debra and I would do our pre-read to digest the results. The reports (created by Glint) were first shared with me, in deck form, of the breakdown. It's a deeper dive into what the numbers and comments mean. What the trend is. All that stuff. (This is what I meant by the need to have a good partner.) We'd meet with George and CEO staff to review top-line trends and determine what we want to focus on before releasing the results to all managers for team planning.

Then there'd be a discussion at the global company All Hands, followed by an email (often from Debra) summarizing the high-level results with a message along these lines: "*We hear you. We see you. This is what we saw. This is what we're gonna do.*" Then we'd disseminate data to leadership, managers, and teams. It was not filtered or sugar-coated. Transparency and authenticity lead to the tough conversations, which lead to faster, better results. So, we showed everyone—the managers, the teams, the CEO staff, and the whole company the good, the bad, and the ugly of the Pulse Survey results. Not just the good stuff. Full transparency. If there were problems or challenges, everybody was going to know about it. In NetApp's case, we let them know, "*We're having various execution problems here, and it starts at the top.*"

Survey's In!

We're now two years into the process, and each time survey results come in, it's a full-court press. Everybody's working on it. CEO staff is focused on their own team results and the larger company trends. Each team is working on theirs—and managers are free to contact the survey staff directly, should they require more detail or guidance on how to interpret data. Over those two years, some teams began asking for more data, and that was when we knew the wheels were really rolling. Ask or not, the central premise remains the same: The managers receive their results, sit down with their team to discuss, and then come up with a plan as a team to address their chosen topic with velocity. 1-2-3 action. Speed and direction. Using the process, they can effect changes locally in ways that best suit their needs.

Bots Won't Ruin the World

Year One was just getting people's brains out of the traditional mindset and going toward QCs and the Pulse Survey. People needed time to absorb and process such big changes. And that was why, during that first All Hands meeting in August 2019, I mentioned a few key points such as, "*I want you to focus on your relationship with your employees and your manager and not focus on filling out forms. Who wants to fill out forms, right?*" I repeated over and over, "*Technology gets you to the table faster and better. It gets you to the conversation, and that's when managers, employees, and teams take over. Nothing will ever replace the table. Pulse Surveys and AI technology speed up the ability for you to get to the real human conversation.*"

It may be less so today (or way more, depending on your perspective), but a few years ago, some people were afraid that the bots would take over the world! At the time, it was a big change management obstacle, to be sure. I often said things to people like, "*All right. The bots aren't coming to take your jobs. Science fiction movies have made it seem like it, but they're not, right? Think about pilots, for example. They're not really flying the aircraft most of the time, right? Technology is. The pilot is just keeping an eye on it. That's what autopilot is, right? They take off and land. That's about all. The repetitive, low-value activities are really what AI is designed to be best at. So you can do bigger, better things. Make us smarter and get quicker, not be less in control. And what is growth mindset? You need a growth mindset to adopt new technologies. And they're all designed to enhance the employee experience.*"

20 · Enterprise-Wide Mindset

Driving Results Through Enterprise-Wide Thinking

From our first team meeting, the enterprise-wide mindset was already top of mind for the CEO staff. Too often, at the average company, people talk and talk about enterprise-wide goals in group meetings, and then everyone just goes back to their own siloed little worlds. That was why Talent Career Week, the NetApp Business School, our Silo-Busting-in-a-Box workshop, and the pre-existing Breakthrough Leadership Program were included in the three-year plan of the larger cultural transformation strategy. The third part of the Wheel: Activate the Enterprise. The mindset we wanted? Think like an owner.

To create an environment where the decisions your employees and teams make work together for the benefit of the entire company? What leadership team wouldn't want this? How do you cultivate this more progressive mindset, really? How do you get your leaders in particular thinking with an enterprise hat? I won't kid you; it's very difficult to do. We made a conscious effort to highlight this during our long campaign.

For the employees, democratization of information is one key in the process. Invite everyone into the conversations about the business and financial sides of your company. Enable all the employees to become more educated and engaged with business operations, provide opportunities to teach them about business, and embed opportunities for cross-conversations between business units. By giving access, you're enabling employees, managers, and teams to think and act for themselves. They grow more invested in the outcomes of the companies in which they work and are willing to have more skin in the game. *"Think of yourself as an OWNER of the entire company, not just your little budget and P and L"* is what I often tell managers and employees alike. Having this enterprise-wide mindset, thinking about making decisions that benefit the enterprise and not just you and your team, is another component of the Golden Thread and another key to change.

Data, Alignment, Action

Eventually, the expression "high-performing teams" became more about having an *owner's mindset* and enterprise-wide mindset. Meaning high-performing teams *across* teams. Improving collaboration to optimize for the enterprise. For this kind of transformation, it's important to tackle from the top of the organization and why enterprise-wide mindset is a key component of the Wheel and the cultural transformation.

Nobody's Gonna Read That

I visited a customer recently and, while waiting my turn to speak, I noticed their values on the wall, such as *Respect Each Other, Grow Together*. But I didn't get the impression this group was particularly aligned. I raised my hand and asked the CHRO, *"Can I just interrupt for a sec?"* She said, *"Sure, go ahead."* I said, *"The way I see it, there's really two kinds of cultures. There's one where it's about: How do we treat each other? How do we expect to be treated?"*

I then suggested that the second type is an *operational* culture and that it's important to bring these values off their walls and into their work lives. To take action and ask questions such as *Are you hiring to these values? How are you evaluating each other?* In an operational culture, the question that is asked is *How do you work together to make decisions, communicate, align, and be accountable?* The truth is most companies suck at this. They're usually good at it with product. And maybe the finance part. But when it comes to building enterprise-wide thinking, they often fall behind. I continued, *"And you putting things on the walls or in teams' chat? Or a blog? No one's gonna read it. Nobody cares. Information doesn't matter. It's Data, Alignment, and Action. That has to happen. You need all three."*

That is the point of exercises such as Silo-Busting-in-a-Box and Dash. Both are designed to cultivate an enterprise-wide mindset. Both are about Data, Alignment, and Action. You've got the data—you share, discuss, compare, stay up to date with what others in the company are doing and working on, and take action based on the totality of that shared information. You then know that what you're doing works for your team but is also aligned with what the larger enterprise needs and wants in that moment.

Then I told them about Dash. About when I first came to Silicon valley, I worked for a medical device company called ADAC. ADAC labs. And we made nuclear medicine equipment. This nuclear medicine was either inhaled or injected with very small parts of radioactivity that went to a certain part of your body and lit it up. Brain. Lungs. Heart. Then the camera read that. It's primarily to find tumors. We were this super small, 3,000 person medical device company competing against Phillips, GE, and Siemens. Three huge international companies. The way that we thought we could beat them was with speed (velocity). We had to be faster than them because they're big boats. We're a small boat. We should be able to turn faster than them. So every quarter we would have what we call *Dash*. (Dash meant two things. This was 1999, and the meetings were quarterly so "99-1," as in "ninety-nine dash one," then two, then three, then four. And secondly, everyone's dashing around madly before that big meeting to get their stuff straight before they present!)

These meetings were powerful. They would happen over the course of 2½ days every quarter, during which the CEO would come up and give the State of the Union. And then the head of sales would talk about where we're winning, why we're losing, what customers are saying. Then marketing would say, "*Here is what we're planning for next year and why, and here's the data we're using. And here's what we're trying to convince.*" Then engineering would come up, and so on.

Part of that meeting would include what was called your Vital Few. The CEO would ask the sales guy, "*What's the Vital Few for sales for this year? And what are your MITs (most important tasks) for this quarter?*" And sales would show it. Everyone who got up there would say, "*Here's what I'm gonna deliver.*" That way, everyone would be accountable, transparent, and aligned every quarter. It would all be put out there every quarter. As you can imagine, there was a lot of opportunity for alignment here. Sharing information. Avoiding waste, misunderstanding, miscommunication, and lost time. The whole company would be working in sync. Made sense, right? But more often than not, companies don't do this well.

I completed my story to this group by saying, "*Honestly, that's a muscle most companies don't have. And if everyone in this room [it was all VPs] did this once a quarter? And you stood up and said, 'Here's my goals.' And this person said, 'I thought one of my goals was one of your goals,' and they re-*

sponded, 'No, I dropped that ball,' to which the first person replied, 'You never told me.' Just like that, you're instantly aligned! That instant! As opposed to going a whole year and then asking, 'Whatever happened to that project?' Just to hear someone answer, 'Oh, I killed it six months ago.'" That's a hard muscle to build, but it's also one of the greatest things I learned when I first got to Silicon Valley. When tasked with improving company culture, a lot of companies simply put money into a fresh marketing campaign, and I just don't believe in it. Operational culture; Data, Alignment, and Action; and enterprise-wide mindset are stronger positions to embrace. That's Dash. The purest form of strategy democratization I've ever been involved in. That version of the method was also a very specific, intense thing that we did at ADAC. But it could take many forms to suit your environment.

Silo-Busting

At NetApp, when I first came in, my team and I invented what we called Silo-Busters. Where we got people in a room and made sure they were wearing a sticker that said their name, their department, and a question that they would need help solving. We had seven stickers and, in a round-robin, people just walked around and talked to seven different people. Specifically, people they didn't already know. As in, not in their department. And they were told to say, "*Hey, I'm having a problem with this. What is your suggestion?*" And they might say later, "*Oh my God, I would never think to go to someone in finance and ask them about this question. But that guy had the best advice for me.*" So, that was our first foray into cultivating more of an enterprise-wide mindset. Then we turned that into an activity any employee could do on their own! All they had to do was go to the website and download—something any team could do. We called it Silo-Busting-in-a-Box.

Emily had done similar things during former marketing leadership meetings. "*We did simulation games...and that was an amazing experience because I got to meet people from other departments. I met leaders from other divisions,* and it was awesome! Some I have stayed friends with for a long time... *So, Larry and Debra did bring in those great opportunities... I've sent a lot of my team to meet with people from other departments. It's that kind of glue that's working and creates that enterprise mindset."*

21 · Owner's Mindset

Earnings Calls: Giving People Agency

At Equinix, I invited an investor relations liaison to come speak at one of our All-HR offsites. Her topic? Earnings calls. What they're about, how they prepare for them, what they mean. You know, the meeting where the CFO talks about earnings last quarter, and the head of sales talks about what customers want, and you get to learn, *specifically,* how the business works. The liaison addressed topics such as, *"What's the street after? What do they ask us? This is what matters."* is the kind of thing she spoke about. Engaging in these is the ultimate in democratization for the employee. And guess what? In the five years of hosting offsites, she was the highest-rated guest speaker we ever had. People's reactions were fantastic. *"Wow, I never knew all this went on,"* or *"I never knew I could be allowed this information!"* were the kinds of responses we got. Instead of employees thinking, *I'm just gonna go do my job,* they began saying, *"Wow, how cool is it to know this? I'm hearing about the business. I'm gonna start listening to the earnings calls."*

But the most powerful upshot for our audience was that it uncovered a thing generally kept secret for *no* reason. Every chance I get, I encourage employees to listen to earnings calls. They're public—anyone can listen (a lot of people don't know this). I tell them, *"Here's why you should be listening, and here's what you should be listening for."* By encouraging staff to jump on, the message is *"No, you should care about what analysts and customers think about this company."* It gives people agency to care. Feeling and knowing that they're part of it.

It's surprisingly easy to turn people's minds around that: *"Yes, you really are a businessperson. You're not just in HR, product development, or engineering."* If you're *not* doing this, I think you're missing a giant opportunity. It's a chance for management to trust that anyone in the organization can really get that kind of information. And it's an opportunity for every employee to feel it's their right to access and engage with it. This is when alignment happens. Cultivating enterprise-wide mindset through democratization of information. Once invited in, people want to know what's going in. Think about it. They're already invested—they work there! Then, when you have that next All Hands meeting, they may actually show up for it—and may even really care about what you're saying. They'll be more engaged—and will connect the dots around how these decisions directly affect them and the company.

NetApp Business School: Aligning Talent with Strategy

Hosting an earnings call inspired me to pursue this idea of doing a business school at my next company. If you're a shareholder, that's *literally* for you, right? You own a fraction of the company and are invested in its performance. That's an owner's mindset. When you're seeking to align talent with the business strategy and address questions such as *Do you really understand how this business works? How our customers look at us?*, a great, all-encompassing solution could be to create a business school. One specifically tailored for *your* company and your particular business circumstances, today. In our case, the focus was (obviously) going to be NetApp business.

Because leadership is highly contextual, right? It's different in every organization—if you're worked at a few you know. For me it was very different at NetApp, Citi, and Equinix. You've got to be mindful of that when you're setting up these programs and providing a learning experience about *your* business. That's why our business school was going to be *homegrown*. All companies of a certain size should consider providing one. The built-from-within kind, with employees with the skills and insights to offer classes and workshops for other employees. So, in the meetings, the CFO would talk about earnings, but we differentiated by having the product development manager step up and talk about how the product road map works here, what decisions they make, and why.

Again, it goes back to the original Dash I did when I first got to Silicon Valley—where you're in a room watching every group provide updates so all the attendees can instantly see how everything ties together. With Dash, you literally sit in on the meeting as an employee, becoming privy to decisions and prioritization. In real time. I still think Dash is the purest form of strategic democratization I've ever come across, but a school could become an expanded version of this. A chance for employees to do deeper dives into business operations across sectors and divisions and get a chance to see how their role fits into the bigger picture. (Launching this school was part of our original three-year agenda and one of the initiatives we were building toward when the pandemic hit. COVID, however, put the kibosh on our plans.)

22 · Training: A Misnomer of Growth

I'm not a training organization,
I'm an enablement organization.

I was once asked if I followed any particular style of leadership training in the course of my career. The truth is, whatever leadership abilities I might possess are just part of who I am. I think it's just the way I interact with people. With leadership, there's no one right way. You could read a hundred leadership books, and you may learn tips and tricks about certain things, right? But how you interact with humans is the most powerful leadership training there is. That's why I don't promote leadership competencies. A lot of companies have them and say, "*All leaders must act like this.*" But I—or you—might respond, "*But I don't wanna act like that. That's not who I am.*" So, how can I tell everyone in this company, "*This is what leadership looks like,*" when every fingerprint is different? No two people are alike. That's why we give training that's situational. As in, "*Here's the unique situation you might have to face.*

What would you do? Let's talk pros and cons." It's based on the circumstances of the moment, as opposed to: *"Act like this no matter what!"*

You might then ask, *"But what about early-in-career managers with potential?"* Wouldn't you want to guide them? Yes—and that's part of the reason for this book. To show you all the elements of Thrive vs. a more generic Leadership 101 kind of package. Having said that, off-the-shelf training can definitely be helpful for brand new managers. The kind of general leadership training that can apply to anyone. And maybe for early career folks as well. It can be a good guide, sets a baseline and gives them an idea of how to approach leadership. But for ongoing growth, it's much more effective to teach people what to do to be successful "here and now"—as in at *this* specific company, in *this* specific industry, at this particular time.

For example, if we're saying (and we are saying), *"You should be doing these Quarterly Conversations on growth."* We're definitely going to give you a bunch of experiences, *basic* training, and tools so you can have those QCs—so everyone is doing them the same way. Let's say, you're doing quick surveys. What's the easiest way to take this survey data? Share it with your team? Build on it? Here's what we do: demo it, workshop it, show you videos, offer examples, sit down and walk through it with you, outline it in emails…whatever it takes. In other words, at NetApp, we're showing how to be successful with the tools here, at NetApp. With these company-specific and newly installed QCs and Pulse Surveys. How young managers go about that with their team in terms of style or tone? That's up to them.

Bazooka Joe Tattoos

Training can also mean different things. When you need to teach a new tool, you can just throw employees into a class, and you're fine. It works if you want to learn how to use WordPress or develop a tangible skill such as working with spreadsheets or creating presentations. But if your plan is to take a two-week training class to learn how to be a leader, don't expect it to stick. It doesn't work like that. You don't get a high-performing team by sending people to training either.

Let's revisit what the ultimate objective was for NetApp: moving from storage to the cloud. In business, that's two entirely different sets of skills. And two entirely different sets of mindsets of people to sell to. I knew that how we looked at talent and how we grew talent had to change. And I got told a lot: "*We believe the primary thing we need is high-performing teams. Teams that work together to grow and transform this business.*" The next thing everyone usually says, once they have an idea about what to do with talent is "*Let's have high-performing team training sessions for everyone!*" And I don't believe in training by itself. In my view, training alone is a misnomer of growth.

Here's an analogy. If someone goes to a training where behavior change is the desired outcome, they may try, but it's sort of like a Bazooka Joe tattoo or one of those other old bubble gum tattoos. It goes on blurry and lasts about two days. That's all you get out of that training unless you're super-duper motivated. The next level is to have a team or division of people who are really committed to learning. And they return to work trying very earnestly to bring that training with them, offering such declarations as, "*We are gonna try to all hold each other accountable…*" That goes on like a henna tattoo. It's clearer, beautiful, and can last weeks or months. But eventually, even it collapses under the weight of the organization because that team or division is the only one doing it. That one might stick a little longer than individual training, but the investment probably isn't worth it.

So, in response to companies such as NetApp who have told me, "*Let's do leadership training,*" or "*Let's do training on this or that,*" I always respond with, "*Throwing people through training is not the answer.*" Because when companies talk about training, they usually mean setting up a course, which people attend and then leave. In some magic way, they're now supposed to be better at their jobs. Again, if you need to learn Excel, go train for it. That's just a skill, and you can readily apply it. But behavior change is very difficult. So, after I mention my Bazooka Joe tattoo analogy, I continue, "*Instead of offering training, I'm gonna change the name of my team to Talent Enablement. I'm gonna enable you, starting with Quality Conversations and Pulse Surveys and an understanding of how that works.*" My goal is to give everybody everything they need to go do things for themselves. And I mean everybody.

Behavior Change = Permanent Tattoos

If I can get everyone in the organization to do something the same way—all doing Quarterly Conversations and Pulse Surveys? If everyone's doing that? That's the permanent tattoo. I have now changed the behavior of the organization because *everybody's* doing it. (Another good reason not to pilot transformation.) All this aligns with part of my continuous messaging, "*I'm not a training organization. I'm an enablement organization.*"

And now (Year Four), instead of training (for example), we started Manager Enablement sessions. "*Hey guys, come on along if you want. We're gonna talk about how to have a great Quarterly Conversation, what the purpose of it is, and how you do it. Why don't you guys go into breakout rooms and talk about how you're doing it and how it was a great experience and engage them in this change?*" as opposed to training them on what's going on. That's how to differentiate. They are doing for themselves. (By the way, we don't make any of these trainings mandatory. Think velvet rope. We didn't force anyone to take a leadership experience—and my general philosophy is, only build things people want to be a part of!) I would tell them not to expect training—we are rolling out a framework that will be accompanied by tools to help you be a better enterprise-wide thinker, build your own high-performing team, and be accountable for this—so you will be enabled to run with it. Through this system, we're saying to the managers, "*This is your team. And we trust you to manage your team.*"

This situation's a bit more complex, right? You're not teaching anyone a new tool; you're asking people to change their mindsets. And letting them know that the way they've managed before is not gonna happen anymore. This can take some getting used to. Vicky recalls a manager or two from one particular QC training asking, "*So when are we gonna get the guidelines? When are we gonna get the brackets?*" Though she kept telling them, "*There are none,*" it didn't always penetrate right away. And that's okay. It's sort of like taking the training wheels off. They were looking for the guidelines. Specifics. We call it a *guardrail*. But there aren't any in this new system. Some then asked, "*So, I can just make decisions? I can just decide?!*" She said, "*Yes!*" To which they still asked, "*Do I need to get approval?*" We let them know that they really could manage their own teams now, and if someone came to them with a question, they were free to field it themselves.

All Levers Need to be Pulled

Again, you don't build a high-performance team by attending training (or trialing with a pilot), but high-performing teams also don't build themselves. This happens in real time, on the job while you work with your team. You build these teams by consciously putting effort into leading individual employees well (playing to their strengths and then *aligning* those strengths, along with each person's talent and interests, with meaningful work), leading your team well (understanding how to weave the collective strengths and gaps together so that the whole is stronger than the parts), having regular Pulse Surveys on the team's health (and understanding the broader organizational ecosystem your team operates within), and by building formal and informal networks for individuals and teams across the business. It's about an amalgamation of all these small and large things. All the levers need to be pulled to truly have a high-performing team. And that can only happen if those doing the pulling are thinking broadly, with an enterprise-wide mindset.

SECTION 6

The End of the Rainbow

We really had a pretty big campaign going on,
a storytelling campaign.

S o, what makes someone prepared for change? More than work or life experience, I'd say it comes from mindset. People often resist change because they can't imagine a transformed future. So, I said to the team, "*This is the end side of the rainbow. Help me figure out how we're gonna get people there.*" Vicky brought so many great ideas. "*Well, before we even do any planning,*" she'd said, "*let's all get in a meeting and talk about that futuristic pot of gold.*" That way, the vision, and any problems with it, could get flushed out. She had us start at the end and work backward. And that's exactly what we did. EM and Vicky had already worked closely for many years. EM offered, "*She really brought her change management expertise, addressing how we were gonna make this happen. This massive, large-scale change across the organization.*"

23 · The Change Narrative

Though Vicky's background is in industrial organizational psychology, she often says, "*It's really understanding organizational life,*" and ensuring that any change management she embarks upon aligns with the goals and strategies of the business. With considerations, of course, for external factors and new research. Especially neuroscience. And her influence on our approach included both art and science. This really resonated with me. She would often say, "*You need to bring people with you to make the change.*" So, when you're trying to implement change, you need to build a compelling narrative so they can imagine themselves being part of the journey.

Or maybe even build their own. In other words, you're not selling the tool, you're going to sell the story. A change story. And I think that is the gist of it, essentially.

So, what was our story? It encapsulated the Thrive vision. The Wheel. Transforming the employee-manager relationship. Embracing the latest technologies and an owner's mindset. Moving with velocity. Enablement. People Powered, Data Driven. In so many ways, NetApp's call to build high-performing teams—this particular challenge—had many layers to it. It was complex. In change management, they identified three levels. The first was organizational. Like a restructuring or a product change such as NetApp's pivot to the cloud. The second was at the team level—how people work together. Their norms and practices. And third was the individual level, as in *me as a single person*, asking such questions as, *How do I do more? How can I be better, more efficient? How can I grow my career?*

This change with NetApp encompassed all three. Like three quadrants of the wheel. At the organizational, team, and individual levels. That's why it was a bit complicated. The changes are simple when you introduce a new tool and new technology. You're just switching from one tool to another for the same task. Super straightforward. But this? We're talking about culture change. About mindset, how we reward people, and how we look at performance as a company. How a manager manages the team and assesses performance within the team. And then, with individuals, how they receive feedback. So, again, all three elements.

This was nothing short of a massive, large-scale cultural transformation across the company. Not something you could pilot, as I've mentioned. Gotta jump in with both feet. We had to build a big campaign. A storytelling campaign. It was also part political, part marketing (although some change management professionals might balk at this characterization)—the whole enchilada. This happened along with the launch of an internal brand: Thrive. Basically "*We planned it as an internal mar-comm campaign,*" shared Lisa.

The Case for Change

To begin, we had to build our case for change. Many clear steps are required in this evolutionary process. First, you have to demonstrate what's not working in the current situation—and how it's not working for the company. In many ways, this was built in because I was hired to address a pre-existing challenge. Even so, it was important to reframe it in our own way. EM and I produced this. Second, you need the right executive sponsorship. We had that with George and Debra, but a campaign was required for all additional outreach. Your stakeholders. Your committees, the work groups, and work councils. Third, you need the right solution. Meaning, how, exactly, are you going to fix the problem? Our answer was the Thrive Ecosystem for High-Performing Teams. Our Wheel. We deployed many strategies on this front, which essentially is what this book is about. And finally, you have to sell it. To the stakeholders, leadership, and the people. Sell them on WHY your answer is the right one.

Our first step was to go to the CEO staff with our case. Lisa, Vicky, and the team helped me put together that story and the messages. Again, ours was not about bringing a tool but about the whole picture. The Golden Thread. Systemic change to the full ecosystem. We presented the challenge before us in this slide:

Net App has a strong culture with employees who care deeply about doing the right thing for our customers, partners, communities, and each other. And yet:

- As we've grown, we've become more siloed, less agile, slow to evolve, and risk averse.
- Our people strategies have lagged behind the market and haven't provided employees with the experiences that allow them to grow, develop, and challenge themselves.
- We must evolve our approach to talent to create a nimble, agile, forward-thinking NetApp where everyone understands their stake in the business.
- To ensure NetApp's success, we need a talent ecosystem that drives performance at the individual and organizational levels.

We Believe

The centerpiece for my presentation would be, as usual, a slide deck. There was one key slide that really reflected our solution to the list above. The Talent Enablement slide, which we worked particularly hard on. It had fifteen boxes, kind of like *Hollywood Squares*. Vicky had been thinking of all the elements that needed to be included for this massive transformation to move forward. We needed videos, graphics, All Hands meetings, the QC trifold, manager deep dives—everything. Each box addressed a different aspect of this massive campaign we were developing. Storytelling would be at the center but also politics—in the good sense. Because it was based in research and facts. My team pulled out all the stops to fill these squares because they were genuinely excited and wanted to be sure my pitch was bulletproof. I was so moved by Vicky's perspective here: *"For me…we had a lot of the marketing elements to it, but we made sure whatever we were selling, it actually had legs. And it was based on data. It was based on research because we were excited. We are believers. So, it's like finding a drug that works! Not only do you wanna, of course, sell it, but you also want to tell people about it."*

We showed the leaders and everyone else: *"Here are the fifteen things we're gonna do to enable everyone. There are comms, videos, meetings. Here are all these assets we're building out for you. These are the fifteen things we're going to do to drive this change."* Once the CEO staff—along with Debra—saw all this, their blood pressure dropped. I got such responses as, *"Whoa, you got it. You have a vision!"*—which I was grateful for. Afterward, George and Debra told me, *"We believe in your vision, Larry."* (Phew!) We just surrounded them with so much enablement that it took the pressure down. Yeah! For our part, this was our way of saying to the doubters, *"Back off. We've got this!"* Our bottle was filling with more than just vapor now. It was becoming tangible. Real.

It was after these early meetings that we really started to chew on the idea of the growth mindset. And wanted to include the basic idea of: *"Just because you haven't done it doesn't mean you can't."* (Which draws on Carol

Dweck's idea: *You can grow no matter what.* So, we tied those messages together.)

24 · Building Seasoned Stakeholders

Then there was the political aspect of our campaign. We needed to recruit executive-level sponsorship. That meant establishing our stakeholders and building out our advisory groups and committees. Many are "best practice" change-management tactics and the kind of strategies I'd been deploying since my early days at Citibank. Our goal was to identify who were the critical stakeholders, enlist some early advocates, and raise the funds we would need. In all of this, we knew George had our backs. Without that kind of readiness at the highest level or his executive sponsorship, this would have been a nearly impossible undertaking. But it was time for HR to transform. It was the last function in NetApp to go through a transformation, and its moment had arrived. Even so, it would take more than just George's support to make this transformation come to life. For it to really fly, the entire company had to embrace the change. This was the task in front of us.

Seasoned, Credible and Skeptical

When I was quite young in my career (my first ever director job), I built a training. I was so proud of it and brought it to the leadership team. And they were like, "*What is this? Why are you bringing this to me?*" I learned in that moment that you should always have seasoned, credible, and skeptical leaders on your side as you're building anything. Because then they become the voice of the business, the voice of the solution. It's never just you, spinning. You're herding the leadership to deliver for them. This has been my mantra ever since.

And that was exactly what I did at NetApp. The model Debra and I brought over from Equinix was a vision around leading change that involved building up groups of leaders as part of the campaign. We called it a Business Advisory Group. That's a key way to operationalize any transformation. Involve the key players and show them how this will get done—together—fast and organized. We also worked hard to enlist work groups, advisors, councils, committees, and subject matter experts.

Then, from an overall change management perspective, Vicky also helped us think through the *how* of getting things done. Namely, the stakeholder engagement plan. Designing the engagement plan for key stakeholders, I asked myself, *"Okay, when do EM and I need to be in front of CEO staff? When do I need to be with the Human Resources Leadership Team?"* EM and I identified all the stakeholders who we thought were important. Vicky also helped us determine who I needed to get in front of. Then we assessed them based on where we thought they were on the "readiness" scale. Next, we identified what we thought their role would be and what impact they would have, positive or negative. We also determined who could "stop the train." These are the skeptics. The naysayers and tough critics. I always like to get in front of those first, early, and often.

Business Advisory Group

So with our Business Advisory Group (which we affectionately called the BAG), we looked to cultivate and build a group of well-heeled leaders. We developed a group of ten or so, primarily VPs and some senior directors from around the world who served in various jobs in different departments. I wanted a mix of experienced and new, to be sure we're covering all the critical pieces. Vicky facilitated around these, helping think through what they needed to know and when we would need to engage them. We used them to bounce concepts around, gave them previews of what we were doing, got their input, and asked for their advocacy. After producing the first draft of the game plan, we went to them for feedback.

The kinds of members you should choose to include in your BAG are those below the C-Suite. They're usually VPs or others who are influential but are actually doing the work. Because after the launch, these people will be using Thrive far more than George ever will. So, we wanted them to help shape it and provide feedback. I knew that if it was a really good BAG, they'd be rolling up their sleeves and helping. They might also ask, "*Okay, can you come to my team and talk to them?*" That kind of thing. Here's the great part in the process: If all goes well, they become your champions. And they did.

We knew that having a BAG would do two things for us. Once those folks were convinced, they became another voice for you—and essentially, an influential team member. Because it's not always me who can do the talking, right? And it won't always be you. It can't be just a one-person band. You won't get very far. Even when I was at Citibank, doing my first leadership development program, someone told me, "*You know, you gotta get the managers involved, or else it's just gonna be a Larry story, and it crests and falls on you.*" Getting others involved is key to the process. That way, when I got to the CEO staff, I could say, "*Here's who's on my Business Advisory Group,*" which speeds up the adoption process. And provides instant credibility. Now, at NetApp, we had these people, our BAG members, actively supporting and broadcasting out on our behalf.

As for the other BAG benefit, I was brand new, and needed to hear what this company was like. *What am I going to have to overcome and how can I get some allies in there?* Vicky helped me identify "friendlies." People who would believe in the solution you're bringing into the company. (In our case, our members included Emily Miller and Anna Schlegel.) And then, when it comes to your next phase, the rollout, you're already off to the races because ten teams already know about it.

Steering Committee

Your steering committee consists of one or two people in the C-Suite. Here's where the true power of the BAG comes in: these one or two add their voices, so when you go into the meeting, you can say, "*These twelve VPs like it and are ready to roll.*" The steering committee's people are more like high-level "influencers," to use today's social media slang. Executive-level and above who will sponsor the program for you. These types of committees are fairly commonplace in corporate life. Everyone has them (as opposed to a BAG) to get top-line input or approval. But don't expect them to do anything for you. That's not their role. The steering committee exists just to make sure that someone on the CEO staff is saying yes along the way.

Once you have your committee, you can then go to them with the ask: *"This may come to money at some point."* To go to a CEO staff with questions such as, *"What do you think?"* is just gonna slow you down because they're not thinking about that stuff. They'd spout out an opinion here and there, but they're not working on it. That's your job. You're solving the problems, not bringing them up the ladder. I learned that the hard way, years ago. I had mistakenly thought, *Well, let's go ask the smartest or the highest-level people.* They usually responded along the lines of, *"I dunno. I'll give you my opinion, but..."* You have to build your world and invite them to play in it.

Whenever I say, *"We're gonna break glass,"* and *"Move at speed!"*? Steering committees are part of that. They can push things along and get things moving. They are usually quick—sometimes one and done—or meet monthly or quarterly, as necessary.

If you're trying to raise funds for your project or initiative, building a BAG to secure a steering committee may be the way to go. So then, when you walk into that room where the money people are? You can build on the credibility you've already established. It's not just Larry coming in here with a pipe dream. It was my vision, but because of leadership support, it was transformed into a much more credible, tangible, strategic initiative.

Topically Focused

Our work groups were subject matter work groups that would go off and do the work between BAG meetings. The key one was a small HR and managers group that really worked together to iron out the details. We also had subject matter experts on call, such as finance, legal, and IT, that we could bring in. That way, we could say, *"Hey, so, we're gonna buy a piece of technol-*

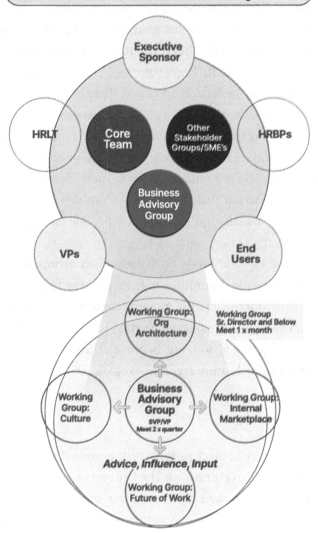

Image 2. Business Advisory Group Ecosystem Slide, Version 2 (roles and responsibilities overview)

ogy. Let's bring an IT person into the business group as a special guest for this meeting." That kind of thing. We kept the subject matter experts in the loop. At NetApp, we had three European work councils (Germany, Netherlands, and France) working with our local HR business partners. We knew they could help us get in front of any issues that came up with implementation across international borders. Planning ahead here was key.

So, we had our BAG, an HR working group, a business working group, our work councils, our experts, and then, on the side, the executive staff. All of this evolved in tandem with the internal brand Thrive that we were building. The brand, the selling, the partnerships, and the business advisor group, tying it all together—that was turning into something much bigger. All part of the Golden Thread that, ultimately, existed to serve the development of Thrive.

25 • Messaging Around the World

Bringing Stakeholders on a Journey

Once I'd clarified who the various stakeholders were, Vicky came to me and said, *"Okay. Based on that, let's use our communication techniques and vehicles to help you deliver our message."* She and Lisa posed the questions: *"How are we gonna get the story out? And in what ways?"* There were various audiences (stakeholders), so each needed to be addressed individually. Our next questions were then, *"What's the message for each? And how are you going to communicate that? And who's going to deliver it?"* As mentioned, we weren't just delivering tools. This was about a whole picture, a full transformation. And knowing change takes time. So, I planned for the communications to go in phases. That way, people could know what was happening and get a good understanding before they could really be committed and (hopefully, ideally) become advocates as well.

So, Vicky and Lisa worked on crafting the Change and Comms plans. Vicky kicked us off by saying, *"Let's break things down by stakeholder."* This is where they used the levels (See The Change Narrative, page 132). What were we going to tell the managers, executives, and employees? Each was a very distinct audience. So, they worked up the following list for each audience:

1. What do they need to know?
2. What do we think the problems are gonna be?
3. Where are they gonna push back?
4. Who should deliver this message?

As I keep reiterating, I'm a great believer in branding. That's why, after we built my talking points, I kept repeating them as we continued to focus on sharpening and shaping that consistent narrative. Even with a receptive audience, *how* you pitch the change should still be where the money is. It's important to be consistent with that messaging—but also listen to the feedback you get and build on that. While I worked on building relationships, I started planting the seeds of what was to come. I always tried to be approachable—more carnival barker than disembodied voice behind a megaphone.

We spent a lot of time hammering these things out. And everyone on the team, with their decades of NetApp village wisdom, would warn me about any red flags ahead and what had been tried and failed. All of which was quite helpful. Even if I'd also usually reply, *"Okay, maybe I'll craft my message a little differently...but we're still gonna DO IT."* I wanted to know where I could push the envelope to make something new. And push I did. *"Let's do that. Definitely,"* I would tell them. Eventually, the communications built up to the launch, but the messaging didn't stop there. That was just the beginning.

And so, we carried on with our briefings to get the information into the people's hands. We also did a lot of briefings with the employees, managers, and leaders, going through content. EM and I had multiple sessions with our HR business partners, who, as NetApp employees were the daily go-between for business and HR, each played a crucial role as a strategic partner and trusted advisor to their business leaders. Bear in mind: It's best to identify and get all your stakeholders on board early (as many as you possibly can) because, ultimately, the message is really for the entire company. And *ultimately*, everyone in the company is a stakeholder.

WIFM: What's in It For Me?

Let's put ourselves in the stakeholders' shoes for a moment. Why would any of these folks want to join my project? This is where a little research comes in. Find out what your stakeholders can get out of your initiative too, and you're more likely to get to yes. Unsurprisingly, this is a key concept in change management. They call it WIFM (What's in it for me?). Understanding that we have our three big stakeholder groups, we now needed to find out: *What's in it for employees, people managers (anybody who has a direct report), and finally, for the executives?* The three levels of stakeholders. Let's tackle the first level. As an employee, why would I care? What's in it for me to change? We had an outline specifically for them, and so on. And, of course, we addressed the entire company overall as well, digging into: *What's it for NetApp?* As we worked to identify those areas and got crystal clear with all three groups, we infused that information into all our engagements and communications. We now had several targeted ways to tell the same transformation story.

WIFM for employees and managers, in the case of NetApp, was mostly about ensuring people had a positive experience. We wanted employees to feel empowered and that they were learning and growing. Overall, we wanted to create a more humane environment, and we knew that the old system was really getting in the way of that. For managers specifically, achieving this meant giving them tools, data, and the trust that they could make the right decisions. For the leaders, the messaging was more around business strategy. You want your people strategies to align with your business strategy. To support your business strategy. There was a HUGE push for the company to perform. To make that happen (referencing what we discussed back at the beginning of the book), we needed to build high-performing teams. So, we made everyone aware that this was the ultimate end of the rainbow.

Skeptics, Doubters, and Naysayers

After going through our stakeholder assessment process, identifying those who could "stop the train," and other potential skeptics, we then asked ourselves, "*Okay, so what are we gonna do about them? How do we bring those people in and have them provide us feedback upfront?*" When looking to increase our adoption rates, our toughest audience was the internal one.

People were used to the old Talent Development process—what it used to be like. "*Give us some trainings, set up our focal review. And then, back to business as usual.*" That wasn't going to be the reality anymore. We had to think about the future of Talent Development (TE) and getting managers to believe in that. Changing an old mindset, starting at the top, is always the biggest challenge—and it often looks like a much bigger lift than it actually is. People will say, "*Well, why can't we just do it the way we've always done it?*" even as they're quick to point out, "*I hate how we do it.*" Focus on unshackling the leadership and the managers. Getting leadership to realize there are better, easier ways to do things is the aim. Give them the accountability and the tools, and I guarantee they will rise to the occasion.

There will always be some skeptics in the room. If you don't get them involved in the process or get them on board? Then it's super easy for them to come in at the end and say, "*Oh, yeah, this is garbage. I don't support this at all.*" Sometimes leaders don't realize the influential power they wield. You could have the CEO standing on a stage talking about a strategy. And a manager in the audience could turn and say something to their employee like, "*This is not real,*" right? And it's gone immediately. That one prick of the balloon blows up the whole story. So, getting the skeptics on early is key.

For starters, I would get to know them. In my team meetings, I would ask, "*Okay, who are the naysayers?*" And I'd go to their meetings. We'd also invite them into our work groups. Doing this was a big piece for us—putting potential naysayers on the committee and getting them talking! During our assessments, we'd say, "*Hey, that person might have feedback,*" or "*We're aware they have feedback. Let's bring them into the loop,*" Or "*How do we get feedback from them early on?"* Then they can start to be advocates for us, which ended up happening.

So again, for the BAG, we chose seasoned, well-known, vocal members. Some were skeptical, and some weren't. But we also went with people who were visible. While at Equinix, there was one guy in our BAG who was quite dubious, and he had a big group. I knew that if this guy were to put his name to it? That would mean eight hundred people would be behind it, right? He was one of those who asked me, *"Why now?"* To which I gave my standard reply. *"There's never gonna be a time where we're not busy. And you know, we go slow now to go fast next year."* He stayed, even though he wasn't sure about this whole thing. He hung in there.

Four months later, it was launch time. We were having these leadership offsites. All the top people were expected to come. I planned a trip down to Carmel, California. You could golf, dine, and we had speakers—some celebration and a little strategy mixed in. That year, they decided to have different groups—somewhat like a science fair. Each booth would be hosted by a different part of the business. Engineering would showcase a new product coming down the pike. IT would highlight a new tool, and so on. Then all the leaders would go around to each booth and learn about the future. That way, at the very least, they could see what other projects were going on in the company. At our booth, we were highlighting the Equinix equivalent of NetApp's Thrive—we called it *GPS. Grow, Perform, Succeed* (which may have been based on the Dell performance management model). And instead of me at the booth, it was manned by a gentleman who, four months earlier, had been one of my chief skeptics. Now, here he was volunteering to host the booth, saying, *"Look how great this is."* My work was done!

There was another guy at NetApp, a kind of self-styled non-HR leadership guru. Which I appreciated. He regularly posted leadership quotes on LinkedIn and Twitter and had a loyal following. When I came in, he was skeptical. Fine. No problem. Somehow, I still managed to get him on our BAG. He would offer comments but never say anything too positive like, *"This is going great."* Three-and-a-half years later, I heard him say, *"There's so many great things that this HR BAG team has brought to leadership.*" That was the kind of mindset change we were after. I mean, as long as you're doing what you say and not just posting on the internet? Perfect. And he actually used the tools and applied a growth mindset. Couldn't ask for more.

We Can Actually Have a Voice Here

For the HR staff at large, I know my leadership style was a bit jarring for some. I wasn't focused on tactical or operational changes, like many of my predecessors. I was taking a big picture, *let's blow this up* kind of approach, and to be fair, they hadn't experienced much of that before.

So many were saying things to each other like, "*Oh, God, what's going on here? What kind of crazy is this? THAT's what he's introducing? We don't operate like that.*" Elise reflects on her initial thinking. "*I had thought, 'Is his style SO different from what everyone is used to that this is going be really hard for people to adapt to? What kind of fallout will there be from this?' But it didn't take long to figure out that shaking things up wasn't a bad thing—it was just uncomfortable. And, wisely, Larry did some things early on, so we had some quick wins. That built credibility and trust. There were growing pains, of course, but as people became more comfortable speaking up, and they felt heard and progress was being made, the consensus was 'Yeah, this is a good thing.'*"

Countering Objections

The NetApp case had another additional challenge: *change fatigue.* When I showed up, they were three years into their business transformation already. The executive leadership was getting fatigued from that because a big bulk of it was cost-cutting. To go to that team and say, "*I need you to have the same rigor, inspiration, and buy-in to this part of the transformation that you just had for the business one.*"? That was rough. Rallying those troops, who were tired and wanted to focus on the newly transformed business, was a big ask. Because even under the best of circumstances, common knee-jerk reactions to this type of change are always along the lines of: "*Why now? It's always been the same. We've done it all the same way,"* and *"What are the tools you're gonna give us?"*

In fact, there's a host of common resistance "myths" you'll need to be prepared for. With more seasoned, senior executives, for example, I wouldn't say they are less savvy to learn, but what I might say is that they're less inclined to change. People don't like change! They want change, but at the same time, they don't like it. And some felt like the storage business was good enough: *"I bought my house and put my kids through college on storage money."* Other common resistance myths you'll likely hear are: *"It's too big." "It's not my job." "We've always done it this way." "I can't see the future. That's what consultants are for."* So, in this massive, large-scale change across the organization, how were we going to make sure that our approach was really going to help increase adoption? At the macro level, BAG was one answer. At the micro level, you just gotta keep talking to people.

Let Me Break It Down for You

During Year One, when we were getting rid of ratings and rankings and going toward Thrive, one question was posed to me constantly, *"How are we gonna know if our people are productive?"* That, I had to answer brutally. *"Well, how do you know NOW?"* Right? Meaning, *"Just because you don't have a rating system anymore, you'll never again be able to tell if they're productive or not?"* (Really, people?) *"You're now getting tools so you can talk about productivity in a much calmer, easier way,"* I'd explain. In fact, I was frequently questioned about removing ratings and rankings in general. My standard reply: *"Do you like doing it the way we're doing it? Do you want to keep these one-through-five ratings?"* To which most people would say, *"No, I hate it!!"* My response: *"That's why!"* None of us really liked the old processes, yet most were so ingrained, it seemed for many like a waste of time to change. That is when you know the old ways of doing things are ripe for transformation.

I really worked to break it down for people, to tell them how it was going to go. I'd say, *"You know all that stuff you used to have to do?"* I'd talk about how super-bogged down the processes were with the rankings and ratings and forced distribution, which was just painful as a manager. I really understood that pain, and I let them know that. I empathized with how frustrating it was for employees too. I was able to then say, and have them hear really quickly, *"This is what's gonna happen. Here is what you can expect, and this is the replacement. Ratings are gone. They're out the window."* These were easy things people could wrap their heads around and imagine might be possible. And then I delivered on it. That quickly turned into a good, quick Year One win.

From-To

Another strategy for macro and micro is the from-to technique—one of my favorites. My whole thing is about showing what the *from-to* is. I really leaned into this, and Vicky and I always joked around about it because every deck had a from-to slide. It seems so basic, but it was huge. *"This is what it is now, and this is where it's gonna be."* *"Do you want the left-hand side of this slide? Or do you want the right?"* And everyone would always say, *"We want the right!"*

There are so many examples of how I used the technique. Addressing issues such as: *"From slow, paperwork-heavy, checking on you, 'You are an obeisance to me or my team...' Do you guys like that? Do you want me to continue to do that? Yes or no?"* Their responses: *"No, that sucks. I hate it. That's why we hate HR."* Me: *"Great. How about if we went to NO paperwork?"* Them: *"Well, where are we gonna put our goals?"* Me: *"Only 8 percent of this company puts their goals in the old system. Eight. Why is 80 percent of the company worried about it?!"* (Just stating the facts can help too.)

I had used from-to at Equinix as well. One guy there said, *"Well, why do we have to do it now? We're so busy."* And I said, *"I want to release you to focus on your job and your team. That's where I'm going."* I told them I was trying to unshackle the company from all these things that get in the way, all this scaffolding that HR had built up over twenty years. That employee relationship with the manager—that was what I wanted to pour all the water and the seeds on to make that grow.

I remember one executive, an old sales guy, saying, "*Thank you for dragging us into the twentieth century,*" which I thought was kind of funny. I love Avery's thoughts on this point too: "*I mean, you know what the past looks like. And if it's not working, if you are not happy, if you're not having fun sometimes, and if you're not being honest? To me, that tells me something needs to change, because why are you still doing this?*"

The Velvet Rope

Another strategy is the concept of the velvet rope. In case you're not up on your hot, '70s midtown NYC nightclub history, truth is, Studio 54 was a dive. But as soon as they put up that velvet rope and said, "*You can't come in.*"? The line went around the block. We design things in the hopes that people will *want* to get behind the velvet rope to experience. That way, it's not us trying to push people in. It's not mandatory. Nothing I do, in fact, is mandatory. If all is working well and as it should, it's a pull. It's coming from them—people asking, wanting to be part of it. Everything that we've done and developed has been through that lens of trying to make it something that people want to be part of rather than something that's being done *to* them.

This mostly came into play around workshops and offsites. I let leadership know early and often, "*I'm not doing mandatory training.*" I don't know how you feel, but for me, the second someone tells me something's mandatory? I'm thinking, *Ah, no thanks.* Because that usually means that whatever it is, it's not as good as it should be. Or could be. So, I said, if we're going to do anything, we're not gonna tell anyone they have to go, but we *are* going to make it so compelling that they *want* to go. And if we've done our job well, we've inspired people and carried them with us on the journey, and they feel they are *part* of the change. Not subject to it. In our first Directors' Immersion Experience in Year One (more about this in Part 4 Section 2), we had an *actual* velvet rope—and a full house. Then we used video and testimonials from those folks to draw more attention so that others would want to go to the next leadership offsites.

26 · The Launch

It was August 16, 2019. Sunnyvale headquarters. We launched Thrive to a global audience of ten thousand.

During our early sessions in April, we began to think about how best to announce getting rid of ratings, beginning Quarterly Conversations, AI-supported Pulse Surveys, and the whole vision around Thrive, the Wheel, and the Golden Thread. We needed to go wide, letting everyone know we were moving the company in new directions. An HR overhaul was underway; big changes were going to begin being implemented immediately. How should we tell everybody? We wanted to kick off this massive campaign with a bang. Make a big splash. The August All Hands felt like the right place to do it. The whole company would be gathered; the timing worked. And treating it like a product launch worked too. Lisa had run many of these in her decades doing PR for tech startups all across Silicon Valley. It was a seamless decision to go that route. In the run-up to the August deadline, we'd built our messaging, grown our internal support with various stakeholders, finalized our internal brand and identity with marketing and the branding team, and planned for the rollout over the fall and following winter.

The launch messaging for the Wheel was the Thrive Ecosystem for High-Performing Teams, as you know. And the tagline, thanks to marketing, was People Powered, Data Driven. Again, there was the *why* of doing it—and George's demand of it. Of *How do we catch up with the cloud business? How do we increase the speed in how we make decisions, how we work together, and how we grow people at the speed of cloud?* The Thrive Ecosystem was our answer to George's challenge of "*We need higher-performing teams.*" The launch would be announcing to the whole company, the "*Here's how we're going after it.*" Our campaign had been in development for months, and now, we were going company wide.

Dear World: Here's My Idea

There were more than a few unprecedented things about this launch. The meeting was super global because tech companies, especially the Fortune 500 ones, are in every major developed country market. And a good part of NetApp's annual income is international. So, there were employees and/or customers everywhere. Thousands were dialed in to watch the All Hands on video. As for me? I've included roughly twelve days of events in my "highlight reels" across my three years at NetApp. This day was definitely one of them. I was the first non-CEO staff to be on stage for this kind of meeting. The first! To date, HR had never really been part of All Hands. Usually, just product or salespeople were present. It certainly raised some eyebrows amongst the legacy comm teams. "*Is that Larry? He can't get on stage. What are you guys doing?*" Nowadays, though, it's done all the time. There are VPs on these things regularly in current times, and in general, there are a lot more speaking series, talks and fireside chats than were seen in the past. Some invite only, some department specific, some anyone can attend. But at the time, this was a bit radical, and was certainly signaling some change was afoot.

So, there I was, the first non-CEO staff to speak at an All Hands meeting, and it was essentially, "*Dear world. Here's my idea.*" The key points I wanted to get across were about democratization, speed, and telling an inspiring future story. When I watched the video playback later, I'd totally forgotten there was clapping and cheering from some in the audience around dumping performance ratings. At the time, my mind was laser focused. And part of that message was how I was doing transformation. Of course, I didn't actually say, "*I'm doing a transformation,*" out loud. The messages were more like, "*We're moving from old school to new school and toward a new answer. And you're going to be better equipped to have these conversations and have data and grow your teams so that you can achieve your business goals.*" And although my intention was to change the way HR was viewed and to redefine what HR did, I didn't say any of that either. Instead, it was more like, "*We're gonna reverse that. It's Talent Enablement. I'm going to enable you to start having better conversations and build great teams.*"

27 · Post-Launch Enablement

The launch of Thrive was a big push. We then immediately pivoted to launching the Pulse Survey. I called it the *one-two punch* of growth. The QCs, then Pulse. We had people's attention at the All Hands. The goal now was to keep the momentum going and have them start to engage with these new ways of doing things right away.

Having just launched the manager-employee conversations—now, we needed to educate people on how to do them. We knew this transformation would be a marathon. In fact, introductions on all these new programs remain ongoing. We had prepared for this and knew we would have to reach out in consistent and sustained ways throughout this campaign and beyond to achieve the levels of engagement we were after.

Email Ain't Enough

Helping people understand, even become advocates, of change...that's what you hope for. We wanted the employees *themselves* to spread these new ways of thinking and doing things. For many, when they think about leading change, they presume people will commit from the beginning to a change. While you can hope for that to happen immediately (and for some, it might), for most, it just takes time. And sometimes people just don't understand what's happening at all. At least not right away. Or they may have questions. They're not necessarily questions around resistance, they're just trying to "get it." You need to take the time and be thoughtful around providing enough information. Just like anyone, before employees can commit, they need first to understand. Then they can be advocates for it. Be patient. And walk people through the journey of what you're trying to do. That's really the point. Because it's never instantaneous. It happens over an arc of time.

And there's a lot of tactics; a lot of things you do. An email is not enough—that's a Bazooka Joe tattoo. You need to do different things. It's conversations. People don't necessarily understand a thing just by listening to someone. Some need to ask questions. Others need visuals. Everyone needs to be engaged with the content. To think about the implications. To repeat processes. All that gets them to a better understanding of what these changes are going to mean—for them, their teams, and the company. One-way communication is not enough *by far*. Sometimes program planners presume sending an email, putting out a newsletter, and presenting at an All Hands is all it will take, but those things are barely the beginning. Vicky partnered with the training team to figure out the most effective solutions to educate the population. (Note: This is a time when training *is* effective because you are teaching how to learn an actual skill—like how to have a new conversation or, in our case, use the new total rewards system. Together, they worked creatively to expand well beyond mere emails and your run-of-the-mill online training classes.

For people to engage with content, they need to know what to do. You see it starting in our school systems now. In K-12 learning, for example, there's been a lot of investment by the Gates Foundation and others in these true, adaptive learning curricula. Every student gets personalized curricula, say, on their iPad, which figures you out as you go and adjusts. For us, we wanted to hit every employee where they were and find what fit best for them by bringing in the most current thinking around how people learn as adults. And that is really what we need in our leadership development, mental health cultivation, or mental fitness, as well as around important topics such as inclusion, belonging, diversity, and equity, or, in this case, inclusive leadership and growth mindset. Already, you're seeing kids in our schools no longer listening to the teacher tell them the content in this passive, asymmetrical form. Kids interact. Vicky's daughter, for example, is learning about the Indian tribes in her city. The school is having them build the huts! And engage with the knowledge. My point is that it's no longer just about listening. Modern learning practices, and changing management philosophies on a group level, include engagement.

Also, some people don't process information with text. Or text alone. For example, did you know that 5 to 10 percent of the global population is affected by dyslexia?[9] Another reason why you can't just rely on email, right? As a communications strategist, you have to have email but also a website, FAQs, various interactive, social, and multimedia of course. The team really tried to embrace the ideas: *Don't rely on just one thing. Try to be broader and more holistic.*

So, as part of our larger enablement strategy, we had a variety of solutions. Vicky contributed a lot in this arena. She was very hands-on, and with Avery, conceptualized and designed the training content, including the decks, infographics, and slides, from a training perspective. They worked to introduce visuals into all our training materials. They really considered how people process information because of how important it was for us to reach everyone. A total transformation would not be achieved without that.

At the beginning, we did briefings during which we would present the specifics of the Thrive model—and all the tools and information they would require at that particular time. In the beginning, it was all mostly about the introduction to the model. Addressing the *what* and *why* of it all. It was less training and more about the briefings in those early weeks. That was live. In our second briefing, we covered resources. We also had white papers, job aids, and infographics. This way you hit both the right- and left-brain type folks. For the QCs, for example, we had the trifold. We also aimed to be multi-mode from training and rewards perspectives. The team went on to develop an online course on the compensation piece as well. Those are just some of the training solutions that we deployed.

Sometimes You Just Gotta Talk About It

There was a whole lot of work around dialogue. Sometimes people just need to talk about it. With a massive transformation such as this, it still comes down to engaging in that conversation. For some, it's an essential part of their process when absorbing new information. Providing forums for dialogue is crucial for a successful change campaign. Some might say, "*Oh, we're just wasting time talking about it,*" but these forums actually help a lot and can move people along. So, take the time to have them, before and after launch. Elaine Marie and I had a lot of those stakeholder conversations with the Business Advisory Group and others, for example.

We also did a lot of fireside chats, town halls, and various employee forums, especially after launching. We still do them to just make sure managers are up to speed on what they can expect around, for example, the end-of-the-year Thrive Rewards (how to navigate from a budget POV, what to think about). I did a ton of these kinds of "infomercials" called *Talking Talent*. EM produced these bite-sized conversations—me as the sort of "talk show" host and a guest. They also served as a spotlight for recapping Quarterly Conversations, Thrive, and Rewards, and what that all means for managers and employees regarding the transformation. There was always a lot to cover. Sometimes they'd get recorded. Elaine had this to say about it: "*That, to me, is so much more effective than a big training program. That people walk away, and they might apply, they might not, but those constant, 'in the moment' quick events that you can listen to and get that insight from.*"

Then we started Thrive Thursdays, which the talent enablement team uplifted. They continue to be hosted monthly, addressing what it's like to master a skill or grow your career at NetApp. On some Thursdays, there are Q&As or activities. Each time, it's a fresh topic about some aspect of the Thrive Ecosystem in detail. In the beginning, these spotlights were often about Quarterly Conversations. Anyone can attend Thrive Thursdays. Once the pandemic began (Year Two, 2020), we launched No Zoom Fridays as well once a quarter. Then Dare to Dream—also quarterly. In our first event, we brought in an external speaker from DreamWorks to talk about her career and what *career* means to her. "*Where have you stumbled? And where have you grown?*" I wanted to know. That kind of thing. All three of these ongoing group events continue to tell the story of Thrive and all its programs internally. The town halls are normally specific to a population. Some are open. Others are not. Some are just for managers or VPs. There are a lot of different populations that these town halls are addressed to, but then there are also those meant for all employees when it's information everyone needs to know.

Office Hours

Another change management tactic we used centered around open office hours. Instead of hosting Zooms with three hundred-plus people, the team offered open office hours and open labs. Smaller groups, where attendees would be a lot more likely to ask a question. Introverts, for example, are less likely to ask questions in a large forum, right? But with drop-in sessions, where anyone could attend, and with a team of experts on hand? A lot of people joined—they could just drop in during the time slot and ask questions. There was a schedule, and people would sign up. Sometimes you'd have one person. Sometimes twenty. Vicky, among others, would host.

We always had a multidisciplinary team on hand. Someone from Elaine-Marie's team, another from the compensation team, and someone from IT. We also had HR services represented. People could speak to the experts and then go into a virtual meeting room (the open lab), where they could share so others could learn. Vicky had this to say about these open hours: "*The sessions were…great because it was time for me to hear directly from managers and employees. That was really good. There was no question that I felt like I didn't have an answer to.*" Overall, my team did a good job providing people with resources, tools, and information to get them acquainted with it. They were very helpful for a lot of people, and it advanced the training campaign.

Selling is Perennial

This enablement is ongoing—and woven into standard practices now. The team will always be broadcasting these concepts and keeping up with the messaging. There's a continuous and perennial need to sell.

28 • No Posters, Please

You may be asking, what does he mean by *culture*? Especially in HR, it's a very difficult question because the idea of culture gets thrown around a lot. Remember that famous Enron story, where they had four values and began with "integrity" and "communication"? You could rip the name Enron off the header, slap another company name on there instead, and the message would be exactly the same.

Traditionally, internal marketing comes up with the company values. Prior to Equinix, I was often approached by business reps who would ask me, "*Hey, Larry, can you help us with the culture?*" But in many cases, what they really wanted was for me to rebrand their existing culture with an internal marketing campaign. Meaning, let's figure out a way to sell back to the company what we believe the culture is (but probably isn't), as in, "*We repainted the building, and isn't it cooler now?*" even though on the inside, nothing's been changed. There are just the same old desks. Rather than doing the work to bring these values about, the focus is often a lot more on posters or videos or other media that are just selling, selling, selling. Most times, these campaigns are done internally, but occasionally, external marketing firms are brought in to build and execute them. From a leadership perspective, this is even more removed and less authentic than hearing it from your own people. If you're not living it, what's the point of any of it?

My role, as I see it, involves not only helping a company identify its actual values (and some may be aspirational) but also then identifying how to *realize* those values. I asked, "*How do you operationalize the culture? And how do you get them off the walls into people's lives?*" While at Equinix, we tried to focus on building values in a more authentic way. We gathered all the executives together for a multi-day *Culture and Values* meeting and said, "*What is the culture? Let's really work on defining what that is, for us, here and now. What do we care about? And what do we think matters that makes this company so successful?*" Over a week or so of half-days, we defined that culture. We broke it down, with our own working definition and with values—and a couple of bullet points on what those values meant.

We had one wonderful addition to these meetings—an artist whose job it was to memorialize these conversations by visually documenting meeting highlights using a sketch note-taking technique. All over the walls, she'd put hand-drawn updates of what we discussed, a very cool way to reflect on the day. It was playfully artistic and way better than simply taking notes. At the end, she condensed all that artwork into a hand-drawn, cartoon-esque one-pager on the values and the mission, entitled The Magic of Equinix (Image 3). Marketing responded by saying, "*You have to put it in brand. You have to put it in brand.*" And I replied, "*Okay, one day we'll put it in brand. But if I put it in brand now? It doesn't feel like the employees have any say over it. We're coming down the mountain and I never want to be viewed that way.*"

No matter where I've worked, I've always said, "*I don't want posters. Don't post this on the wall.*" Just like making training mandatory, if you're not living it, it doesn't matter. Instead of turning it into a marketing piece, we brought the image to the All Hands meetings. Then, I did a bit of a world tour. I took that one-pager and went around the globe, to Singapore, Australia, Amsterdam, London, wherever our big hubs were. We put people in a room, showed them a video, and then I handed them that piece of paper. A laminated cartoon! Yes, to this culture of serious data center people...a cartoon. But one which reflected the conclusions of executive leadership. And I said to them, "*This is what we think. I'm coming around the world to hear what you think. Is this real to you? Is this authentic? What's wrong with it? And if you feel it's authentic, please give us examples of how you see this expressed in your work life.*"

I was not trying to define a new culture. I was trying to define and illuminate the one we had, to breathe even more life into the best parts of it. To give employees an opportunity to participate, give honest feedback, and choose to own that messaging...or revise it to reflect the micro-culture of their particular location. Or the culture they'd like it to become. What I was trying to get them to answer wasn't "*Do you like the values?*" but "*Do you see evidence of these values, and are these values you'd want to follow?*" Meaning, "*Is this something that you want this company to be?*" At best, I figured these employees might then say, "*This is an example of when I've seen this value*

Image 3. The Magic of Equinix (*The People's Document*)

happen, and this is the benefit of it." By giving them a voice, we created an opportunity to turn that whole campaign into a People's campaign for Equinix in a way. And in the end, it did become a kind of People's Document!

For fun, we printed T-shirts that reflected regional differences—the front was an artistic look at whatever city they were in; down the sleeve of one arm, it read, *The Magic of Equinix*. People began buying and trading T-shirts from other cities, and it became a fun way for everyone to connect. We then provided a way for employees to publicly recognize one another through the internal website. People could select one of the hand-drawn icons and then write on their profile why/how that person was living this value. And while, yes, from one perspective, this hand-drawn thing looked sooo unprofessional, from other perspectives, it made our message real. And authentic. Finally, we redesigned all our All Hands meeting agendas to reflect the structure of the culture document as well: Mission/Vision, then Business Update, then Values. In doing so, the culture document's message became more and more embedded into the actual culture of the company around the globe.

Throughout, marketing and I did not see eye to eye. Their position was "*Everything's gotta be in brand. This is not going to work.*" My response was always, "*If it's in brand, it doesn't mean anything anymore. It's not the heart and soul. It's just another uniform that we all wear. It's gotta be the heart and soul.*" With Debra's help, we prevailed and kept the internal website in that look (the hand drawing) the whole time. Those examples represent just a few ways you can operationalize culture and get all your employees to feel they are part of the messaging. Find ways to engage your workforce directly. Expose them to the values' *development process* and the thinking, give them a voice in the messaging, and build ways for them to connect and talk amongst themselves. These are some of the strategies for actually bringing company mission and values into people's work lives.

Since the pandemic, ideas about what corporate culture means and how to build and maintain it have been radically evolving. How do we stay connected and inclusive? New entrants from college to the workforce were never planning on going into offices, for example. How do you onboard those folks? Going forward, we all need to rethink what culture is and what the new world is going to require of us.

A Human-Centric Work Culture

Hybrid, all in office, all remote, no matter what arrangement your company has, you can still aim for a human-centric work culture, as we did. It was everything that we'd been aiming for. It was an uplifting and inspiring company statement: *People Matter Most.* A human-centric work culture comes down to making decisions around how to maintain, iterate, and grow that culture—and that includes listening to the employee voice and acting upon integrated data. It also means consistently showing and telling your people that they are valued.

The greatest measurement of human centricity is when employees say, "*This company cares about me.*" Caring is the ultimate measure. Among the wealth of information we collected from surveys and BetterUp, the most significant finding was that our employees did, indeed, feel cared for by NetApp. That was amazing to see and feel. When an employee feels cared for by a company, it's like a breath of fresh air in their work life. They feel valued and appreciated, which boosts their overall engagement and enthusiasm. Like getting a pat on the back or a high-five from their employer; they feel acknowledged and motivated to give their best effort. Feeling cared for also leads to greater job satisfaction. Employees experience a sense of happiness and fulfillment because they know that their well-being matters to the company. It's like finding a work environment where their needs are considered, whether it's through flexible work arrangements, supportive policies, or opportunities for growth and development.

This type of caring atmosphere fosters trust and teamwork. Employees feel comfortable expressing their thoughts, concerns, and ideas, knowing they will be heard and respected. Such open communication leads to better collaboration as colleagues are more likely to support and help each other, creating a positive and productive work environment. Ultimately, when employees feel cared for, work feels less like work. It becomes a place where people can thrive, find purpose, and enjoy their professional journey. It's like being part of a supportive work family that values their well-being, leading to a happier, more engaged, and loyal workforce. And when they feel invested and engaged, they're more likely to seek out resources for professional development. Ideally, it becomes a self-fulfilling upward spiral. A tech-inspired, human-centered Golden Thread.

Part II

The Year of HR Technology

SECTION 1

Choosing Tech

Remember that great line from the movie *Field of Dreams*, "*If you build it, they will come.*"? That may be true for cool baseball movies, but not when it comes to buying and propping up a piece of technology. Any piece of tech you introduce to your company's ecosystem must be connected to, and in support of, the larger transformational strategy. Your talent strategy. It's got to be Golden Threaded. In this section, I'll talk about the appropriate use of vendors and tech. How to find them, integrate them, get the most out of them—and build the muscles of continuous adaptation and change. For us at NetApp, the year 2020 (our Year Two, which fell in tandem with the start of the pandemic) was our Year of Technology. This also happened to parallel the very beginning of the Golden Age of HR Technology. We have more insight available to us now than ever before in the history of HR. As AI-integrated platforms evolve, the options are only getting more and more refined—and all the more essential for being competitive in a democratized marketplace of the future.

29 · You're a Technologist Now

I tell everyone in HR, "*You're a technologist now! And a transformation expert!*" In other words, don't wait for someone else to try to do either of these things for you. You've got to keep up with what's out there. And whatever tech options are on the horizon. You've also got to know how to make transformation happen. These are the new required skill sets for almost everyone in business today. And with the rise of AI, as we know, especially Generative AI, this has become all the more true. For those of us in HR, we're also in a golden age. Technology for our needs has finally caught up to all the other technologies out there. In the past, we had to wait for the monolithic HRM companies to gradually iterate and innovate their platforms. Now, we have a myriad of small companies building AI tools easily bolted onto those HRMs. There is no way one tech company will be able to invest and advance its tech, in so many different areas across the employee experience. So many HR tech companies—thousands, in fact, are now focused on specific AI-enabled tools, from candidate matching to candidate coding assessments to internal talent mobility to enterprise-wide coaching. We will dive more into Generative AI later. We have a chance for a do-over. To build anew from the ground up. Let's take it!

So, YES, there's a need to keep up with the AI-driven boom now upon us. But please—never be fooled by even the shiniest new toys. How do you embrace technology? As I've been saying, it's never tech alone. Begin with the Wheel. And your Golden Thread. Build your talent strategy, then propel it with tech. Tech can be an accelerant to your plans, materializing your vision with the aid of AI-driven data processing. It can also solve problems unearthed by implementing a strategy, but you can't rely on tech to figure them all out. Just turning technology on and hoping for the best isn't the right answer. (Well, you *can* just do that, but I wouldn't recommend it.) I don't claim to be an AI expert. What I do claim to be is a talent strategist who takes advantage of tech because I recognize its value—but I can't tell you about every aspect of AI. Nor should I need to. Nor do you need to know everything about it. Our job is to identify the right vendors and build the enablement that will make our chosen product(s) work within our companies. This book is designed to close the gap between making use of yesterday's state-of-the-art tech and tomorrow's.

Anyone can say, "*Oh, I know how to bring in a piece of technology.*" But can you bring in a piece of technology that's Golden Threaded to your version of the entire Thrive Ecosystem? That's the key—getting to the point that you can say to leadership, "*Here is our talent strategy, and here's how this carefully chosen piece of tech fits into it and why.*" A lack of Golden Thread is what kills people's tech dreams. What causes initiatives to flounder. To never get properly adopted. You must be able to explain how it's driving the talent strategy to achieve better business results. And be certain it's the right fit for your company at *this* time—and for the next two to three years.

Year One was about getting people's heads around the idea that we were making sweeping changes. It gave them time to adopt QCs and begin to see the power of regular Pulse Surveys. To begin to understand the whole idea of Golden-Threading it. Year One, the Year of Execution, was when we jumpstarted a transformation in the entire culture and how the company worked. We were after quick wins and landing every plane. In Year Two, we started focusing on introducing technologies for every quadrant of the Wheel (including the 3rd and 4th) and building on all our newly planted talent strategies.

Tackling the Fear of Technology

As a tech and tech-adjacent company in Silicon Valley, in the NetApp culture, there was perhaps less resistance to the idea of embracing the intelligence of Generative AI than other industries. Because we're in that milieu and it's not as foreign, incorporating tech was, I'd say, perhaps less of a change management challenge than it could have been (or might be elsewhere). It was more inspiring and exciting for many, as in, "*Cool!*" But whether your company is generally tech-savvy or not, if you give people reliable data, so they can draw a line from A to B, they'll likely not care how you got there. Probably, they'll just be thrilled to no longer need to sift through all that data themselves. But before you get that far, to the phase of demoing new software platforms, you will likely meet some resistance. If nothing else, your audiences will reflect our current global conversation—the hopes and fears about how AI is going to change our world.

When I do my talks just on artificial intelligence, or even just on technology? I usually have to address those concerns (as I've mentioned before). "*Hey, the bots aren't coming for your jobs, okay? They are coming to take some parts of your job, which encourages us to look at our jobs differently. We have to see ourselves as tech-enabled.*" Fear, uncertainty, and doubt. FUD. There will always be ethical issues we have to face, but, in my view, it's the people who are the ethical or unethical ones. It's not the frickin' machine. It won't be artificial intelligence that takes over, it will be the misuse of these new technologies in ethically questionable hands. Again, my job is not to become a tech philosopher or policy consultant. My role is to find the best tools available to improve the ecosystems and the culture of the business I'm working within. The benefits and competitive edges to be gained are unassailable.

A Future Without Tech?

You may be wondering, can you go through a transformation (these days) *without* AI? Is it AI-dependent? Did technology, more or less, facilitate this NetApp transformation? The bottom line is, AI does make us smarter and quicker, but it isn't necessarily *everywhere*. Because technology is so much better than it used to be, we could say that this was a much more *productive* transformation. Think of it this way. The QCs and this whole idea of getting rid of rankings, and all that? We could have done that without any technology whatsoever. The core change of mindset can be achieved without any technological interventions. But bringing in Glint for our Thrive Pulse Surveys, for the voice of the employee, and bringing in BetterUp for growth at scale? Yes, they both have AI tools (even though a coach is a coach is a coach). That old-school survey (the one we all used over the last forty years) is not as great. It's tougher for the managers to process. Now, the managers can just *BAM!*—get right to the discussion immediately. They don't have to do any analysis because AI is propelling the transformation. Sure, you *could* cue up a whole bunch of coaches—meaning old-school coaches—but they're expensive, and there's no visibility to it. I don't get any of the background of what people are asking for. So, this idea of propelling people and moving at velocity was definitely dependent on the newer technologies in some key ways.

But it's true; we could have done Year One without any technology. To get the company to think about how they frame interactions, change mindsets and rewards programs, and give voice to the employee? That was tech-free enablement. But as for Year Two? The way the technology is now, it's made everything go faster. As I often say, "*Technology gets you to the human connection much faster and with more actionable data.*" And it's a self-fulfilling loop (Golden Thread) where you're getting data you never would've gotten before in a way you couldn't have digested before. That then informs what we're gonna do next. These days, if you can't get the tech, I think you're in for a slower development no matter what you're trying to do. You aren't gonna get to "dynamic career pathing" without technology (for example). I'm saying, if you can build your talent strategy and build things out around that talent strategy, you'd be better than you are now. But NOT with as much gas in the tank as you would have with technology to accelerate it. For instance, before we brought in Fuel50/Mosaic (which we'll address in detail in Part 3), QCs were based on the guidance we provided and access to open job requisitions for the manager and employee to talk about and align. By using Fuel50, employees can now talk about the next three roles they may want to take, what their gaps are regarding those roles, and suggestions on how to close those gaps: for example, taking a gig, signing up for a training, or talking to a subject matter expert. Those conversations became so much more fruitful, actionable, and real.

AI as an Accelerant

We already had our strategy in place with Thrive. We didn't think continuing to do ongoing enablement alone was going to accelerate that strategy any further. The question we were looking to answer in Year Two was *How do we use technology to go farther, faster, higher, better?* There were two arenas, two pillars of the Thrive Ecosystem I was looking to kick into overdrive: (1) matching up talent/bringing people in (4th quadrant, Activate the Future) and (2) moving employees up in their careers (1st quadrant, Activate Yourself; and 2nd quadrant, Activate the Team). I felt confident that some form of AI-enabled data processing was going to give us the kind of high-powered engine we were looking for in these areas because everything to date at NetApp was, on some level, done by hand or memory or through conversations, good recordkeeping, good data tracking, follow up, or follow through...everything long form with traditional tools. All "best practices" for an analog world. Again, you can grow and improve without AI, but not exponentially. Not without the kind of tech that is just now exploding in the marketplace.

The Evergreen Field of AI

Late in Year One, I told my team, "*Let's bring in a bunch of vendors. Let's see what kind of career pathway software is out there.*" After checking out a handful, we said, "*Whoa! It's really WAY, way better than we expected.*" Which was daunting but also exciting. This is why I'm advising you to keep up on technology. I remember my mind-blowing shock at the array of options out there when we really began diving deep into this process. My team and I were saying, "*Oh, my God, I'm not up to speed with what's going on in HR technology. Look at all the different ways you can go. All the different things you can do. And how all these fit together.*" And that was in 2019!

This is what I call my scare slide below (Image 4), but it's really a Call to Action, where I tell folks, "*Do you realize all this technology that's out there?*" (And *this* slide's from 2021!) "*Look how far behind you guys are. Get on it!*"

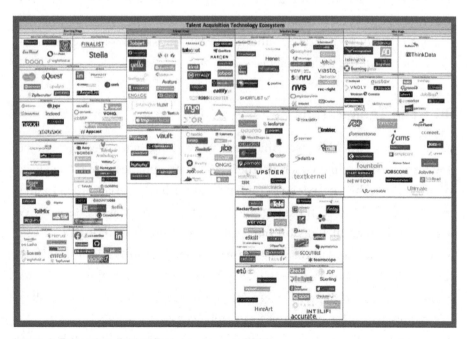

Image 4. Talent Acquisition Tech Landscape, 2019

And then I tell them, *"You can look at that slide I just showed you. A year from now, the face of that slide will be totally different. And then the next year is gonna be totally different again. So, it's always going to change. You just gotta pull the trigger. Pull it because, if you're NOT doing it, your competitors are ahead of you by THREE years. Because it takes a year to implement and get it going, right? Then to hone it and so on. The cycle continues."*

The development of technology is inherently iterative (mostly) and sometimes it just leapfrogs. So, yeah, it flies by. If history's any indicator, it'll never not be that way. So, there's no reason to wait. Yes, at some point, the product you purchase may become obsolete. And/or it will become integrated into another piece of software you are considering. Stick with short-term contracts and always watch the horizon for more robust platforms. The less you have to customize, the more you'll save money. With so many of these businesses popping up all the time? You'll be more exposed to it because you're getting bombarded with it. There are emails in my inbox all the time about yet another new technology. And every year, it's probably less of a sell. But your strategy, and how it ties in, is always the key element. No matter *what* the technology is.

30 · The Tech Parade

Early in Year Two/2020, we canvassed the field and narrowed our choices down to our most likely tech partners. We heard pitches. We interviewed. We brought in the top sixteen potential vendors, having asked them to present. We called it the Tech Parade, and the vetting process was extensive. We had several different folks on our evaluation team, from HR to IT to the business. We all agreed on what we were trying to solve, used a uniform scorecard, and asked questions like, *What's the most essential service your company is focused on, and where are you headed?* A lot of these small AI companies had a lot of promise but not necessarily a lot of delivery. So, yeah, we vetted these guys a lot. They all did something a little different. In the end, our biggest challenge was deciding between the best of them.

Selecting the Right Technology

I developed certain guidelines for the review process, which I'll share with you here. I used the slide above (Image 5) as part of a presentation to TA leaders about becoming a technologist as an HR person. Of course every company's different, I'll stick to some core principles I believe could be useful across most environments. First and foremost, know exactly what problems you are trying to solve and how any given tool under review might accelerate your talent strategy. I can't highlight this enough. If you are not clear on what problem you are solving, I feel very certain you will not solve it—leaving you stuck trying to jerry-rig some new tool into your tech stack. Guaranteed lower adoption.

Ours was such an exciting process because I had been dreaming my whole life about the kinds of tools that were now becoming available. Ways for *true* career pathing—historically just a myth—to become available. That was the Holy Grail "problem" we were looking to address. Ways to connect skills with immediate business needs and make the best use of the resources already within your company—talents and capabilities that you might not have known were there, available and waiting to be tapped. Here are a few other criteria to consider:

- Only half-believe the future roadmap of the vendor.
- Check references with peer companies.
- Tie the performance of the tool to the contract.
- Use comparative demos of different technologies.
- Understand the limits of your current tech focus (what you can bolt on to supercharge what you already have).
- Have the employee experience top of mind.
- Get a complete scope of the tool's "custom" integrations.
- Pull the trigger; there's always going to be another great technology around the corner!

In those early review sessions, you want to focus on solving your biggest problems while also concentrating on implementation, functionality, and

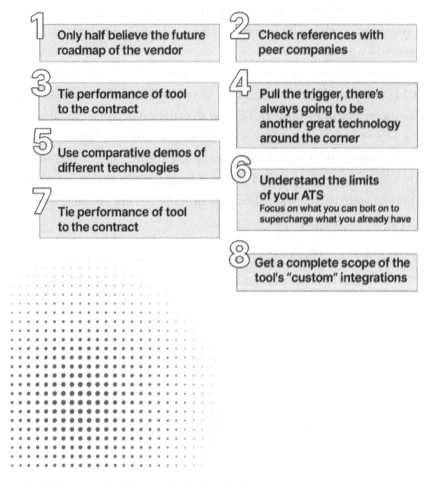

Selecting the Right Technology for You

Global, cross-functional team representing HR and the business Partner and Collaborate to Inform and Design

1. Only half believe the future roadmap of the vendor

2. Check references with peer companies

3. Tie performance of tool to the contract

4. Pull the trigger, there's always going to be another great technology around the corner

5. Use comparative demos of different technologies

6. Understand the limits of your ATS
Focus on what you can bolt on to supercharge what you already have

7. Tie performance of tool to the contract

8. Get a complete scope of the tool's "custom" integrations

Image 5. Tech Selection Guidelines for HR and TA Leaders

the potential vendor's future roadmap. Find out where they're headed and/ or where they want to go. And you certainly want to ask if you can speak with their other customers. Then dig deeper. Get curious about how the vendors see their futures and where they're headed with questions such as: *"How are you visualizing this product? What are you trying to do with it? What are you doubling down on? What's the most value we could get out of this?"* So, it's them telling us how they use it, why they do it this way, and what they think the benefits are. At the end of all this, you can then determine, *"Yep, that hits our needs."*

Again, we knew what we wanted, but the vendors also contributed to the final shape of things. It's a conversation. And this was no small undertaking. *"Huge,"* as EM once described it. We were looking for the vendor to fulfill our vision, but what we learned from the vendors through the Tech Parade also helped shape how we approached implementation, usage, and adoption. We knew what we wanted to get, but we really framed how to approach it with input from the vendors—and the vendors' clients too. We ended up choosing four new AI-driven tools to launch in Year Two: Eightfold, HireVue, Fuel50/Mosaic, and BetterUp. (In addition to Glint, which we were already using.) BetterUp is a virtual coaching tool. Then, we worked on using AI matching capabilities to (1) bring people in (talent acquisition/ recruiting) with Eightfold (a candidate sourcing tool) and HireVue (a video interviewing platform), and (2) move them up in their career with Mosaic (a career pathing tool). Our headline was "Accelerating the Business with New Talent Tools."

By the way, even though our Tech Parade came and went, our vetting never really stopped. It's good to build the muscle for continually canvassing the landscape. That's really the only way to stay current. The landscape continues to morph and roil at an unbelievable clip. Keep conversations going with those you've already met. Throughout my time at NetApp, I constantly brought in other companies and said to my team, *"Let's check this vendor out, meet with them, see what they've got."* If a vendor called me up, and I liked what they had, I'd bring the team together just to familiarize

FY21 Focus & Beyond   What is AI Doing?

What is AI Doing?

eightfold.ai

- Match and stack rank internal and external candidates to our jobs
- Improve the candidate experience with a streamlined UI, Chatbot, and easy ways for TA to follow up with candidates using full CRM capabilities Reduce time to evaluate candidate profiles
- Easily identify diverse candidates to increase our diversity pipeline

Hire·Vue

- Video interviews enable managers to view candidates on-demand
- Eliminate phone screens & reduce on-site interviews less interviews, reduced travel and fewer scheduling conflicts

fuel 50

- Activate internal talent market place
- Talk about your talents – what you love to do, want to develop and are great at!
- Define career paths aligned to employee interests
- Develop & grow role-specific skillsets & forecast future skills needed

BetterUp

- Unleash the potential in yourself and others
- 100% virtual, 100% personalized expert coaching
- Whole person approach

GLINT

- Formulate and administer an anonymous survey
- Uncover the psychology of human motivation and its under lying emotional drivers
- Helps us understand what actions need to take place for us to move the needle in our business

Image 6. Internal New Technology Orientation Slide (2021)

everyone with the technology out there. We no longer needed to do a big parade going forward, but we did consider it good maintenance.

Above (Image 6) is a slide of what AI does inside each of these products. So when you wonder, *What is AI really doing?* There's always the definition of Generative AI you can fall back on, but this slide shows the practical uses of AI based on each company we utilized.

31 • My Twenty-Minute, Million-Dollar Ask

It's one thing to select your list of licensable products. It's another thing altogether to finance them. So that was my next step—to present my case to HR and CEO leadership. It was a million-dollar ask for Eightfold, HireVue, and Mosaic/Fuel50. (BetterUp was getting charged back to the business). So, I was walking in there with a six-figure ask *again* during cost-cutting years.

The task before me was to present my plan to the executive staff. And that plan was investing in the chosen technologies that would best support and accelerate NetApp's internal Thrive Ecosystem for High-Performing Teams. The ecosystem was for every single employee, but leadership had to believe it. They had to fund it, to stand on stage with me. They also had to tell their teams: "*We're doing this,*" right? So, they were partners too because ultimately, we were all on the same team.

I told you how I raised the funds for the Glint survey license. I did the same here. Present the problem, describe the benefit, and explain how this amount of budget is going to be used to make it happen. Pretty straightforward, right? The biggest aspect of successful sales pitches, in my experience, is those magical from-to slides. First, we say, "*This is what it is. This is where we are now,*" which describes the central, current company challenge, or barrier, of the moment. Then we say, "*Wouldn't it be better if we could be here?*"

I really had to go to bat to get the budget for these. Typically, HR doesn't receive a very big budget for technology, and we were also still belt-tightening. We'd been given a target, our "efficiency task" for the year, to bring down the budget dollars. So, for us to go in with an ask for all these major tools and technologies was kinda bold. (And to be clear, we had to make asks for most *everything.*) What was working in our favor was that it was actually the *only* ask that we had that whole year. It was JUST the technology ask versus a lot of small requests.

I presented it to the CEO staff team and a few of the finance folks. My pitch included, "*This is going to be big for us, and really help us progress in this space. If we don't do this, we are falling behind. We won't be able to develop people without tools like these. Our competitors will beat us to finding and hiring the best talent in the market, and our employees will start to see we are not on the cutting-edge of development, mobility, and well-being.*"

Surprisingly, we did get the budget for all of them—although it did require some priority tradeoffs. By the time I went in, they actually seemed very keen on it and replied, "*Oh, this completely makes sense. This is a great idea. We'll help figure out a way to get you guys to fund it.*" The main reason why it didn't feel like such an "out-of-left-field," *What are you talking about?* budget request was because the Thrive Ecosystem was so well known by this point, and so much a part of the culture, that these technologies were an obvious next step. And it took twenty minutes. So, that was one of the top five big days of my tenure at NetApp! I call it my *Twenty-Minute, Million-Dollar Ask.* The pandemic was well underway when this conversation took place. Confusion reigned around the world as epidemiologists and governments struggled to understand the nature of what we were dealing with and how to respond. And the tech we were delivering came at a time when we were looking for solutions for an isolated, stressed workforce.

32 · Delivering on Values

In my view, culture and leadership are naked during a transformative event like this. This pandemic provided this shining moment for companies to deliver their values—to take them off the wall and bring them to life. It's times like these when people are very perceptive. When they feel it and will remember it most. People can talk about culture and leadership all they want, but when a pandemic is happening, the battle is on. You can't fake it when people are scared and looking to you for guidance. Great leadership drives a great culture, which drives performance. So, what's the ultimate goal? How do you measure your success? Through Leadership. Culture. Performance. And technology can help you with that. *"Thrive speaks to the values that the leadership team has espoused for a long time but had not yet acted on,"* Elise, long-time head of TA, generously offered. *"In some companies, CEO staff will pound the table and say, 'We need more diversity! Make it happen!' But Larry and the CEO held each other more accountable and realized that it can't just be a mandate—it has to be a culture shift, and the executive team has to be truly accountable. Verbal support is terrific, but we also needed financial support. Larry partnered with Estaff to provide that so TA could dedicate resources to support the diversity initiatives. That made a big difference, and we saw tangible results."*

33 • Enabling Tech Partnerships

A final note on why we chose these specific tech companies. There's the obvious reason—that the solution each provided met our needs. The second was their willingness to partner. As Anne Fulton said, *"You should seek out enabling partnerships."* My philosophy, which I tell vendors: *"Hey, for me to HAVE a good partner? I know I have to BE a good partner. So, let's hold each other accountable in making sure we're better."* This goes for production integration too. The truth is, a lot of these new technology firms aren't necessarily well-versed in explaining how to sell into your company. It's something you've got to figure out. But if you've read this far, you likely won't be surprised to learn that I believe it's also our job, as the receiving company and licensee, to build the enablement to make the product work. I just feel that's my role. *The company's* role. Integration is 90 percent on us; it doesn't go on the vendor's shoulders. Now, some vendors require more attention than others. Some can be relatively plug-and-play.

With others, such as Fuel50, for example, you have to do more implementation work so that it fits your company. In this case, one size didn't fit all. Quite the opposite. So, we staggered the implementation into three phases. And prioritized. We had to wrangle through some issues: *How do we message this? How do we roll this out? Which services and components should we focus on first?* Fuel50 did have an implementation team and a customer success team that helped us as we continued to evolve. (Good partners.) I believe it was adopted quickly *because* we took that time to plan ahead. *Because* we took that time to plan the rollout and integration. And we wanted to prepare for how to sell Mosaic into the company. You've got one shot at this, in a way, and we wanted to do it right.

34 · The Employee Life Cycle

The next step, now that these technologies were on board, was to sell it into the company at large. We prepared our slogan: *Empowering Employees to Transform Their Experience Through Data* to present to all the staff and demonstrate how these specific technologies were going to fit into the larger picture, the Wheel, and our talent strategy. And how folks might engage with these day-to-day. During our rollout of these platforms, what really piqued everyone's interest was my *"You no longer have to..."* list. It's an example of the kinds of content we used to get everyone excited and engaged. As you might imagine, this list was popular and well received!

PRACTICAL USES OF TECHNOLOGY IN HR

New Tools and Tasks	You no longer have to...
Survey Analysis of Feedback	...be an amateur data analyst.
Chatbots (Eightfold)	...answer repetitive, easy questions.
Digital Interviewing (HireVue)	...do tedious phone screens.
Recruiting (HireVue)	...guess if someone is going to reply to your call.
Career Pathing (Fuel50)	...use artificial career path documents.
Mobile Coaching (BetterUp)	...spend a lot of $$ on a coach for difficult-to-measure ROI.

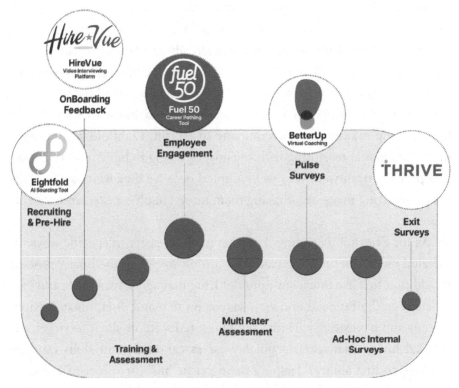

Image 7. How New Tech Enhances the Complete Employee Journey

When selecting our tech partners, we had in mind to build out a formal, unified, and more uniform global hiring process—at that point, NetApp didn't have that. In our aspirations to hire and develop for the future, our lack of standardization across the globe was another area of improvement to tackle. Specifically, one area of focus was to help smooth out the process of TA, because it was our belief that the way we bring people into NetApp sets the stage for the employee experience and business results. We wanted consistency in our hiring and recruiting methods, and up until now, and we didn't have technologies in place that could assist in achieving that. This was our vapor in a bottle for Year Two—a long-term vision for the 4th quadrant, Activating the Future, and workforce planning with a three-to-five-year horizon. It was the beginning of our transformation efforts in the TA space. Ambitious in the midst of COVID, admittedly, but a good start.

So, this slide above (Image 7) presented the idea of the employee life cycle. It said, "*Here is what we brought in,*" tech-wise. Eightfold, HireVue, Fuel50, and BetterUp. (Again, Glint was already in.) The squiggly line is the employee life cycle, which shows how I'm using technology across it, from end to end. This lifecycle included AI-powered talent/candidate-matching with the goal of supporting more consistency and more access to talent, thus making it easier for the company to recruit. Eightfold and HireVue supported global recruiting with the goal of trying to build a more consistent process. Both were very well-adopted because they were layered onto the pre-existing processes, making them more tangible, faster, and easier to use.

As for external recruiting, HireVue made it easier in specific ways. As a digital video interviewing platform, it took weeks off the hiring process. In addition to a live interview option, hiring managers, recruiters, and candidates could all upload and view videos on demand. It eliminated phone screens and navigating calendar bookings, reduced on-site interviews, and enabled hiring managers to quickly assess candidate soft skills (and for NetApp, coding ability). Helping them get to "no" (or "proceed") quickly. Many candidates worked on this process during off-hours, recording answers to a handful of questions, including, say, a thirty-second recruiter video asking things like, "*Hey, tell me a little bit about yourself.*" For internal recruiting, Mosaic (a tool for both talent enablement and talent acquisition) gave us access to all our internal talent pools. Within NetApp, we did not know what skill sets people actually had. We could say generally, *Hey, this person is in IT, so they have an IT skill set*, but they might have other skill sets that we are unaware of. But now, we get access to that information, making it easier for us to also recruit internally and have access to more talent.

These are just some quick examples of what these newly implemented technologies could do for us, accelerating the power of the TA team to identify and recruit the best talent available, from either without or within the organization, locally or across the globe. Mosaic was implemented in three phases, beginning in the latter part of Year Two and much of Year Three.

35 • Data: The Future of Talent Strategy

Ideally, we wanted to be able to synthesize data from all our AI-enabled technologies (along with HCM). Nowadays, we're just beginning to take advantage of these possibilities. Already, we're seeing this concept in the consumer products space. The Internet of Things, where everything's connected. The point is that you can turn on your lights from your phone. And your security and washing machine. When you can program your car to turn the heat on ten minutes before you go outside. Anything with electricity connected to it? That will become part of the internet. In our personal lives, the future is already happening.

In business, and in NetApp's case, we're talking about data from Mosaic, BetterUp, and Thrive Pulse Surveys. If we start automatically getting and using AI across that? That will be incredibly powerful. As Josh Bersin, HR Industry Analyst and Thought Leader, says, "*Companies still want integrated HR systems, but what they don't want is complex, integrated ERP software that makes everyone's life more complicated. In fact, they want life to be more simple.*" That's the goal—to use technologies to make our lives better. Faster. Make working more streamlined. Using AI to do all that heavy lifting of data processing for us. And, as I say repeatedly, "*The way AI technology works is it speeds up the ability for you to get to the human conversation.*" And to strengthen a human-centric work culture. Nothing's going to replace the table—sitting with someone for human interaction. Pulse Surveys and AI are just getting you more quickly to that table.

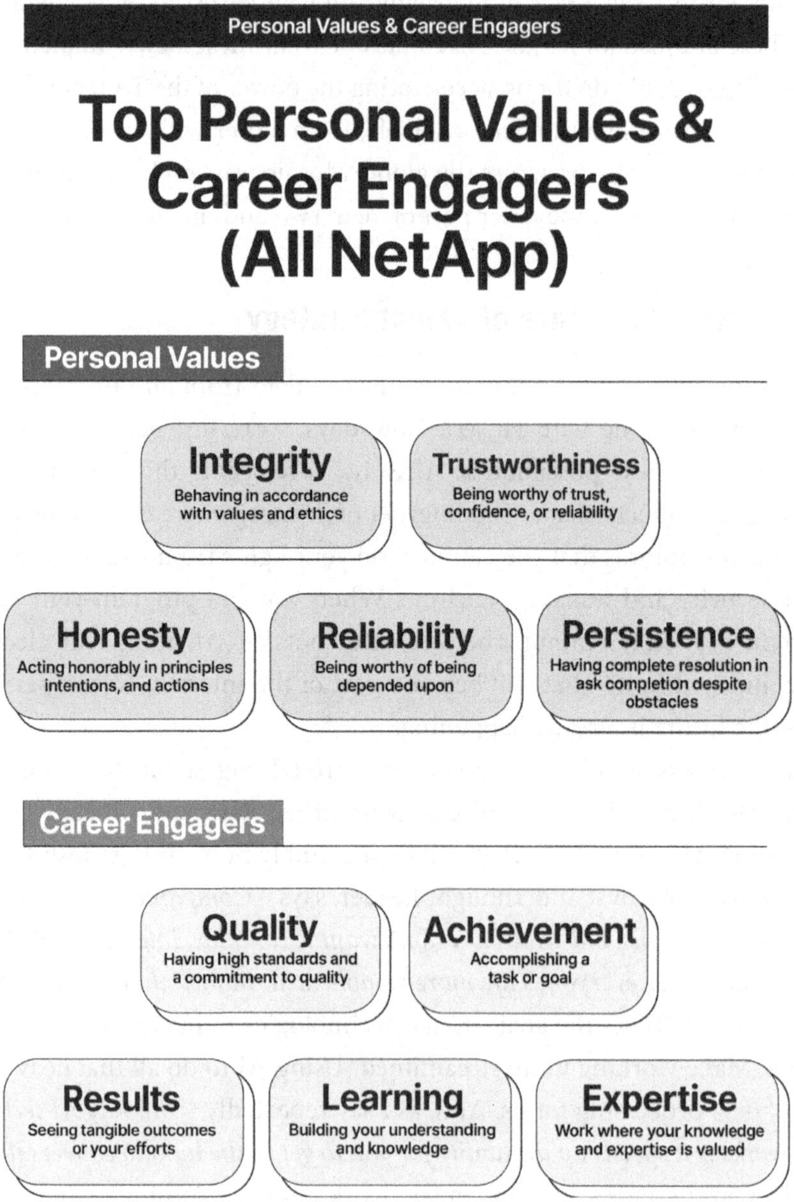

Personal Values & Career Engagers

Top Personal Values & Career Engagers (All NetApp)

Personal Values

Integrity
Behaving in accordance with values and ethics

Trustworthiness
Being worthy of trust, confidence, or reliability

Honesty
Acting honorably in principles intentions, and actions

Reliability
Being worthy of being depended upon

Persistence
Having complete resolution in ask completion despite obstacles

Career Engagers

Quality
Having high standards and a commitment to quality

Achievement
Accomplishing a task or goal

Results
Seeing tangible outcomes or your efforts

Learning
Building your understanding and knowledge

Expertise
Work where your knowledge and expertise is valued

Image 8. Fuel50 Report, Administrative view on what matters to employees (top 5 things they care about), 2021

We already do some of this data aggregation. This slide below (Image 8), for example, demonstrates what we can now do inside Mosaic. It tells us that these are the top five values and top five *career engagers* that our employees want to grow in. This is what they care about.

Once people start reflecting and putting their motivators in, that builds the engine. It builds the AI. It builds data. As talent folks, we have so much more data now than *ever* before. The point isn't the words that are on the screen. It's that we now *know* this. The software spits out timely and concrete information on employee preferences. *"Here are the top five personal values of the employees who have gone in during these reflection periods,"* and *"Here are the top career engagers."* We talk about all the AI data on the back end. We can now see: *This is what our employees care about. This is what they want.* Wow!

So, you tie in the Mosaic data with the Thrive Survey data and the generalized BetterUp feedback. The future is to incorporate them all to inform the talent strategy moving forward. This level of confluence would provide us with *exponential intelligence* and offer the opportunity for HR's pivot to be complete. This kind of synthesized data can enable any HR team to be more strategic and become more of a true business partner rather than a catch-all functionary. We could then become a more targeted engine to help the business enable its employees to meet their full potential.

SECTION 2

Pandemic-Affected Work Culture

A lot of good lessons came out of the pandemic.

Ialways used to say that the cell phone broke our work-life balance. Pre-pandemic, I'd hold up my PDA in various town halls and employee forums and talk about how it had blurred the demarcation line between personal and professional life. *"This is what's killing your work-life balance,"* I'd say. *"Now, any time of day, you get a text from your spouse, then a voicemail from your boss, then a notification that your dinner is about to arrive."* During the pandemic? COVID eviscerated any lines that may have remained. They were eradicated because you were never *not* around your phone, and now, you were sitting in the same chair for everything. Work-life balance? Gone. No more town halls or big All Hands meetings to commiserate together about it either. In a matter of months, the boundaries between home and work were completely erased—in much more significant and enduring ways for all working people across the planet.

36 · Handling Crisis

In the NetApp case, the pandemic couldn't be divorced from our Year of Technology. Because the Thrive Ecosystem for High-Performing Teams was introduced *before* COVID, and our transformation was already underway, I dare say we fared better than most. We were already listening to the voice of the employee. Thrive went live in August of 2019. We ran our first Pulse Survey in September of 2019, and were scheduled to run the second in March of 2020, at which point, we were in lockdown. Because we were already down this path of transformation, we were better positioned to pivot when chaos and challenges arrived. Because we had established transformation and change muscles. And we were able to build on them in a much more meaningful way.

You never know when you're going to be thrown into a transformation. But if you've already established enablement, democratization, and ways for people to feel that they belong and have a voice, whatever hits your business, you'll be better prepared to pivot. Not to suggest that we didn't scramble during the pandemic. Everyone scrambled. We all freaked out, us included. In those early days, no one had any answers. But how we *responded* was based on the tools and data we had and the way we talked and listened to the employees. I'd like to think that it put us ahead of the game. We saw a lot of other companies stumbling out in the open during this time and having to backtrack. But since we'd talked about growth mindset and whole person approach *before* the pandemic, we already had that messaging out there and could double down on it, even as the pandemic's reach began to mushroom across the planet. As Debra commented at one point, "*We are also very sensitive to the fact that there's been many (unfortunately, in a global pandemic) silver linings in terms of our resilience, our ability to adapt. How we've stayed productive and connected—but also having to have compassion and understand that this has been a tough time for a lot of us. Juggling family, diminishing boundaries between work and home life.*"

The shutdown was easier for every company to process because, like everywhere else in the world, everyone's light switch shut off at the same time. Suddenly, everyone began working from home. Everywhere, simultaneously. The disease forced it upon us all. The harder part was coming back. Returning to work. Companies continue to struggle even now on how to frame workforce flexibility going forward because that light switch in the sky doesn't work anymore—there is no one, single switch to flip everything back on. Our norms have been irreversibly fractured, and the world is exploring all kinds of variations to take its place. Everyone understands that we are not going back to the "normal" of before, and flexibility has to be part of it; the footprint has changed.

So, how do you do transformation now that everyone has their own personal light switch? Where one blanket policy no longer works for everybody? We had to discover, individually and collectively, what worked best. Again, we'd already begun focusing on the individual, atomized level.

And the team level. Because ours had been a *human-centered* transformation. And individualized development at scale. From the very beginning of introducing Thrive, it was ALL about building and re-humanizing the relationship between the manager and employee. We had been busy working on the manager-employee relationship and a growth mindset. And to have a transformative mindset during this return to work? It was a time of corporate distress, but our more human-centric approach actually helped us through it. We were prepared to bring a transformative mindset during this return to work. We were ready. And we had a key piece of the data at our fingertips during this shift that made all the difference.

Well-Being Survey Results

In March of 2020, at the beginning of the shutdown, we shifted from engagement to a series of well-being surveys—with a 91 percent response rate. (Yes, that's really high.) Now, with the advancement of AI, and because of our great partnership with GLINT, we were able to ensure we were asking the right questions. So we switched to the likes of: *"Hey, we're a year into the pandemic. How do you feel about it? How do you feel about the company?"* These revised questions were shorter and all focused on, *"How are you feeling? How can we help?"* But also, *"How do you want to return to work?"*

The response was overwhelmingly: *"Thank you for taking care of us, for putting the person first."* And there was a lot of data around: *"I feel taken care of during this very rough time."* What else did the survey results reveal? Strategically, I always knew where we were headed, even with the massive curveball of the pandemic, but I felt fortified by this survey data—and in some cases, surprised. Because we also saw overwhelming evidence that people didn't want to come back to the office. In fact, only 9 percent of employees wanted to come back in full-time. (Less than 10 percent!) I would not have guessed such a low number. Perhaps a third at most, I had figured. When I saw 9 percent, my head kind of exploded. (And my next thought was *Wow! Everyone feels like me!*) Then, six months later, after the vaccine shots started, that 9 went down to 7. And some of the comments we got were basically: "*If you make me come back, I'm quitting.*"

Those became the arrows in my quiver. *This* is how the voice of the customer and data influences talent strategy. All this backend data changed the way that I was able to talk to the CEO staff and plan an informed response. Before, it was a guessing game in a lot of ways. Around this same time, George was planning to announce a three-day-a-week return to office policy. It was already in his all hands deck. But the people had spoken! And I felt it would be irresponsible not to deliver their message. At that point, I was thinking, *Why say that? Let's not put that ultimatum out there!* I pleaded my case: "*George, please cut that. The pandemic's really changing people. We're not going back to where we were. We're never going back.*" So, as unpopular as I knew my words were going to be, I had to go to George and the CEO staff and tell them what the data was clearly telling us. And because George is a caring, people-focused, and data-driven CEO, I had the courage to be bold. I knew he would understand that forcing folks to come into the office was going to blow up in our faces. So, I dug an even deeper hole for myself and continued, "*Okay, we're not telling them to come back for a certain number of days. We're not gonna do it. It's gonna go bad.*" (Some days are indelible, right? This was definitely another one of mine.) I believed in the data, and, turns out, so did George.

But it took me longer than twenty minutes this time to get *everybody* on board. And several meetings of back and forth. Some people were incredulous: "*What do you mean we're never going back?*" Our data was putting us ahead of the national conversation. It wasn't out there yet, and again, we were all struggling through these challenging times with limited information. Even so, I repeated, "*People aren't gonna come back. They don't want to. The impromptu well-being Pulse Survey suggests that they aren't gonna return.*" If I hadn't taken that survey and didn't have access to the results? I would not have had a lick of data to stand on. No arrow in my quiver.

How Will We Know?

I got a bit of pushback. No surprise. We were still contending with old school mindsets in some ways, and again, a lot of unknowns. Not one person had the perfect answer, including me. Once employees began working at home, I was already getting questioned. *"What?! We're gonna let them work from home?"* Some leaders came to me and said, *"Well, if we're not back in the office, how do I know if my people are actually working? I wanna see the whites of their eyes."* I remember another guy asking me, *"If I can't see what people are doing, how am I gonna know if they're being productive?"* to which I responded, *"How do you know now? How have you ever known? Were you literally watching them all day long? Were you standing there watching them in their cubicles? You were not. You were waiting for them to deliver. You were having meetings to talk about progress."*

What this transformation helped managers understand is how to focus on more helpful questions. Questions such as: *Are they achieving their goals? Are they hitting their priorities? Are they getting their projects done? Is the coding written on time?* If you think about it, most workers at every level are largely self-managed on a day-to-day basis, anyway. Even when they're in the office, they're self-managed. Of course, if you have a bunch of sixteen-year-olds in McDonald's, you probably gotta keep an eye on 'em. But in this context, we're talking about suuuuuper intelligent people. And we now know what happened. Yes, there was a lot of trepidation around productivity. *"No one's gonna work now,"* became the presumption among many. But what happened was the opposite. Everyone worked twice as hard during the pandemic. They actually leaned the other way and overworked. (In fact, as was proven to be the case in many companies across many industries, NetApp probably had two of the most productive years on record. Productivity never suffered a beat at NetApp.)

And then we all finally agreed, and George cut it. I was thinking, *Thank you, Jesus.* And then, during the next week or two, Apple announced, *"We expect everyone to come back,"* and were derided. Then Google did the same thing. *"Three days a week."* Up until now, we couldn't compete with Google, with their bikes and their free, all-you-can-eat salmon buffet. And soon we realized: We can get things done. So, we met with marketing, pivoted our talent brand, and said, *"This is going to be our new differentiator! Work in the office when you and your teams want to—or not."* Our focus was on individual and organizational success. I wanted to work together to figure out which occasions we *did* want to come in for. Brainstorming sessions, perhaps? Team building?

We had proven to ourselves that we could get work done remotely. I knew *I* wasn't going to (that's just me, Larry, the employee, talking). I was never going back! So, I was right in there with how most everybody else was feeling. I told my team we'd find ways to get together, but I was not gonna be sitting in commutes twice a day, five days a week. It's barbaric! We just didn't know any different!

37 • Thrive Everywhere: The Hybrid Work Model

BetterUp launched in May of 2020. By late summer/early fall, BetterUp began reporting some common themes that were coming up in coaching sessions. What were people asking for? Before the pandemic, when we looked at aggregated data, it was mostly focused on leadership, teamwork, work/life balance; a wide swath of all those factors—a lot of variety. After the pandemic, the themes were very common and consistent. Fear. Health. Family. And *What will the company do to help or hinder me?* (As we got a year into the pandemic, the pendulum started swinging back to more varied focuses on success.) But for now, what I heard was *"The employees are saying they don't wanna go back to work in the office unless it's on their terms. And they're scared."* We could now go to NetApp leadership and let them know, *"Hey, a thousand of our employees are saying that they're getting burned out. The survey is saying this, and the coaches are actively working on these same themes. What are we gonna do?"* By combining this data with the voices of our employees in different contexts (one from a whole person context with BetterUp, the other addressing work/home life through surveys), we could build a more nuanced plan of action. Our ability to access this kind of synthesized data allowed us to continue to focus on problem-solving these acute, pandemic-related challenges hitting the staff all across the company.

And NetApp leadership listened. They listened to the data and to the workers. And it all began with the *voice of the employee*. With, "*We're Never Going Back!*" Our HR leadership team held meetings and began to consider the hybrid work model. Instead of looking out at the world at all those other companies also struggling to find the right path forward, we kept our own council. And those conversations became the vision for what eventually became *Thrive Everywhere* (so named with help from marketing). In January of 2021, the beginning of Year Three, NetApp officially embraced Thrive Everywhere, the pandemic hybrid work environment. As data kept coming in, this hybrid work model continued to grow more flexible than many even wanted it to be, but for now, it was a start. Elaine-Marie recounts a story that reflects how things have been going since Thrive Everywhere began:

We launched a new manager program that supported our new Thrive Everywhere hybrid work model. We had a fireside chat with the VP of engineering from our core engineering group in India (a very large percentage of NetApp's overall population), talking about how, just weeks prior to the pandemic, and in response to some concerns, they'd piloted a four-day work week. He said, 'We're going to do one trial run to see what it's like. Everyone across the organization is going to be working from home.' And we haven't been back since. And in the face of productivity concerns, 'we've probably had two of the most productive years of our career…and we realized, in the two years of the pandemic is: We can get things done.' And he continued, 'Now it's all about…learning to manage our work around our lives.' To consider where and how we work most effectively…showing up and being in your seat doesn't equal productivity. It's not the same, right? It's your output and your results. I thought that was so great. And finally, he said, 'And this is what you guys are driving with Thrive.' And I said, 'Yes! Thank you. Thank you.' That was awesome.

Is It Worth It?

But deeper than all of this, as we all now know, people were reassessing their lives. I wasn't able to articulate it that day the way I could, say, a month later, when we'd realized that, during the pandemic, human beings in this world had fundamentally changed. Because we were all stuck at home. And people were dying. At the beginning, everybody was afraid. We didn't know whether we could leave our houses. We didn't have all the information that we now have about transmission. Looking back now, you could almost say it was inevitable that people would re-evaluate their priorities. At the very least, they were going to be reluctant to go back to an office—or back to the way things were. The Great Resignation was just beginning. People began quitting their jobs and began wondering whether all this effort was worth it. *Is it worth it to me to put all this energy into work and the rat race when I could die? When my family members could die?*

As horrific as the pandemic was, it also became a catalyst for change and a window of opportunity to really reboot our way of thinking about work in general. About our life priorities and life balance. And, really, you should always be moving forward anyway, right? As a business, we should all strive to be more future proof. And not go back to the way things were just because. I believe everyone saw the pandemic as an opportunity to make change—and be visionary about what we wanted to do so we could try to work toward that. It was an accelerant, forcing us to rethink situations that weren't quite working anyway. We all saw that this was going to happen on a cultural level. And on a global one. So, for our situation, we began to say, "*Well, this is also an opportunity. We're on this transformational journey, and we've been wanting to change things, but this could be our chance to make big shifts in the workplace.*"

Offices Are Open

Two years into it, NetApp sent out an email that said, *Offices are now open.* But there was no mandatory follow-up saying, "*Okay! Everybody, come back in now. You have to be in the office two to three days a week."* If people wanted a break from their living situations and to return to the office, fine! I wasn't stopping anyone from going in. But I also was not going to tell anyone to come in unless we all agreed "X" was a good time to do it. It continues to all be based on personal choice, and that's part of the essence of the Thrive Everywhere hybrid work model.

Transition Based on Hard Data

With NetApp, because our human-centered transformation was well underway before the pandemic, we were able to navigate those waters much more easily. We could use that baseline and our ability to listen to build Thrive Everywhere. And because of our Thrive tools, we were able to make better decisions faster.

Specifically, we reframed our Pulse Survey questions around the most pressing issues (well-being and hybrid work). The data we got back (which were our best scores to date) included, *"Thank you for giving us choice," "Thank you for not dictating,"* and *"Thank you for making us feel we have control over it."*

Where we saw big companies out in the market saying things and then retracting them, over and over, our employee listening data fed out to our Thrive Everywhere strategy. And we never had to retract anything because we had solid, relevant intel on how our employees were doing. And because QCs were already established, we could adapt those conversations and lead with grace. Employees said they felt cared for during this time, which was a big win.

The pandemic is over. But inevitably, something else is going to happen to your business. It won't look exactly like any challenges you've faced to date, but there'll be something. If you already have in place some kind of agile, closed-loop system, with enablement and ways for people to feel better and understand there's a vision in place and that they belong, whatever hits your business, you'll likely weather the storm better because of all the positivity-minded preparations you've made along the way.

38 • Well-Being vs. Productivity? Or Both?

NetApp's reaction to the pandemic reflected its human-centered, whole person approach. The change of mindset, the focus on the individual, the democratization of the management process. Inclusive leadership. Growth mindset. First Thrive, then Thrive Everywhere. First surveys and QCs, then virtual coaching, career pathing, an Internal Marketplace, and AI-enabled recruitment strategies. Using cutting-edge technology, tools, and programs to activate powerful employee experiences throughout the life cycle. And a long-term vision to build a universal hiring process. But with the pandemic, for the first time, and in a sweeping, global way, companies began to realize that the psychological well-being and the psychological resources of their workforce were something they had to consider—possibly even manage *beyond* just reducing healthcare costs. This is what BetterUp calls your *performance potential* as a knowledge company. Are you managing that potential?

To borrow an Alexi metaphor, imagine that potential as a barbell, where well-being is at one end, and productivity is at the other. At the start of the pandemic, and for the first time in corporate life, the emphasis was heavily weighted in the direction of self-care. *"We care about everyone flourishing,"* and *"We want well-being."* So, a lot of employers picked up one side of the barbell, to which leadership applauded, *"Mental health benefits! Flourishing!"* But until we began to get COVID under control, no one was focused on performance and productivity. They were focused on preventing people from dying. And generally speaking, economic productivity was strangely high—or at least it *seemed* to be at the time. As the world began to normalize, many dropped well-being as a focus and picked up the productivity and performance side instead.

There were a lot of great lessons that came out of the pandemic, and I'm hoping that this is one of them. That well-being and productivity are not mutually exclusive. That leaders don't have to choose to invest in one or the other. They aren't forced to make impossible choices because the data now shows that even a pandemic-affected workforce can be extremely productive. Imagine your employees' performance potential when they're not isolated and/or in a state of distress.

If the future of corporate life is in fact headed in this direction, perhaps we'll stop asking boardroom questions like, "*Should we invest in the well-being of our people or their productivity?*" And leaders and managers alike will come to understand that to maximize the potential of their employees, to achieve high-performing teams, they need to manage both. Productivity *and* well-being are two sides of the same barbell, so to speak. And we can start noticing instead, "*Hey, people aren't performing? That's actually a symptom of poor well-being.*" Or the opposite. "*People are performing. That's actually a sign of positive well-being.*" They reflect a symbiotic dynamic, a Golden Thread, and there are solutions available to regain this balance, should it ever get thrown off.

Again, the conclusion I hope we arrive at, eventually, is that well-being *and* productivity are needed to realize your employee's performance potential. You're missing out if you're only picking up one side of the barbell and dropping the other. Alexi reflects on this essential idea in this way,

> I think…the future is getting more scientific to understand that there's not a social psychologist in the world that is confused by this. The only people confused by this seem to be executives in business. You call Adam Grant. He's not confused. You call Amy Edmonson. She's not confused. None of the scientists that truly understand the research are confused. It's both. And I think that is where business is going. As we're catching up with the science, but also with the wisdom traditions which knew this the whole time, that peak performance requires peak mental fitness, and they are the two sides of the same thing.

BetterUp Coaching & Good Data

We're not trying to manage performance.
We're here to go from good to great.

I'd given up on coaching. That was what I told them on my very first day at NetApp. In the old days, a typical coaching scenario meant choosing one very pricy coach for one high-performing but troublesome VP. Leadership would say, "*Go get them a coach*"—which is, pretty much, the completely wrong thing to do. How about saying instead, "*If you continue to behave this way, we don't care what your performance is. You're outta here!*"? Instead, we'd hire those executive-level coaches (the only kind you could or would hire) who'd meet with the exec in question to talk about who knows what. And typically, at the executive level, employees don't really even want to be coached anyway. Whenever I went this route, I'd get a limited response back, even after I'd just dropped $100K. And what was I learning from the coach? I wouldn't get any data. Coaches never told me anything. The ROI was impossible to measure other than to say that, more often than not, the investment didn't actually fix or change anything.

Discovering BetterUp was a breath of fresh air. This platform (which "*delivers transformative coaching experiences to drive productivity, engagement, and retention at scale*") was such an individual-by-individual development opportunity. It was very logical and easy to show how it fit into the *Activate Yourself* quadrant. We made sure leaders and employees knew getting a coach was not a punishment or a "fix this person" approach. The purpose was to move employees from good to great or from great to greater. Any employee. Anywhere.

After bringing them on at NetApp, I spoke on a panel hosted by Josh Bersin at a BetterUp conference. I was asked why I chose BetterUp. Not in terms of my talent strategy, which we'd discussed before. This was more about: "*Why'd you choose us? How do you plan to use us?*" I told them their company had helped me believe in coaching again and that I believed it should be a benefit for all employees. But you have to want to have a coach, right? You can only get good coaching if you want it. I believe we should make it available to everyone, so those who want to can seek it out, regardless of circumstance.

39 • Dreaming the Same Dream

When BetterUp came around, saying, "*We produce all this data in the background. We can tell you what people are working on. They'll be self-assessed on how they're improving. Our coaches are vetted [and] world class,*" I thought that was pretty fabulous to hear. You get to choose your coach, and it's tied to what you want, and I get backend data out of it? That was leaps and bounds ahead of what executive coaching did. BetterUp went on to describe their approach: "*Coaching is not to fix you. If there's a performance problem, you deal with that as a manager, not a coach. We're not trying to manage performance. We're trying to go from good to great.*" That was when I knew BetterUp and I were dreaming the same dream.

Founded in 2013, Alexi Robichaux is the co-founder and CEO of BetterUp, and a former executive at a *Fortune* 1000 company at the tender age of twenty-five. Widely recognized as a leadership development innovator, BetterUp is the first leadership development platform to connect coaching to sustainable behavior change.

Like me, Alexi believes the changing relationship between employees and employers "*will be key to future human flourishing and innovation.*" That's what we're all after: growth, innovation, and enterprise-wide expansion! They were the first vendor I approached only months after joining NetApp. I knew if I was going to be successful, I needed to have BetterUp in our corner.

In its second year at NetApp, Thrive Ecosystem for High-Performing Teams was focused on bringing in technologies to further develop our cultural transformation. That included BetterUp because I knew their approach was the right one for where we were taking the company. At some point, I spoke at their BetterUp sales kickoff, and as part of that talk, I said, *"We're putting the 'human' in human resources, as opposed to the way it used to be—resources first, humans second. We're leading with talent. We're leading with the whole person approach."*

The first time I spoke for BetterUp, their topic was resilience. *How do you fill the tank? How are you resilient?* That was before we even really started thinking about resilience in the way that we do now. They were way ahead of the game on that—another reason we chose them. I knew that together, we were going to drive the idea that: *The fuel in your tank is your energy and your resilience. And if you're not looking at your whole person, your tank's going to run low.*

What Is BetterUp Virtual Coaching?

BetterUp is virtual/mobile and on-demand coaching made available for every employee and manager at NetApp. It's a tech-enabled solution for the 1st quadrant (*Activate Yourself*) and the 2nd (*Activate the Team*) on the Wheel and a growth platform for organizational transformation through individual transformation. It's individualized development at scale, meaning, for NetApp, it was an individual-by-individual development opportunity.

As a company, BetterUp is an innovative market leader. They're constantly adding to their suite of services and resources and, well, as you can see, I remain a huge fan. In 2020, we started out with these options for supporting employees' development journeys:

- **Dedicated Coaching**: Meeting 1:1, focusing on highly personalized growth areas, and includes:
  - ▷ 1:1 expert coaching
  - ▷ Feedback and progress
  - ▷ 24/7 messaging with a coach
  - ▷ The creation of a development plan and setting of goals
  - ▷ Personalized, curated, micro-learnings for twelve months

- **Specialist Coaching:** Access to an on-demand, extended network of coaches to support additional needs
- **Development Library:** Over three thousand learning resources in the BetterUp platform

I began speaking with BetterUp about partnering in early to mid-2019. We ran our first virtual coaching pilot in November and signed a contract with them the following April, one month into the pandemic lockdown. May 26, 2020, was the official launch date. It couldn't have arrived at a better time as we needed wellness services for our distressed workforce—as well as detailed feedback on how they were feeling and functioning as COVID raged across the planet. The idea was to provide all employees with a platform to access coaching from wherever they were. With mobile coaching and our whole person approach, you could talk to your coach about whatever you wanted—your spouse, health, or management style. It was delivering precision development at scale.

Life-Changing

Since the launch, nearly 1800 NetApp staff have gone through coaching with BetterUp (over 15 percent of the company). Out of the one thousand-plus employees who participated in the first cohort, 76 percent of them said there was a moment or session that was life-changing for them. (Life-changing!) Where else in this company do we provide tools that could generate a reaction like that? We were just hoping they came back tomorrow. Never mind changing their lives. And then we started getting feedback like, "*BetterUp has helped repair my relationship with my daughter.*" "*I have someone dying in my family, and my coach got me through it.*" "*I can so much better articulate my vision to my team because of my coach.*" These kinds of quotes are not normal corporate answers. All for 1,500 bucks?! These stats and comments have been mind-blowing. And powerful. While I expected positive results, the feedback was, quite honestly, off the charts.

September 2020 Insights from NetApp's May 2020 Coaching Cohort*
100% said it was worth their time.
96% said they were more productive as a result.

Member Satisfaction
76% Rated as "Life-Changing" or "Amazing."
98% Agreed that "BetterUp is a valuable use of my time."
88% Agreed that "Working with my coach has made me more effective at my job."
96% Confirmed that, "My coach helped me make meaningful progress toward my goals.
64% Executed against objectives .
74% Helped themselves or direct reports with career growth .
83% Grew in their ability to adapt to change.
73% Built relationships and internal partnerships .
80% Focused on creating an inclusive work environment.
81% Aligned others around a clear strategy.

*Percentage of sessions is based on 1,363 rated sessions with 330 unique members.

40 · What Do You Mean by Whole Person?

Years ago, we tried to beat the personal part out of people in the workplace. You could *never* say something like, *"Oh, I'm feeling depressed."* That would be a black mark against you in the corporate world. Why do people think that they only have to focus on their physical health? Why are we proactive about our bodies, but the only time we think about our mental health is when we're in crisis mode? Your mental health should be given as much priority as exercising and eating right. Health. Well-being. That's the whole person approach. As in, we look at you as a whole person, not just employee number 52, not just telling you to, *"Just shut up and get your work done."* We believe you can't separate any part of yourself into work and life. You need to approach work and life as an entire person, as a whole one. And that *whole* means feeding our body, mind, and emotional life. The work parts. The life parts. All the parts. Because they're parts of a whole. That was what we were trying to get people to think about. Which was why we brought these tools in. Why we brought BetterUp in. Because, ultimately, Thrive is really about well-being.

Health As Fuel

Your health and energy are what fuel your productivity. Let's say you're a knowledge worker (which most folks are these days). Employers used to be able to just ask, "*Do you have the stamina to stand on this assembly line for eight hours?*" To which, if you wanted a job, you'd reply, "*Yes, sir.*" And you would build up the stamina to do that, no matter how unpleasant an experience it was (and hopefully, not get carpal tunnel or whatever in the process). But *now*, as knowledge workers, you can't shut off your brain. You can shut off an assembly line, but that doesn't work on a mental level. Speaking personally, I'll wake up sometimes with some panicked idea and think, "*Oh, my God, I forgot to do this (or that), or I have this big meeting, and I don't think I'm properly prepared.*" How you handle that is the productivity and the fuel of your life, which includes how well, or poorly, you perform at your knowledge worker job. So, that's a slice of the whole person concept. This concept also speaks to your level of resilience. Don't expect to be able to put in your best at work if you're not taking care of your health and energy all the time.

Such a Grind

Not that my thinking on this front started at NetApp. My "humanist" approach began in reaction to managerial styles I was exposed to early in my corporate life. When I was at Citibank, it was such a grind. I was in phone-based business development—with thousands of phone reps to manage at a time. Not that being on the phone is a bad thing, in general. But in the '90s? If they were cleaning the bathrooms, they would put a big "X" over the entrance and say, "*Don't even think about coming in here. The bathroom is off limits.*" The stress was crazy on these people. And the per capita of miscarriages at Citibank in those days? Unreal. That was when I began thinking: *Why would anyone treat people like this?*

Back in 2015, we brought a program into Equinix called Archimedes. It was designed to help plan business improvement proposals. As part of my talent management team, Donny Przygodski was hired to build executive development programs, and what he added to that was the idea of pitching these proposals to *Shark Tank*. He then suggested another fresh idea: the Corporate Athlete. The way it worked was we'd have all the directors participate at an offsite. After presenting them with a business challenge, they'd have to work as a team to develop it—and then go on the TV show to see if their idea would get funded. During those two weeks, staff from Corporate Athlete would come in and talk to them about diet and exercise, make them do jumping jacks, take walks, and talk about health, well-being, and how it's all connected to their work performance. Nothing like today, but for that time, it was a move in the right direction.

HR and the corporate world have not been ready for this idea of a human-centric work culture, but that's beginning to change. The pandemic was a big catalyst for that. For the cultural correction, which includes both sides of the barbell. Now, I think every culture has its own view of time off or resilience. And Carol Dweck's *Mindset* book has been popular, but I think, overall, corporate culture has only *juuuuust* recently really started to embrace the idea of whole person. Even if they don't call it that. Equinix, for example, is a data center. And their workers sit in a locked building that uses retina scans all day long. Not necessarily the kind of environment that lends itself to conversations about whole person. Adding in the Corporate Athlete really introduced some new ways of thinking, for sure. I love being a trumpet for this kind of thinking. I was on these panels, think tanks, and product development councils, but even there and then, surprisingly few of my colleagues used terms such as whole person, well-being, or growth mindset...yet.

Individualized Development at Scale

By introducing BetterUp to NetApp, I was once again looking to challenge the old assumption that training is going to help every single person in the same way. There's really no practical way to do that and make it stick (remember the Bazooka Joe Tattoo story). Now, each person gets their own coach. Their own self-tailored career planning with time-out for reflection and private feedback. With mobile coaching, BetterUp completely embodies the whole person approach and individualized (but scalable) development. You get your own personalized development. A supportive listener, co-strategist, and accountability partner. You're not going to some off-the-shelf training designed for the masses.

Not a Spa Day

As part of the BetterUp process, you work with your chosen coach to develop yourself. An approach that fit right in with our Thrive Wheel. This, also, is where the enablement part comes in. We can provide the tool, but it's up to the employee to reach for it. And make the most of it. As I've often said (with a line I stole from someone who stole it from someone else), "*Going to a coach is like going to the gym. It's not like going to the spa. You have to put in the work.*"

Well-Being: The Center of the Next Wave

As influential public figures such as Prince Harry and athletes such as Simone Biles, Naomi Osaka, and Serena Williams de-stigmatize the ability to speak publicly about mental health issues, it grants more permission for the rest of us to prioritize self-care. There's room now for all of us to lean into these methods for maintaining personal well-being. And that means at home and at the office, which, for millions more than ever before, is now the same place. I think we can all agree, hybrid is here to stay. The pandemic may be over, but that's just the way we are now. Being in the office all the time is probably never going to be the expected norm again. That means protecting your personal life and managing healthy boundaries will remain ongoing needs and challenges. And that means well-being is going to be the next big wave.

Mental Fitness

At the center of all these discussions—and throwing around terms such as *whole person, well-being, resilience,* and *growth mindset*—is the idea that work culture is beginning to accept the idea that we get to be fully human in the workplace. That we can bring our *whole* selves and be transparent about the actual truth of the matter, which is that to give our best at the office, we must take care of ourselves and our loved ones, and that includes our and their health—physical, emotional, and for some, spiritual too. And that self-care is best done *proactively* rather than reactively. "In the workplace" means building in systems designed to care and provide support for the whole person—and that thinking is at the center of Thrive, along with philosophically aligned partners such as Fuel50 and BetterUp. We know that to produce our best work, healthy bodies and healthy lifestyles are a must. That includes eating right, exercising, getting sufficient rest and sleep, and downtime. We need room for play and relationships. Now, we're beginning to embrace this thinking for our minds as well. To reference Alexi on this, he says:

> We're talking about proactive, preventative mental health. We're talking about shifting the lens from mental health being the removal of mental illness to mental health being the proactive cultivation of one's psychological strengths and capacities. And so, that's where fitness comes in. We really think of mental fitness as the psychological strength and resilience of individuals and your ability to proactively cultivate that. Whether you call it mental fitness or preventative care. The reason we like fitness is because it's action-oriented and pulls on these metaphors of physical fitness, right? Which is, Hey, this stuff is hard work, but it's

rewarding, and it's a muscle (it's literally not a muscle; it's your mind), but in the physical analogy, it's a muscle that you can build. And so that's why we use the fitness analogy.

BetterUp also uses the analogy of what it takes to perform at the level of an elite, Olympic athlete (a like-minded descendant of the Corporate Athlete!). An Olympic athlete doesn't just receive coaching in the realm of their chosen sport. They rely on a whole bench of coaches who look at their nutrition, sleep, and well-being—physical, emotional, and mental. You have to focus on all those aspects of yourself to achieve peak performance. That's where we're beginning to go beyond just coaching, and addressing all aspects of achieving full potential.

Coaching Democratized

How does coaching work at NetApp? From day one, the kind of coaching we introduced at NetApp was democratized—by design. It was no longer just for the C-Suite. I opened it up to anyone who wanted to do it. I'd long been a huge proponent of coaching for all. Yes, there is a place for executive and manager coaching. It is important (and again, not all executive coaches are bad!). But what about everybody else who wants to BE a manager or an executive someday? How are they going to get there—and be of greater value to the company—if they don't feel supported? Let's enable newbies, interns, and first-level careerists and provide them all with tools and resources that they can use in their career ambitions going forward. As EM shares,

Coaching is such a powerful way to grow. It meets you where you are. We want to bring that to the masses. Right now, if you look at typical executive coaching engagements, they normally cost around $30,000 for six months. So, naturally, they're reserved for a very small number of people. But you can use something like a BetterUp that we've been partnering with and make it available for $3,000 for six months. That's a tenth of what it costs now, and it's accessible to more people.... So, *when you look at it at that 'per employee' level, it just makes sense to make the investment.*

Thanks to advances in technology—pushed forward all the more by the pandemic—now democratized and with improved access, enabling us to video conference from anywhere in the world to anywhere in the world, we could easily reach everybody and anybody with customized, one-on-one coaching. An entry level NetApp employee in Bangalore can have a world class coaching experience from their phone. We believe any employee who wants to get better by working with a coach can go from good to great. And the service is now accessible on your device. It's in the flow of work, and there's a platform with curated content as well. Of course, in any company, you are going to run up against budget. But this is an investment in your own. It's that two-sided barbell. What was once $200,000 for an executive coach for one high-level staff member now costs $1,500 to $3,000, meaning every level of staffer can enjoy the benefits. And again, it's not about performance problems or designing a system around underperformers. This is about everyone going from good to great. So, we pushed really hard on that.

Coaching Sessions: Action-Oriented

This is not therapy—it's action-oriented. And there's some level of accountability built in. Not for the purpose of your manager policing, however. This is really about you, betting on yourself. Setting your own goals and then asking, *How'd I actually do against what I said I wanted to do?* And if those don't line up, it's not wrong; it's just an opportunity to reevaluate. In this vein, coaches often provide assignments or tasks. There's also an online database with thousands of resources members can access. So, at the end of a session, the coach might also say, *"Hey, here is a masterclass you should go look at,"* Or *"Here is a talk, or here's a paper or a book."* They'll give you these resources to consume between coaching sessions. Coaches also have many other tools at their disposal to help members advance their career goals.

Optimizing Human Performance

As BetterUp says, "*When your employees are thriving, so does your organization. It just takes a little dose of transformation.*" In today's volatile world, leaders are coming to appreciate that in order to thrive, they need to embrace transformation and build more trust in their communities. And building the muscles of transformation means changing behaviors—which comes down to individuals. That atomic level of behavioral transformation. Human transformation means investing in your employees' productivity *and* well-being while also fortifying your workforce with the tools and resources required to achieve their full potential. Yes, that means recruiting, but it also means investing from within. A process that includes developing not only skills and capabilities but also mindsets. Building resilience to optimize human performance. Coaching is a cost-effective way to achieve all these things, and the stats don't lie. BetterUp Labs studied what transformation looks like in the workplace. With coaching, employees are seeing these kinds of results. In fact, percentage increases[10] have been reported in the following areas:

Stress Management	90%
Emotional Regulation	92%
Productivity	2.1x increase
Resilience	149%
Intent to Stay	68%

And finally they're also seeing a 35 percent decrease in burnout.[11] Since bringing BetterUp on board, over 10 percent of employees have gone through it—and it's all voluntary. Their feedback has been genuinely moving and exciting. Specifically—after the six months were up, the coachees were surveyed, and, as the client, we received a summary of those comments from BetterUp. Here's three:

What skills do I need to demonstrate to get promoted within the next year? Learned about leadership styles and am more conscious of what style I'm demonstrating. Have a "sounding board" [now] to help me prep for conversations with my boss, colleagues, etc.

Oh, my God. To tap the coach like this? That cares about my whole life? Thank you. Thank you. Thank you for giving me this opportunity.

My coach helps me explore...how empathy can help my career. She asks great questions that get me to think about how other people might look at situations in ways I don't naturally explore. Through these sessions, I felt more willing and excited to reach out to my coworkers and to open up personally to them. If we weren't working at home all the time, I'm sure I could put these skills to work even more.

I took this summary as a good indicator that we were really onto something here. BetterUp's no longer a startup. As a more established market innovator, I believe one of BetterUp's home runs is that it has shaped itself into a complete well-being platform for organizations (and it's the future that companies need). It's no longer just about coaching. They've been an exceptional partner. The staff is well-educated, and I've loved working with them. Their accessibility, responsiveness, and desire to collaborate have been exemplary.

41 · Data in Aggregate: Where Else Would You Get That?

Most people buy AI platforms for the front-end features—dynamic interactions, friendly user interface, the flashy state-of-the-art features. What's often overlooked is the back-end data. But this is where the game-changer information can be found. Where, as I've been saying, you can hear the voice of the employees and act accordingly.

The BetterUp data came to me in a hard copy deck quarterly (the coaching sessions themselves are completely private, just like medical records). There's also a year-end review "slick," as I called it. What we got was strictly

NetApp's—our data for our people who'd gone through the process. The coaches enter into the platform, for example, that, *"People are asking a lot about 'X.'"* The platform puts it all together and reports, *Here's what your people are concerned about. Here are the top three issues.* Trends begin to appear. And unlike surveys, in coaching, the discussions are unique. You're not answering twenty questions like what I wrote with the Pulse Survey vendor. Every data point is unique. There's *no* view to that anywhere else. It's data that's completely different from any signal I get from any other source.

As the pandemic marched on, we noticed a significant shift in our employees' concerns. People were scared! In retrospect, this progression may seem logical, from leadership and growth to fear and safety to what future work was going to look like. But in the moment (and always especially true in crisis moments like those), there's nothing like real-time, data-driven insights to fuel strategic decision-making with solid information. And it became a powerful tool when discussing budgeting or making changes with the CEO and leadership. The impact of that data was undeniable.

Praisidio: Building an Integrated Narrative

The power of integrating data is crucial in building a narrative that prioritizes employees. In this era of Generative AI, tools such as Praisidio (full disclosure, I'm an investor in this company) make the process even easier. Praisidio leverages AI to bring together and analyze data from various sources, providing real-time, insightful analytics that support critical decision-making—including, for example, predicting individual turnover and suggesting ways to prevent it. For example, you might be wondering, *Who on my team is going to turn over?* Using natural language processing, this company can deliver a list of high-risk employees. Praisidio is a leader in integrated people analytics. With instant insights about your employees, it allows you to:

- Improve employee performance and retention
- Simplify workforce planning, performance management, and talent risk management

Praisidio is truly remarkable. All you have to do is ask it a question (like ChatGPT), and all of the employee data (from as many sources as you care to include) is tapped, giving you powerful, synthesized analytics and exponential intelligence in real-time to enable you to make critical decisions.

Imperative: Fixing What's Broken

There's a new vendor worth mentioning that I'm quite excited about. It's called Imperative, and their mission is to "fix what's broken" in today's workplace, meaning the lack of connection and sense of belonging among employees. Talk about dreaming the same dream! The idea is to build buddies across the organization, with whom you can commiserate—and be held accountable to.

I love the structure they've introduced, and it's all app-based; so, it's very accessible for any employee, anywhere. At NetApp, we chose a pilot for our directors. What Imperative does is automatically match up two people (all directors in this case) located in the same time zone. Ideally, it's someone new to you. They could be in a different job, but they're at the same level, so the responsibility vibe is the same. The pair meet five times for an hour or so and have a conversation using the prompts provided in the app.

The first question they ask each other is: "*How are you feeling today?*" And the answer is usually some version of: *Burned out, stressed,* or *overwhelmed.* Then they type in responses, helping each other with those questions. The last question asked is always: "*How are you feeling now?*" And the data that they showed us revealed a singular answer: "*Relieved.*" In an hour, you can go from feeling hopeless to peaceful! And now you also have a partner somewhere else in the business with whom you can continue these discussions. There's no "training" going on here, but we do hope to go from a Bazooka Joe to a henna tattoo on this platform and that some positive behavior changes stick.

PART III

The Year of Growth

Year One of Thrive was foundational and monumental, but it was still very instruction focused. As we moved into Year Three, we focused more on breaking down silos and cultivating an enterprise-wide mindset. During this next phase of Thrive, and this pivot to quadrants three and four on the Wheel (Activating the Enterprise and the Future), we were all about focusing on human connections, talent, and new ways of looking at career development.

As many statistics show, companies that drive a great employee experience are better at customer experience. The Thrive Ecosystem defines a great employee experience as doing things *with* and *for* our employees, not *to* them. If employees are engaged? They feel purpose, and that commitment drives productivity and connectivity.

In the past, work culture was typically developed or handed down by HR. Employees were expected to sit back and wait for news or direction as if it were something to be bestowed upon them. But Thrive is about all of us creating experience together. And continuing to cultivate culture together. NetApp's goal through this transformation became intentionally cultivating an employee voice and employee advocacy. It became building a positive employee experience and pathways for employee growth. The focus of Year Three, the Year of Growth, was on *career* growth—from within. And the start, finally, of true AI-driven career pathing. For the first time in the history of HR, we were able to begin to develop a tech-enabled, human-centric ecosystem. One with the ability for personalized development at scale.

Beginning in late 2020 and into 2021, the next iteration of the new normal at NetApp was going to be: *How can we create an environment where employees are happy, inspired, and feel that it's easy to work here?* Debra said it herself in her opening keynote of our inaugural Career Week, 2020, "*If there's no collaboration or career path, or there's a lot of politics? Then people are going to make the choice to go work somewhere else. I know I would.*"

NetApp was seeking to change how they thought about and treated their talent. She continued,

> *The importance of enterprise talent now is: We know, and as a CHRO, I'm gonna say it: Without customers, we don't have a business.... So, we have to make sure that, in this world, where the war for talent is real, we are not only attracting and retaining the best talent; we are cultivating and developing and encouraging and seeing the potential in everybody at NetApp. And so, that's why that enterprise mindset is so important.... At the end of the day, talent means connection. Transparency. Communication. It means respect—and sponsoring our employees to develop their careers at NetApp. And so, the word Thrive in Year Three? I would like to see that come to life in terms of how we really give everybody at NetApp an opportunity to do their best work and feel their best about it.*

George reinforced this message during his keynote: "*There are so many times in my life where I had to take a growth mindset. And a growth mindset, simply, is where you are excited to learn something new, but you are also scared about the risk that you're taking. Without those two, I don't think there's truly a growth opportunity.*"

Mosaic
A Career Pathing Tool

My whole life, I've been waiting for this idea of
true career pathing—it was a myth.

We could have saved that employee. That was what I told the assembled crowd during my FuelX keynote. It hadn't been in my script, but I realized that morning that it was the right story to tell. It was one of those situations where we just really didn't know what we already had. He was an up-and-comer who had just up and left. A young, black employee who said he quit because no one knew who he was. "*No one knew that before I came here, I raised $10 million and had an enterprise-wide startup.*" And that was when I realized, *Oh, my God. We don't know! We are flying blind.* This was a perfect example of how the implementation of new technology could shine a brighter light on our employees and build a more competitive workforce. How it could show what their goals and skills were so we could better enable them and provide tools for them to build out and grow their careers. And by strategically deploying a tool such as Fuel50 (an AI-powered, talent experience platform), this kind of situation and missed opportunity could be a thing of the past.

42 · Skills-based AI Tools

Gone could be the days when I'd sift through a mile-high stack of perfume-stained resumés, and my staff would wade through outdated employee work histories or need to rely on opaque reports. Yes, the story above is about inclusion, but it's so much more than that. Now, with AI-driven, skills-based data and genuine career pathing tools, we would have known about his background in advance. We would know that people have entrepreneurial skills or selling skills, even though they're engineers. We would know what their aspirations are and what skills they're looking to acquire. Let's face it—would you rather have your employee looking at LinkedIn or Mosaic? Because sooner or later, they are going to look at one of them. Now, we have *internal* pathways to retool and match up existing employees with new opportunities—with all the up-to-the-minute data at everyone's fingertips. No external recruitment required. And no reason for a capable employee to leave to pursue career growth.

My core message to leadership on this point was that we had no visibility into our internal talent pool and that our employees had unseen and untapped potential. I conveyed a reminder about the overarching strategic truism (and a reminder from the 2023 BetterUp Insights Report) that, above all else: *"Transformations fail because they aren't people centric. A broad study of transformation initiatives found the central thread that unites organizations who pull one off: a focus on their people during transformation."*[12] We needed to maintain that laser focus, even in the midst of an initiative as large as Fuel50. After all, it was *because* of this "people" focus that I nominated Fuel50.

Specific to this story, this year, the Year of Growth (and the pandemic), and Part 3, my message was that it was our job to create that visibility into our talent and then provide that talent with opportunities. To build an Internal Marketplace for our people—and encourage adaptive mindsets to make the most of that marketplace. Meaning, we could have SAVED that employee—and built a stronger, more competitive workforce in the process. As Anne Fulton, founder and CEO of Fuel50 describes it, *"The real benefit of AI for our customers is where we apply it to our workforce architecture and the skills architecture. A robust skills library and architecture underpinning an [internal] talent marketplace, an opportunity for validation of skills, and clearly defined levels of proficiency. Now we're using AI to support that workforce architecture mapping in a way that has reduced years of effort. There's lots of technology enablement into NetApp with the talent marketplace."*

The Obstacles

As we said at the outset of this book, the urgency for NetApp (and every other technology company in California and around the globe) is about competing for technology talent. And if NetApp couldn't retain people, grow talent within the business, and attract the right talent? They were potentially going to fall way behind. We really had to be at the top of our game with hiring, developing, and retaining our people or face some serious business risk.

Also, the rate at which new, specific skills are retired and replaced has outpaced the traditional cycle of role-based retire-hire. For better or worse, the marketplace has pivoted to skills-based hiring. Within NetApp, our Year One and Year Two data also supplied ample evidence that a platform such as Fuel50 would help us get where we needed to go. There were common threads from both the Pulse Surveys ("*I don't see a career here.*") and QCs ("*We want more tangibly visible careers.*"). We were able to use the data to tell the story that, "*NetApp employees feel they can't see where the next step in their career is here. And because they may lack an internal network, I fear that underrepresented minorities may feel left out.*" It's becoming all the more important that employees understand the broader picture of the company they work for. When they do, they stay longer, are more likely to feel they have growth potential, and can take back ownership of their career path by acquiring new skills and opportunities for NetApp. Fuel50 could provide a gateway for solving all these corporate challenges.

Internal Talent Intelligence

Fuel50 could also fill this gap in our internal talent intelligence. As I said, we were flying blind, relatively speaking. We now had the possibility of answering questions such as, *Who has what capability to be able to support the business? Where are the talent gaps and talent risks? Could we now match and align our employees' current skills and talents with what NetApp requires going forward? Are they well-prepared and enabled to thrive through these transformations while meeting future business needs and demands?*

Fuel50 could provide a pathway for transforming our talent practices at NetApp and begin to enable answers to these questions. So that the employees could be completely empowered to understand their skills and talents. And could understand their future roadmap and what capabilities they would need now and into the future, and could go on that "re-skilling journey," as Anne describes it. *Self*-enabled because the employees will have been given all the tools they could need. Getting matched to a coach, a mentor, and to a learning need—so that they would have a broad array of opportunities to pursue career growth and development.

What else could Fuel50 do for NetApp? That was the answer to a host of industry-wide challenges NetApp—and every business like it—was facing in 2020. Our talent strategy meant supporting the company to evolve on many fronts. Helping the business accelerate and reach its goals—including adapting how we thought about nurturing and developing our employees while adapting faster to this new, pandemic-fueled, virtual work environment. The millennial-plus generations' expectations of career growth and learning on demand (for example) had changed—and hiring managers needed to respond. To retain and attract the critical talent NetApp needed, we had to provide experiences that challenged employees, truly embraced diversity and inclusion, supported a "work from anywhere" environment, and enabled NetAppers to grow and turn their "job" into the best work of their careers.

Connecting with Anne

I first met Anne Fulton while still at Equinix. We were both attending a conference on HR and career growth. In terms of seeking out similar mindsets, Anne generously described her first impressions this way: "*I loved the career vision that Larry presented.... I'd never heard any HR practitioner thinking about careers in that way. Careers is my total passion, and my life dedica-*

tion is to the career experience. So, of course, I was talking almost the same 'talk track' [as Larry]. There was a strong vision alignment between what was needed at NetApp and what Fuel50 could bring to the table." Anne and I had multiple meetings after that, and I was impressed with her vision of the future. Fuel50's core models strive for a democratized talent experience and careers for everyone, accessible to everyone, across the business. What's not to love about that?! I explained to her that NetApp was going through the middle of a business transformation and needed to transform the people experience and the talent experience to map and support that transformation. Through the Thrive Ecosystem and the Wheel, we also wanted to help activate people in shifting mindsets to support that transformation as well. She understood instantly—and I knew immediately that this could be a business partnership with legs. The main objective I was after with this AI-fueled Internal Marketplace? Anne put it quite succinctly:

Transforming the people experience with talent matching so that people could be matched to opportunities. Projects. Gigs. Vacancies. And giving the managers that intelligence as to who had what skill and capability [while also], putting that same matching intelligence into the hands of employees. So, if they wanted to target an opportunity, put their hand up for a project, they knew exactly what skills were needed. So, creating real talent visibility, or 'opportunity visibility' to employees.

Once onboard, my core message to leadership and to our employees was that although Fuel50 is a platform, for it to come alive, we had to make it our own. That was why we didn't call it Fuel50 internally. Once again, we partnered with the internal marketing team to come up with our own name: Mosaic. A word and a visual which, to us, represented different avenues to growth. And so many different ways to *connect* with growth. I wanted to convey the idea that this would now be how this company *thinks* about growth. Tech enabled, but people powered. And again, I was looking for everyone to adapt to this new approach as opposed to, *"I just bought this piece of software."*

43 ◆ Solution: Building Talent from Within

Among other things, Mosaic was designed to increase the amount of internal hiring as well as the retention numbers of NetApp's top talent. When I said at the beginning that we were moving from a traditional storage company to cloud? Our recruiters were telling us that only about 20 percent of the people in the company could take the cloud jobs. Twenty! That meant we would have to go outside the company and hire for the cloud. Mosaic enabled us to say instead, *We can grow people into those jobs.* How would we move people across the chasm? In the past, it would have been a bunch of guesswork. We would have had to say, *"Well, we assume everyone is at Level One. And this is how we get to Level Four."* With Mosaic, for each individual employee, we could now build a career path to get to those jobs—and that was mind-blowing. I believe this is the future of talent strategy. But our leaders needed to embrace the enterprise-wide mindset to make this a successful reality.

We also brought in this AI-enhanced tool to respond to employee criticisms. We'd been hearing they felt there were no pathways to career development at NetApp. The idea with Mosaic was that it could provide employees with a foundation for career development and mobility, boosting employee engagement and a positive experience. It was the start of true career pathing and individualized development at scale.

And we were able to tie it to Thrive. My whole life has been about tying all efforts together, into the bigger story. Making each piece more relevant than a one-off. The Golden Thread. We're not just buying a piece of software that helps you with career advancement. This is part of the way that we're going to grow this company too. Is NetApp still getting there? Yes. But now the company's talent is more visible than ever before. And NetApp now has more insight than it ever had in the past.

We called the Mosaic platform the Opportunity Marketplace. It helps employees across the globe be found by hiring managers and provides managers with visibility into the diverse workforce, connecting the right talent with the right opportunity.

Now, we have the ability to measure in the market who's matching up to your jobs today and who can match up to them in the future. Seventy is the new 100 percent, and technology is going to help us understand what that is. What does this mean for opportunity seekers? Matching up to jobs internally, *real* jobs, so that when workers say, "*I want to be this in ten years,*" it will tell them, *Here are the next two or three jobs you should take. Here are the skills you need to build on, and here's a mentor in the company you can match up to and a gig you can tie it to.* So, the AI is actually helping them understand and build a plan. Followed up with Quarterly Conversations with their manager? Those can be so much more real and authentic now! And so much more tangible as opposed to when I was coming up and career paths were in a binder on the shelf—and didn't really mean anything. Now, it's an *actual* deliverable. Mosaic delivers a completely circular way for people to think about their careers.

This was the first thing we brought to CEO staff, saying, "*If we bring in Fuel50, here's the value of an AI-driven platform to our employees and teams and to the company. Here's the value of an AI-driven talent experience platform for NetApp.*" Below is the list of what NetApp stood to gain from launching an Opportunity Marketplace. By embracing Fuel50, our existing talent strategy gave the company the opportunity to:

– Gain visibility into our workforce to support company strategy
– Boost employer brand and employee engagement
– Tap into employees' underutilized/unseen skill sets
– Address shorter shelf-life of future-oriented skills
– Build up scarce, in-demand skills in-house
– Elevate skills—not job title—as the "new currency"
– Support redeployment, gigs, and agile career growth to drive cloud growth
– Promote conversion of contractors to FT employees

– Keep cost down and minimize attrition cost
– Promote equity and inclusion and increase diversity

Shrinking the World

Inclusion is the future. And Mosaic breaks down those barriers of distance, gender, and race. It has the power to drive inclusivity across entire companies and shrink the world. The agility that this provided, being able to see what talent is already there? Unprecedented. We would no longer be flying blind! Imagine Emily (for example), a NetApp engineer who lives in New Zealand—the opposite end of the world from Global HQ. Traditionally, she might be thinking, *I'm so far away from headquarters. Nobody knows me. No one knows what I want. They don't even understand my country,* right? Now we do.

Then there are the underrepresented groups. We often think of females, or LGBTQ, worrying over such issues as, *I don't know the right people,* or *I don't look like the right people. So, I don't have a future here,* or *Well, I need to be in the "in" group to understand what jobs are there.* Right? Fuel50 crushes all of that. The entire world is now on one platform. With this technology, anyone in the company, in any country, can see what jobs they fit with. And their internal visibility goes way up. By design, Mosaic focuses more on the skill level than a person level or diversity level. (And there's nothing in the platform that specifies gender at all.) The platform makes it much easier to connect from around the world, from wherever you're sitting, no matter your background.

On the back end, we can track and determine: Are underrepresented groups moving at the same time? Are they applying to the same number of jobs? Anne said it well: "*Our purpose is to be a democratic inclusive, fair, equitable, transparent, talent matching marketplace. So that nobody is excluded.*" Mosaic has democratized the hiring process so that *everyone* has a fair and equal opportunity to participate. We believe technology is the number one way to get to a positive employee experience and that it's a very big driver of how we get to better inclusion.

Put It on Paper? It's Already Dead

My whole life, I've been waiting for this idea of career pathing. It was a myth. For thirty years, we've been putting it on paper and in spreadsheets, but the second you put it on paper, it's dead. Because the dynamism of the organization is always moving and changing. The technology we now have *knows* that. This was the first time in my career, as an HR person, that technology enabled this ancient industry term to actually mean something tangible. Actionable. Relevant. We had them in books and sort of assumed you could go to A and then to B, but it was never *BAM!*—there it is right in front of you.

Personalized Career Journeys

What else did the employees gain? A variety of career growth opportunities at their fingertips. We wanted them to find *personalized* career journeys. Every single person is an individual and needs their OWN growth plan, not a manufactured artificial growth plan that fits everybody, right? And to be able to connect to learning opportunities and other people in the organization. A place where employees are enabled and encouraged to build strategically relevant skills and experiences inside the organization. Where they can grow with the business and build vibrant careers. The ability to:

- Showcase untapped skills and experiences
- Match skills to internal jobs
- Find gigs and stretch projects
- Discover skills gaps
- Connect to learning opportunities
- Access expertise across NetApp
- Gain diverse perspectives

Technology can also help employees have conversations about what's in their way. Through implementing the Mosaic tool, we focused on helping them aspire to think more tangibly about their futures. It's not just the next job. It's a landscape of thinking about career and skills and development. We often said, *"You should be able to grow in your company using technology."* By providing increased internal visibility into career opportunities, employees can also feel more empowered to *own* their careers.

SECTION 2

Using Mosaic

There are two pathways in Mosaic. Managers seeking talent and employees seeking opportunity. Our main focus, especially that first year, was on the employees—while we were getting data uploaded into the system and tweaking the platform to suit. The plan was to build on our first quarter focus in 2021, and, as more data entered the system over time, it could mushroom into a more powerful, fully fledged, robust global talent management tool. So, HR continued its campaign to introduce the Mosaic tool to all employees and encourage them to engage. It was a multipronged approach and was ongoing.

44 · How it Works

Once Thrive's Opportunity Marketplace was up and running, users gained access to a host of things they could explore to activate their own personal career pathing. As a 1st quadrant tool on the Wheel, I encouraged everyone to Activate themselves by building their profile in Mosaic. They could discover—and highlight—existing talents, strengths, and skills: "*Talk about what you love to do, want to develop, and are great at!*" By exploring new roles and career paths, they could build a greater understanding of strengths and development areas. By taking on gigs, they could try out new roles. Such gigs would build skills and experience, and they could home in on relevant career paths that aligned with their interests. Or they could develop role-specific skill sets and forecast future skills needed—or find a mentor to strengthen relationships, gain career insights, and build up an enterprise mindset. All encouraged and supported by NetApp management.

It starts with a self-assessment, including what motivates you, what skills you have, what skills you want to have… It includes layers of detail—work style, talents, interests, preferred work environments, and so on. Others can critique what you enter into the assessment if you wish. Once completed, you're live in the AI-powered Internal Marketplace.

Job Searching

Mosaic isn't like LinkedIn, Indeed, or ZipRecruiter. It's the opposite of universal. Mosaic is peculiar to NetApp, specifically and exclusively. It's tailored to the company, based on NetApp's profile and all its current openings. For example, if someone comes in and says, "*I wanna be a controller,*" Mosaic then links to NetApp's open jobs and shows all the controller jobs that are open. (Then it will show, in a percentage, how fit or qualified that person might currently be for that job.)

Career Pathing

If someone's looking to build their career and use the more robust features of Mosaic, they can have it help explore possibilities.

There's *Find a Journey,* for example. They can plug in, "*I wanna be…,*" and suddenly, they gain access to all these suggested skills and capabilities. The definitions and the coaching in that entire library can be delivered in a matter of seconds. Or they can also click on a button that says, "*What would be an obvious next job for me?*" It takes everything entered, looks at all the jobs available, and reports, "*Here are three or four that you're generally qualified for.*" The AI literally reports, *Here are your next three jobs.* Automatically. That's *true* career pathing. Make no mistake, this is why we wrote the check. Right here, this aspect of Mosaic. When it showed me that you could see your next three jobs, I was sold. You're next ten years of your career in one place. With directions on what it would take to get you there. Up until now, you would have had to go look at open job recs while wondering, *Can I do that? I don't know if I could.* This was radically new.

Let's say someone's an early-in-career person. The platform includes questions such as, *Where do you want to end up in the next five years?* Or six years or ten years…whatever. Or they might want to explore some stretch roles. So, either just for fun or in all seriousness, they put in that job. Say they're an Engineer Level 1 and want to be a Marketing Manager Level 5 one day. The platform will tell them, *Here are the next three jobs in this com-*

pany that you could take to get there. It could take thirty years, or however long. It just opens up the mind to possibilities.

Or perhaps someone entered, *I want Larry's job.* Getting there may not necessarily be an obvious or linear path. There could be any number of ways over many years to become well-prepared for that role. The platform will spit back, *You need these three jobs first.* More specifically, it will show the skills gaps, the things they'd need to learn, and the experience they'd need to gain along the way. It's a brilliant way to explore a unique career journey. That's the real value of an AI-driven platform—for employees to find *personalized* career journeys. Individualized development at scale. The ability to plot out an entire career inside this tool, to map out potential trajectories for the coming years and decades. And to continue to revisit and revise over time.

It's also not always about what the next role is but, *How do I grow my current role?* Mosaic can make it easier to find training, mentors, and gigs inside the company. Ways that employees can continue to build their skills without leaving the job they're already in while still preparing them for the next role down the line.

Gender? Race? Location? AI's Agnostic

In general, we know women applicants won't apply for a job if they feel they are not very qualified (meaning their skills don't fully match up with those in the job description), while generally, men will apply to jobs where they have fewer matching skills. The AI currently being used doesn't look at gender. It doesn't even know it. It just says, *You're close enough to apply for this job! (Woman!)* And/or it will even recommend a job that an employee may never have thought to apply for before.

Alternatively, people can find the contacts they want. Right now, people feel they need to be connected to corporate or to someone "in the know." Mosaic shatters that, as we've said. Now, a hiring manager on the other side of the world can see anyone in the system. Internal recruiters see everyone too. Inclusion cuts across silos, taps into talents and skills people may not have known they had, promotes diversity, and powers teams with fresh perspectives. It fuels the Opportunity Marketplace, making the invisible visible.

It's Not a Ladder Up. It's a Jungle Gym.

Overall, Mosaic has introduced a new way of thinking about career development. Careers are no longer as linear as they were in days gone by. It's a new paradigm for employees. Instead of imagining climbing that classic vertical ladder, I encouraged everyone to start thinking of careers more flexibly—both in terms of the diversity of paths people take and the nature of that development from fixed jobs to more gigs and project-based work. *"Over my time at NetApp,"* shared George, in his inaugural Career Week keynote, *"I have seen so many examples of people that have moved from one role to another. From the field organization into technical marketing and product management. Engineers that have rotated into product management roles. People in operations that have moved to IT. They have really brought fresh thinking. I would encourage each of you to think broadly about your career."*

If the future of work is about *experiences* rather than jobs, skills are employees' bargaining power and how they buy into new experiences. We're constantly trying to help people understand: *"It's not a ladder up. It's a jungle gym. You can move to a lateral job or just go work on a project."* This kind of diversity requires higher visibility, right? People can't pick you if they can't see you. *"Managers often don't know that we have talent in different parts of the company,"* George continued. *"And talent don't really know that there are managers in different parts of the company who are looking for that help. I've personally been an internet router for connecting many people. Now…we have these applications that can help."*

45 · Closing the Gap

When it comes to recommending long-term futures, if an employee comes to a manager and asks, *"What do you think I should do next?"* It's unlikely that manager will say, *"Why don't you go into marketing?"* That'd be a rare discussion. It just wouldn't enter their mind to say that. But now, when the time comes for your QC, you can go in and say, "*Hey, I just did this in Mosaic. Here's the next job. I really wanna do this. I just wanna make sure you're cool with these three gaps, and…how do I close these three gaps?*" That's a *much* more authentic conversation. More tangible and immediate. As opposed to, "*I wanna go to my next job. What do you think, manager?*" And then the manager answering, "*I don't know. What do you think?*" This gives both an opportunity to bring new mindsets together and radically increases the impact a manager can have on an employee's ability to grow. The process just *closes* that gap so much quicker. And provides some great data for the conversation.

Self-assessments can also be great conversation starters between employees and managers. It's a time when managers can ask questions such as, *What are your top values? What are your top career engagers?* Elise shares her insights.

> I think where Mosaic is really helping is in saying 'Here's something you might not have thought about. If you want to be that person, you're going to have to take these additional steps. And here's what you need to do to get there.' Maybe you need some additional education. Maybe you need to talk to a mentor within the company. Maybe you need to do a gig. Whatever the case may be, Mosaic can help you to think through that.

But I did continue to tell people, "*This is just a tool.*" Of course, it's great. It gives you a bunch of information, but if you don't have those conversations or do anything with that info? It remains a window you've just peeked through. It's quite useful in getting you to the right doors, but it's then up to you to knock on them. You need to take it into the real world with your team, manager, or a mentor that you seek out.

What Success Looks Like

If I were to distill Mosaic down to its essence, I'd say it proved to be the answer to the single most commonly expressed sad emoji all HR people have heard since the beginning of HR: a lack of advancement opportunities. And that's what Mosaic offers; what this tool is trying to get people to do. To advance. And if they're not actually advancing in short periods of time, to at least feel as though they are. Meaning, "*I understand my gaps, and I'm addressing those gaps and growing in the ways that make me satisfied. And not just because my manager did it or thought I should. But I'm actually growing. And I feel NetApp cares about me.*" I want them to be aware of the many resources available for them to grow in the way they want to—and that doesn't even have to mean getting a different job. But the *ultimate* would be people being able to say, "*I'm growing,*" *and* that they are using this to find new jobs right now.

If you get a gig? That's a thumbs up. If you get a mentor or attend a LinkedIn Learning? That's all growth to me. But for people to be able to say, "*I looked, and Mosaic helped me find a job internally.*"? To me, that would be a big one. Out of all of it, internal mobility is the biggest piece. Creating an environment where people stay because they feel they have career opportunities and growth and can achieve those things *here* instead of having to go to some other company to get that promotion? And for this to occur regularly? Our hearts would just explode! I hate the idea of someone having to leave to get to their next level. All while not knowing *why* they did. Was it that they just didn't understand the gaps? That they didn't get an opportunity? What was it? The goal is AI-driven tools, such as Mosaic, which can help bridge that gap.

How? By helping employees acquire new skills, take short-term opportunities, secure mentors, and work around those they can learn from. To create gigs and actually generate experiences for employees. *Experience* is the key thing here. That way, we can map potential jobs people want and start pulling the experiences out of those jobs to give to people before they're ready for that role. Even if that role's not available, they still get the

244 I THE POWER TO TRANSFORM

experience. That's a win. And when the job does come up, they can move straight in. Because we can track satisfaction levels, we can see how well we are accomplishing that goal—and/or how to pivot as needed—as we dig deeper with Mosaic. Again, to me, the ultimate success is that people are growing and *feel* that they're growing. That's the most basic milestone of success.

Okay, so that helps the employee. What about the company? If someone feels they have a pathway in this company? They'll stay. It's a great retention tool. All the stats point to the truth of that. If they move around within the company, they feel even better. Their engagement goes up. Then we have someone who knows our culture and our company, filling another job internally. Bringing someone in from the outside? By the time you speed them up? There's launch time, development time. And it's not always the right fit, so you may need to start over. With internal job mobility, the employee is already aware of how the company runs. They know the building, they know how it works, and now they've taken a bigger job. So, nothing but upside.

SECTION 3

The Global Launch

Installing and integrating Mosaic into NetApp, technically, adaptively, and culturally, was no small feat. What we wanted was for people to get it, love it, and use it versus being overwhelmed with TMI. The challenge for the team was as much about *how* we rolled it out as the fact *that* we did it in the first place. We knew where we wanted to go, but we also knew launching in one big bang would be counterproductive. There were too many components, too many layers and modules to tackle all at once—for us as much as the users. Success was going to be measured by engagement—and I dare to boast here that we had the highest engagement rate of any Fuel50 customer to date. In fact, our strategy became a model Fuel50 pointed to going forward.

46 · Career Week

What did we do? We staggered implementation and rolled out Mosaic over three key launches, plus a pre-launch Career Week, all in less than one calendar year. My TE team and our change team developed a host of content around how this works ("*resources at your fingertips*" we told them: videos on demand, presentations, quick reference guides, infographics, online courses, and FAQs) for Career Week and for Mosaic, which went up as it was ready, starting in the run-up to the global launch of Career Week (November 2020). With any new platform, you have to do some implementation work so it fits your company. It was a huge success, but there was a lot that went into it, and after it launched, there was the whole getting the word out, getting people to buy into it. Sure, anyone could just turn it on. But we wanted to do the smart thing: figure out what was most important first. *How do we message this?* We believe it got adopted so fast *because* we took the time to make those plans and integrate the platform with the pre-existing Thrive Ecosystem and the Wheel.

Phase One

Mosaic (Phase One) went live with our first global launch in February 2021. With every phase, different aspects were rolled out. The first phase was very generic and still lacked the full capabilities that were possible (it was just about getting the basic taxonomy in there), but it got people informed and excited about what was to come. We were ramping up on the communications campaign while still in COVID lockdown. "*What if…you could build your ideal career journey from your kitchen table? With Mosaic, you can!*" we told them. Our modules included "Reflect. Explore, and Grow," "Goals and Quarterly Conversations," "Gigs," and "Mentors," among many others. EM recaps our thinking well: "*With the first launch, we just focused on 'Reflect, Explore and Grow.' There were* Reflect *exercises. You could grow by finding a LinkedIn learning class or a mentor. Many things were presented in that first bit, but we knew we wanted to start there. To raise awareness and get them thinking about* What can this do for me? *It was a great way to begin.*"

Within the first three months or less, half the company visited and 55 percent of those who did came back, which meant we had shattered Fuel50's previous benchmarks. Because we had the fastest adoption of Mosaic in the history of Fuel50, Anne held us up as *the* model of how to do the implementation. We believe Career Week (a major launch in itself) and the Golden Thread of Launch Week had a lot to do with that. I got the opportunity to speak at Fuel50's next customer conference, sharing (with potential and new customers) how we did it I didn't hold back—I showed them everything, including "*Here's how long it took.*"

Phase Two

Phase Two launched in May, which we picked because it was the beginning of NetApp's fiscal year. The focus was on QCs, plus setting up (data-rich) goals in the tool—and beginning to track them. "*It's a brand new year! Good time to set your goals.*" Between May and September, I began to tell listeners, "*Imagine a world where it all comes together. The richness of what this ecosys-*

tem does for you. You can get a mentor, find a course in LinkedIn Learning, take on a gig—now you're part of the NetApp career experience—a rich ecosystem with many ways to grow."

Phase Three

September was the big bang. The final brick in the wall as the Opportunity Marketplace truly came to life! Where all jobs were open to everyone. Career journeys, gigs, part time projects, were all turned on. The key for us throughout was always to get back to basics, to think about the user experience. (The added benefit of three separate launches was the opportunity to reinvigorate, to bring them back in. That was a silver lining, for sure.) And to remember that our company goal was for this platform to be a key part of how we recruited and grew talent within NetApp while remaining people-centric throughout this third year of our transformation. The strategic challenge was more than just a communication or a single approach. It was about creating a holistic approach to excite, build anticipation, and engage. Which is why we preempted the launch with an all company Career Week.

Self-Enabled Career Growth

In Year One, I often said Thrive was a big mindset shift for everybody. No more ratings, Quarterly Conversations, enablement. Then came coaching, Pulse Surveys, and, of course, the pandemic. Then we unleashed Mosaic, the Internal Marketplace. People first needed to understand how it worked before they could begin to really take advantage of the full possibilities of the AI engine driving it all underneath. It was going to be an even bigger mindset shift, which is why we started off with Career Week, a mindset shift "primer," in advance of the launch.

You could say Career Week was, in a way, an enterprise-wide version of having strategy first and introducing tech later, just on a bigger scale. It was *"NetApp's first-ever Thrive Talent Career Week—and a chance for employees to get excited about growing their careers."* And it was all about career growth. Career Week was hosted from November 9–12, 2020 (coinciding with the transition from Thrive into Thrive Everywhere), and, as we said, was designed, in part, as a run-up to the launch of Mosaic (Phase One) the following year.

We brought in internal and external speakers and held executive panel discussions as well as employee-led Q&A sessions. I told them, "*We're going to have experts come to tell you about the importance of growth and their career.*" And who doesn't love to learn about how to improve on their career growth? Our keynotes included Josh Bersin, Alexi Robichaux, and Angela Duckworth (author of *Grit*) who each addressed what careers and technology can mean. We brought in CEOs from different companies, including *The Happiness Advantage* author Shawn Achor. We did some internal executive speaking as well, with the goal of helping people change the way they think about careers. It was the moment to say, "*This is what career really is now. We're in the middle of a pandemic, but you can still do the best work of your career at NetApp from your kitchen table.*"

All told, we programmed nineteen separate live sessions. We also did a ton of enablement around open sessions with teams, including repeated live demos designed to walk everyone through how to use the platform. All in all, it was one full week of presentations, webinars, and interactive sessions focused on the employee and their growth and careers at NetApp. Thematically, it was a great way to open people's eyes to our message of: "*We're gonna do something different here.*" What was most important was to convey, "*This is coming,*" and provide people with some primers for how the company was thinking about growth, even in the midst of the pandemic. CEO George Kurian generously opened the top of the week with many guiding words, including this snippet from our kickoff: "*I'm super impressed and excited at the work that [Larry] and Deb [have done] around the digitization of our talent management capabilities…. Now…we have these applications that can help people get that visibility.*" I'm pleased to write that it was one of the most well-attended events across the company outside of All Hands. And we got some pretty fantastic feedback from attendees as well.

That was what we were after. Shifting everyone's brains away from how they thought about careers before to how it was going to be. And the lever of that was Fuel50. Showing what Fuel50 could do. It'd be fair to say that Mosaic was the opposite of a plug-and-play kind of platform. Instead, the key here was the Thrive strategy we already had in place. Without it, the statement made by the company with Career Week (which became an annual event) wouldn't have functioned in quite the same way.

SECTION 4

Mindset Shifts

Career Week was also a good reminder about one key Thrive transformation maxim: *Unless you can bring people on the journey, whatever you're doing is not going to be effective.* In Year One, launching Thrive required a big change in mindset. And that was where we began to build the change muscle throughout the organization. In Year Three, igniting an internal Opportunity Marketplace was the next wave of our talent transformation—requiring even bigger changes. This was our chance to build on those muscles and inspire even more agility, resilience, and a culture of continuous learning from the NetApp workforce.

47 · Talk 'n' Learn

When introducing a new platform, you always want to ask, *"How do you get—and keep—people involved? How do you continue to tell your story internally?"* During Career Week, we launched "talk and learn" events to help bring people along with the changes being implemented. You can't just introduce a tool and just hope for the best...right? We needed to program continuous, ongoing enablement. To that end, we hosted a series of monthly and quarterly sessions (See Sometimes You Just Gotta Talk About It on page 154 for additional details.) We began with Thrive Thursdays, followed by the quarterly Dare to Dream speaker series—designed to inspire employees to think differently about their career journeys by highlighting speakers from outside of NetApp. The most popular question? *"What was a mistake you made in your career, and how did you overcome it?"* (People love a comeback story for its authentic feel and inspirational answers!)

48 · For Employees: You Own Your Career

The Year Three transformation was also about helping employees understand their talents, skills, learning needs, and learning opportunities (aligned to business goals). And getting to that individualized development at scale. Anne summed it up well. *"Yes, there's lots of technology enablement going on at NetApp, with the talent marketplace. But that's got to go hand-in-hand with education and people enablement, the mindset shift, and the culture transformation."* A key message from our first Thrive Thursday, which I did my best to drive home repeatedly, was *"You OWN your career. Never doubt that. My job is to give you every tool, every asset for you to understand how to manage that."* Because ultimately (I continued), *"My job is to help you in your career, but YOU are in charge."* And as Debra mentioned during her keynote, *"All of us have to know that we are the masters of our career."* With their own unique path—not a manufactured, artificial one that fits everyone. *"It's new."* I continued, *"And it may be uncomfortable, but try it. Embrace it. Match your dreams with internal jobs. Showcase your skill sets. Find opportunities. Use technology to enable your career to take off. Look at this as an investment in yourself and your career."*

Our Kitchen Table Moment

Then there was the pandemic. Talk about a mindset shift. I told my team, *"Despite the hybrid era, I want people to be able to progress and grow their careers—from anywhere. With employees looking for more flexibility and hybrid work environments, we need to equip them with the ecosystem, platform, and mindsets to make the most of this time."* Thrive Everywhere and Career Week both launched in the fall of 2020. My main message at that moment? *"Don't think you can't grow here just because we're in the middle of a pandemic."* During the pandemic in particular, Mosaic was a very positive way for employees to still feel connected with each other and to their potential for career growth, even during lockdown. To all assembled, I continued, *"I want you to do the best work of your career at NetApp from your kitchen table."* With Mosaic, employees could now also plot out the next three steps of their careers at that same table. *"It's a great time to reflect."*

49 · For Managers: Net Exporters of Talent

The second you start curbing people's growth for
your own benefit, you're failing as a leader.

With AI-enabled tech tools, we all had the ability to move faster and make decisions as we were simultaneously hiring from the market and developing talent internally. These were exciting times, but they pushed all of us to think differently about how we developed, retained, and hired the right talent. As part of Career Week, we hosted a speaker series dedicated specifically to internal mobility. The goal was to encourage managers to think more company- and enterprise-wide about their talent. As belonging to NetApp at large and not just to them or their teams. And to help leaders think of themselves as *net exporters* of talent. (Again, this was not about training managers but about enabling them with tools and information.) We had begun talking about this in Year One, but by Year Three, this idea of internal mobility had become a reality. So, when it came to hiring, we began to say, "*Don't just look externally. Start using Mosaic as an internal mobility tool and look internally.*" But it was a whole different mindset shift—because the AI-generation tools we were beginning to deploy were unlike anything we'd used before.

Internal Mobility Recruiters

Recruiters look externally. It makes no logical sense, but that's what most companies do because, in their words, "*Eh, a known quantity,*" or "*She couldn't possibly be ready for that.*" There may be no quick fix, but this still needs to change. Once Mosaic launched, our talent acquisitions team hired two internal mobility recruiters and directed them to immediately begin looking for matchups. This turned "recruiting from within" into a competitive strategy. Leaders and teams could now access expertise across

NetApp—and know what talent might be available. One of the goals was to see the number of open job requisitions filled with internals go up (which meant increases in retention as well). That included an executive recruitment team (added later) as well, targeting VP and above-level hires. And since Mosaic functions on both the talent enablement and talent acquisition sides, it also highlighted a vision for thinking of TA, TM, and talent mobility together—vs. siloed separately.

But the platform didn't replace the human factor of recruitment. It still came down to people…and mindsets. Just as in a lot of companies, employees at NetApp thought, *It's easier for me to go find a job outside of the company.* Employees could now see what was available, but internal mobility recruiters could still supply the necessary segue to help them do something about it. So, at NetApp, the recruiter's job mainly involved interacting with the employees who were interested in looking but hadn't considered openly shopping internally until now. Some of that had to do with managers and how they viewed their talent. Thus, we led a fair amount of change management around internal mobility—and built more permanent tattoos around changed attitudes and growth mindsets.

Go Ahead, Kick the Tires

There are many reasons why, traditionally, there's been so much friction around internal movement. We used to just hear about new jobs word-of-mouth. "*Oh, this position is open.*" There was no real way for you to actually know for yourself. Now, anyone can go into the tool and see, *Hey, this is what your job is aligned to. What your next step is aligned to, and these are the current jobs open.* When McKenna came to me and said, "*Hey, this is where I want to go next,*" the challenge was for me to be okay with that. If another team sweeps up your employee? The shift is to look at it from a growth mindset versus, "*I don't want that person to leave my team.*" The next tricky bit is the mindset shift for managers needed on *both* ends. The manager receiving the employee and the one giving the employee up. Current managers never had to deal with that before because there was no visibility on it. Again, Mosaic blew that up.

Managers are also sometimes scared to talk about next steps because they might be thinking along the lines of, *I don't know if I can get you the next job. I don't know where they might be.* Or they might be reluctant to promise a promotion or a transfer for similar reasons. Now, employees can just bring that Mosaic-generated list to their managers (like McKenna did) and say, "*Well, this is what I want to do. And here are my next steps. How do you think I can get there?*" It's so much more powerful, real, and tangible. It's seeing the unseen. Growth made visible. (Can you imagine having that twenty years ago?)

But then, often managers also think, *You can't take my talent. These are my people! And if they look for another job, I'll have to backfill, and that causes a hole in my organization. That's not gonna work for me. So, I'm gonna make it hard for people to move or discourage them from moving, or I'll make them feel that if they want to move, they're somehow making a move against ME and being disloyal.* Sometimes workers butt up against that kind of mentality, which makes them afraid to move. They'll hesitate to interview with another manager, even just to kick the tires out of fear of what might happen if their current manager finds out. They're looked at as being disloyal when really, they just want to explore other opportunities.

Some employees may also say, "*Well, I don't wanna tell my boss I'm looking for another job because she's gonna get mad or not let me go.*" In the past, it wasn't uncommon to see employee comments such as, "*I have to get written approval by my manager to move.*" At NetApp, we began working to move away from that and encouraged employees to own their careers. They would still want to talk to their manager first, of course. But the thinking, and our approach to talent strategy, meant wanting everyone to be given opportunities. (And for the managers to consider the possibility of bringing fresh perspectives into their teams as well.) "*One of the most positive things Mosaic does,*" shared Elise, "*is it says to employees, 'We want you to be able to explore. We're investing in you as an employee.'*" And for managers to not just be okay with that but also applaud that.

Be a Net Exporter of Talent

Lots of people say, *"If you work for me, you're mine,"* vs. *"If you work for me, I want you to be better than me."* As a manager, I believe you should be a net exporter of talent. Not a talent hoarder but a talent exporter. That should be one of your traits. Either within the company or outside of it. *"As a manager, one of the things that I think you should be proud of,"* recounts George during his Career Week keynote, *"is that you are a steward and an exporter of talent across the organization."* And the more you export talent, the more silos break down and the more connections grow. You're putting the right people in the right jobs to do the right work to make NetApp successful. If you see one of your people in the job you once had? To me, that feels good. And just remember, that person may hire you sometime down the line or connect you with another position! You know you've done your job well when you're able to find your replacement. My team absolutely has the knowledge and drive to expand on our existing vision and continue to make it better. You can make an impact at work, but making an impact on people is so much more rewarding. During her Fall 2020 Career Week keynote, Debra addressed the topic this way:

> We are doing a lot of work on leadership mindset as well [as] around being flexible because a lot of internal movement does involve the conversation between the employee and the manager—not just the receiving manager, but the manager who may be losing or sharing that talent with somebody else. I know that CEO staff members have been talking to their leadership teams about Career Week around the Internal Marketplace, around understanding that it's NetApp talent, not 'my' talent. We're going to continue to cultivate that mindset.

A good leader, as discussed, is a net exporter of talent. If we had a scoreboard, and you moved more people outside of the organization than you brought in? You're winning! You're growing this company; you're an owner, an enterprise-wide thinker, and a better leader. You have more influence and know more people around the organization. NetApp continues to work on that. It was an ongoing campaign, and I brought it up at every meeting. *"Let people leave your team."* This was why changing mindsets was the biggest challenge of Year Three while promising the greatest potential upside in growth for employees, managers, and the company at large than I had ever seen in the history of HR. AI-driven tech enhancements are making for an "inflection point," as Emily says, and a very exciting time to be pursuing transformation.

The Power of Data: Building the AI

It's very easy to see the front-end features and functions of the tech platforms we have discussed. What's often overlooked is how, on top of the traditional engagement data, the back end provides vastly more nuanced insights around the whole person. It grants the ability to see the unseen. And simply put, good data means knowing and understanding your workforce better. By listening to our employees in these more detailed ways, we were better able to remain human-centric at NetApp. The voice of the employee became more defined and actionable. And as the tools and platforms become increasingly able to synthesize disparate sources of data, your HR strategies will become more and more refined.

50 · Skills Mapping

I may not agree that skills are a new *"currency,"* per se, but it's definitely a bigger focus. Meaning skills (vs. resumés) for presenting a potential candidate's merits. Not *"Oh, you were an engineer for ten years, so you should be good for this job,"* but *"What are the skills that we need aside from programming languages?"* Mapping a skills architecture used to be quite rarified work and would take *years.* To do one job could take a month of HR practitioners and subject matter experts in a room trying to argue and debate what skills and capabilities were needed. Now, we're using AI to support that mapping in a way that has reduced those potential years—and fuels a more democratized talent market. This is one of the arenas in which AI is at its most powerful.

And necessary. In just five years, 35 percent of the skills that we think are essential today are going to change again.[13] We need to be constantly learning, accruing new skills and new opportunities. Both companies and people alike always want to know, *What are the top skills we should be investing in to stay future proof?* The sense of urgency, and need for fast timing, is real. Especially in technology, where skills change quickly. AI-powered platforms can help build the *right* skills (there's even a "Hot Skills" button) to keep employees marketable and assist businesses in building skills internally (and avoid that ol' "build" versus "buy" conundrum). And if you are already growing from within, you know the best approach to use—and the right questions to ask: *"Here are the key skills for this job. Let's talk about how you do them and where you'd learn them."*

AI-Driven Voice of the Employee

So, what's the real greatness of taking the time to enter skills? The AI keeps learning. Once employees go through their assessments and continue to engage with the platform—building conversations, feedback loops, future searches—the AI's database gets more accurate and refined. It builds the engine and the AI.

Historically, whatever we could glean was just based on people talking to one another. Completely anecdotal. Today, we have access to Mosaic's back-end data in real-time and to an organizational architecture program that gives us a better and better definition of the skills we want in these jobs. We can start building out specific career paths for people. Specific! And when I look at it? I can't help but smile from ear to ear. Ultimately, though, the point is not whatever words and numbers are on the dashboard (as I mention in Section X, *DATA: The Future of Talent Strategy*) but that we now *know* this. As talent folks and HR folks. And from that strategic point of view, this data is even MORE reliable and nuanced than anything I might get from, say, a Pulse Survey. Here, people are engaging for *themselves*, pondering their futures and career aspirations. (I trust the Mosaic data more because it's the kind of detail we get more authentically than anywhere else.) And as more and more people do that? We'll get an increasingly layered view into the voice of the employee, learning, *Here's where they want to grow. Here is what they care about.*

51 · Our Inflection Point

There are so many components of Mosaic, it could take years of development for a company to make full use of its potential (such as workforce planning). That's yet another element of this ever-evolving era of AI-enhanced technology. This is a few step changes away from all the kinds of cookie-cutter, third party licensing products you would have needed to acquire to enhance your department's services before now. Five to seven years ago, any single component, say, for example, the work style exercise, would have been its own (expensive) stand-alone tool, available for license or purchase. Or just an off-the-shelf tool like 360 Assessments, or just the Myers-Briggs (MBTI) self-assessment—and that's *all* either would have been. You would've known something more about yourself and then maybe you could go to a class and talk about careers in some generic way. Now, it and a host of other supporting components are completely baked in. Mosaic, for example, now has a whole understanding of Christine Huntley's work style and what matters to her. That feeds the AI, which builds out one possible trajectory for her whole career. Before, all you'd get is feedback. Talk about a massive step change!

A Tech-Enabled Ecosystem

As mentioned in Part 2, this arena of HR and technology will continue to evolve at an increasingly rapid clip. The ultimate point isn't about the magic of any single platform or how many services are bundled into it but that you are building the muscle of engagement with where the business is headed. That you are staying on top of whatever technology is out there and learning how to keep your company—and, ultimately, your employees—ahead of the curve and bringing them along for the change. At one point, I had the opportunity to ask Avery what Thrive meant to him. He complimented us with this reply, *"To me, Thrive is our journey that Larry started. It's an entire ecosystem of working on the individual, and then your team, and then the enterprise. To me, it's just an opportunity for me to think about my career.*

Whether that be [at] NetApp or somewhere else. NetApp is providing a safe space, a safe environment for me to explore that. And, you know, they hope that I still reach those goals at NetApp. And one of the most amazing things that Larry purchased for us was this tool called Mosaic."

In Year One, we planned to grow awareness. Year Two was about starting to use the data to really learn what we have in the system. And the goal of Year Three was to drive strategy with that data. As we rounded the corner into 2022, Thrive, Mosaic, Eightfold, and BetterUp were all in use. Once NetApp starts getting all that data working together? And using AI to cross all of it? THAT will be incredibly powerful. It will be like Dash but way better. That's Data, Alignment, and Action working harmoniously in a networked Golden Thread.

PART IV

The Year of Well-Being

Leadership:
A Long Term, Inside Job

Nowadays, we're seeing discussions about well-being and mental health more out in the open. Can you imagine ten years ago, saying, "*Dude, I'm so stressed out. I'm getting depressed at this job!*"? You know what the response would have been: "*That sounds like a personal problem,*" or "*Go on, leave. I don't wanna deal with this.*" With Thrive, we began to open this idea that everyone could talk about their well-being, and managers could express care for their employees—leading with grace instead of demands. The pandemic really accelerated the need for this as COVID took its toll. Burnout was on the rise. We needed to take immediate action.

That was why our message in Year Four was well-being, well-being, well-being, and leaning even more into the whole person approach. This naturally aligned with one of my career-long aspirations: *Let's put caring back into the way employees are treated.* We'd been working toward a more human-centric work culture from day one. Embracing the themes of Carol Dweck's *Mindset* and both sides of Alexi's barbell—productivity *and* well-being. Because it's the future of business—and the right thing to do.

52 · Work-Life Balance

While responses from our Thrive Pulse Surveys about caring and listening consistently came back great ("*I feel taken care of during this very rough time.*"), the other feedback we were starting to get was "*I don't wanna do another thing today.*" Like NetApp, Glint was reporting lower response rates across the board with their customers and told us, "*We think it's just fatigue more than disinterest.*" All of which hurt our Fuel50 launch, just as we were ramping up with gigs and special projects. As the pandemic progressed, when we surveyed around the question, *Can you separate life and work?* The AI-driven analysis revealed the highest negative sentiment was around nights and weekends. "*My boundaries!*" people cried. "*I'm burning out.*"

We had our work cut out for us because most employees didn't know how to resurrect those boundaries between work and home and/or didn't feel empowered to build them. They'd take every meeting, despite Zoom fatigue. Health and energy, and the energy of a leader's team, are the fuel of productivity. Leadership's responsibility was to help everyone figure out how to manage—and let them know it was okay to do so.

Which was why we wove those themes into our Year Three Career Week programming. As George said at the time, "*We need to balance and build sustainability, [even happiness], into our work lives.*" He continued, "*And we need to have confidence and toughness and grit and our commitment to a growth mindset.*"

In my Global Talent All Hands "fireside chats," where our programming usually addressed "top of mind" themes, we'd been talking a lot about culture. Then we pivoted to themes about boundaries—how to instill and set them. So, I was very excited to weave ideas about well-being into our evolving corporate culture as well. And be able to tell every employee to, "*Make it as important to reclaim yourself in this world,*" and to "*protect your energy and your time,*" because your health is your fuel, especially as knowledge workers.

Although triggered and aided by the pandemic, NetApp's long-term commitment to the employee experience became a competitive advantage as well. As Debra said, "*It's a differentiator. We can all go accept a role at any company that offers us title or compensation…and those things are important. They are. I think what's MOST important is how we feel about that and the connection we feel to the company and the work that we are doing, and our colleagues, and that sort of collaboration. That's why employee experience was important then and going into Year Four as well.*"

Well-Being and Executive Enablement

As mentioned, during COVID, our coaching data said that employees were worried about themselves and their families and their safety. Our leaders needed to care more than ever. That was when we began introducing more enablement around *How do you lead in this new world? How are you still inclusive in a hybrid environment where everyone has different needs?*

Even without tumultuous events such as a pandemic in the mix, pivots in cultural transformation can take years to fully realize. To achieve these changes, you've got to tackle the culture from various points—with patience and consistency. When I first joined NetApp, I did democratization, right? BetterUp for all! The data from the Pulse Survey for all! Thrive Everywhere—*you* decide how/when/where. And I'd flipped the Talent Development script to focus on all eleven thousand employees with Talent Enablement. By Year Four, we'd come to feel that the executive level wasn't responding as quickly as leadership wanted or needed. They'd not yet embraced enterprise-wide thinking. And having teams working with other teams was needed more than ever at this time. So, we focused on the top of the organization (VPs and above), where people were still often retreating into their silos.

We'd done some director immersion offsites at the end of Year One, but now, we were very focused on encouraging these high-performing teams *across* teams. On working toward that enterprise-wide mindset. And as was the case elsewhere, doing so continued to tie together the larger message— and this year's emphasis on well-being. Which was relatively seamless for us in terms of programming because the concern for well-being had always been a core part of the Golden Thread. In many ways, well-being is at the heart of Thrive.

Let My People Shine

My view on leadership is it's a lifelong journey. You're not gonna go two weeks to learn how to be a leader—that's not how it works. That's a henna tattoo. And leadership challenges present themselves in all kinds of manners along the way. Take, for example, someone who is unsure of their abilities as a leader. Who puts walls up. They often tend to be more of the "command and control" variety. They micromanage. And they are afraid that their people will outshine them. Yet, the best-case scenario is quite the opposite! You want to showcase those star performers and make them visible because they make you look good. They drive results for your team. They grow. So that's one sign that a leader may need to learn.

So, we asked ourselves, *How do we create forums, materials, engagement, and experiences where leaders can interact with each other and with subject matter experts and external speakers?* It was really about, *How do we create the right conditions for leadership insights? Those aha moments that will click?* Again, outside consultants can be helpful when attacking business structures, but when it comes to changing culture, it's an inside job. We strove to provide enablement, giving NetApp's leaders the tools to learn for and help themselves. We looked to provide different modes of sharing, learning, and coaching to create opportunities for those aha moments. We strove to drive expansion in their worldview of leadership and how they show up as leaders. And help them to realize that you must let go as a leader and provide that runway, that air cover, the support, the coaching and the guidance, and, like the situation above, let your people shine.

53 • Being Successful Now. Here.

I've mentioned throughout this book how allergic I am to short-term training, so I'd like to take a moment to talk about my approach in a situation like this. HR is as vulnerable to blind spots as any other leaders are in a company.

And I think, a lot of times, there can be a bit of "unconscious unconsciousness" around what HR can actually do. Again, it is my belief that results come from an education process as opposed to delivering some program. Everyone's so used to "*process*," and "*mandatory*," and "*following rules*." Sometimes, when you talk about leadership development, you'll often see HR put a list of leadership competencies together or say things like, "*They need EQ*," or "*IQ*," and all sorts of buzzwords that really could be used for any VP in any company, ever. As opposed to taking all that out and simply asking, *What's the most powerful, quickest and easiest way to get our leaders or talent aligned to what we're doing* <u>here</u>?

My job was to get the leadership team to start asking the right questions, having the right conversations, and demonstrating the right behaviors. Together. Instead of some off-the-shelf leadership development, I believe you should be teaching experienced leaders what to do to be successful here and now. And narrowing the focus onto what matters in this particular business with this group of people, not just a theory about what a vice president is. To be asking, *What does the business need to be running or understanding? What does it mean to be a successful VP here for the next two years? What's the impact?* As I've said, many companies choose to implement leadership competencies that are generic and typically not specific to the business challenge, even though it may make them feel like they are developing leaders. I've seen this over and over again. That was why cultivating these kinds of conversations in a collaborative way, in which we could have authentic, pointed dialogues, and getting people focused on delivering on the current strategy (and less on a definition that could be used anywhere) was our aim.

Thrive As a Leadership Model

We'd already long established Thrive as the leadership model within NetApp. Now, you may be wondering, with qualities such as growth mindset and rigor, *How can you teach that? How do you assume these competencies are going to appeal to every leader?* Well, you can't. Instead of pointing leaders to generic, bland, difficult-to-execute competencies that fade into the background, we were helping all employees live and grow inside the Thrive Ecosystem. We used the Thrive Wheel as our leadership model, a kind of template or cheat sheet because it contained an entire context for everyone and was immediately actionable. And it was everywhere. Activate Yourself = Have your Quarterly Conversations. Activate the Team = Sit down with your team and action plan your specific Pulse Survey results. Activate the Enterprise = Encourage your teams to do the self-assessments in Mosaic and then discuss that data in your QCs. Activate the Future = Use AI to plan for future organizational needs. Now that's a leadership model everyone could easily grasp and execute.

Building Operational Rigor

Year Four was one of those corporate junctures where we wanted to build on our Thrive ideas and push leadership even further. Some of the remaining challenges at NetApp were around collaboration and cross-accountability at the leadership level. And there was a general consensus around improving operational rigor at NetApp. It can happen when you've worked in the same environment for many years. Sometimes you don't know what you don't know (*unconscious unconsciousness*), no matter how long or short your stint with a company has been. We saw it as our job to help shake that rigor up a bit.

We've talked throughout this book about cultivating an enterprise-wide mindset with silo-busting and implementing Dash exercises—where each leader gets up and talks about what they're up to (instant alignment). And remodeling, overall, how leadership and employees work together. I wanted to motivate NetApp leadership to work with employees in even more growth-oriented ways—mindsets, technology, the Thrive Ecosystem. This included getting our NetApp leadership to act even more like owners—planning collectively and working out business problems together. It is my enduring belief that you can get a lot more done, much more quickly, when your focus is on improving these connections and relationships. Which is not easy (I'm not saying it is. It's not.) But it's important to always work at it—because it's central to fully achieving true cultural transformation.

With all that in mind, EM and I went to a meeting of just the senior people, and I said, "*Although I came in to democratize, we need Executive Enablement here because there's no enablement focus at the top. We believe the time for this is now.*" We were definitely looking for accelerated, high-quality results. We wanted to know, "*How do you build operational rigor to get that instant alignment at the top of the organization?*" It was agreed that a return to Executive Enablement was an essential next step.

SECTION 2

Executive Enablement

The two leadership development events we produced were a culmination of all that I'd been striving for these past four years. With the executive offsite and the Directors' Immersion Experience (the first since Year One), we were also making good on the promise of the best of what the Thrive Ecosystem aspired to become.

These two events were hosted in the first half of 2022, leading up to NetApp's fiscal new year in May. An appropriate time for leadership to be working on goals—so the company could kickstart the next twelve-month cycle with a fresh start and some clear direction. Although similar in intent, these two events targeted different populations. The executive offsite was comprised of the top twenty leaders in the organization. The Directors' Immersion Experience was just that—for over one hundred director-level leaders within NetApp at that time.

54 · Executive Offsite. Whose Goals Are They?

Like most corporations, George announced company goals once a year. They were aspirational and often fairly similar from company to company. Slogans such as *Grow Our Business in Cloud* or *Break into New Markets*. The traditional presumption was that they'd sort of organically disseminate out into the workforce as global mandates. That regional and divisional leaders and managers would pick up their respective batons and run with them. And the CEO is expected to circle back 12 months later to report on how well we all did.

But during those intervening months, who *actually* takes these goals on? Who is held accountable? Honestly, after thirty years in business, I can confidently say, nobody. As mandates, they don't work. And I think most people already *know* that. You walk the halls, see the banners and posters and placards, and think, *Oh, there they are. They're on the wall... And who cares?*, you know? It's as if a spaceship landed, but you can't get near it because you're too busy doing your own stuff. But if someone feels, *These are not my slogans, they're George's*? That's a huge disconnect.

Our VP Pulse Survey data was finally backing this up. The feedback overwhelmingly indicated, *"When we get corporate goals, they're George's goals, and we all go back to our jobs."* Meaning no accountability. No planning together, no follow up. How could we get to an enterprise-wide mindset, or owner's mindset, if these were the true conditions? But now we knew! And now I had data I could bring to George. And to be clear, this wasn't a George problem; this was a company one. (And it's an *every* company problem.) Once I brought it to his attention and suggested solutions, he was 100 percent behind it. *"Yes, let them come help with this,"* said George.

So, early in 2022, we extended our pre-existing, bi-annual talent review sessions (see *Be a 21st Century Manager* on page 99) and hosted our first in-person, executive offsite since before Omicron had hit. We called it *Sowing the Seeds of Growth Mindset, Building a Community of Leaders.* The objective? It was a team-based, goal-setting exercise. EM and I had been looking for ways to build a little bit more of that muscle within NetApp leadership. More enterprise-wide mindset, more cross-functional accountability and planning. This was it.

The two-day executive offsite was a gathering of the top twenty leaders in the company (all CEO staff and senior SVPs), all of whom voluntarily put themselves in an uncomfortable spot in a room together; none of our meetings are mandatory (I don't make anyone sign up for a leadership experience). So, their attendance was a good sign!

I set the tone, saying, *"Today's a gym day, not a spa day."* As everyone gathered in groups, instead of talking about traditional corporate competencies, we asked our leaders to help craft, deliver, and communicate the corporate goals. George announced, *"Here's what I think our new goals are. So, let's us, the top twenty people in the organization, develop and drive them."* I reminded the assembled that as NetApp senior leadership, they needed to take off their functional hats and don their enterprise-wide ones. That they would not just have the opportunity but the responsibility to comment on their team members' ideas, and that cross-team collaboration was how innovation happened! And finally, after the fact, it was going to be up to them to break down silos and champion their group-chosen goals.

In the past, when we would come back together (at a VP forum or whatever), George would tell everyone how we were doing against these goals. And I said to them, *"You know, I've heard before that these are George's goals. These are not George's goals. Not anymore. Leaving this offsite, these are your goals. And when we return in six months, I want you to come in and report on your progress to George!"* I followed that up with, *"Never take that hat off again."*

While mingling afterward, I asked them how it felt to work this way. Responses included, *"It's so freeing,"* *"It was great to hear things I never heard before,"* *"I made new friends,"* *"This was needed,"* and *"It was worth my time."* Another asked, *"Can I bring this to my team?"* to which I replied, *"Uh, yes! Indeed!"*

Post-exec offsite, follow through was the next big hurdle. What we worked on was: *How do we keep this on a cadence? The transparency, responsibility, accountability, and execution? How does this become integrated? Automatic?* This would become EM's focus as she pivoted from Talent Enablement into her new role in Executive Enablement. I'm so excited for her.

55 · Director Immersion Experiences

Around the same time we were working with the executive team, we worked with NetApp directors as well. The intent was the same—to develop more of an owner's mindset in that community. We had done a Directors' Immersion Experience around the cusp of Year One/Year Two (at which we had an actual velvet rope—and a full house!). This was our first since. Held late in the pandemic via Zoom on March 14, 2022, the Directors' Immersion Experience was specifically for senior directors and directors.

In addition to our own programming (largely architected by EM), we blended in business simulations delivered by a company called BTS (www.bts.com) whose expertise is around leadership readiness and development. As we had done in 2019, we worked with them beforehand to plan some really worthy challenges. We focused on issues and themes we felt these guys needed to get better at such as cross-functional working together.

We used the word *immersion* in the title because that was the mood we were going for. This was not a training, it was designed as an experience. I'd aimed for this all these years, and this was finally it.

Immersing a group of directors into a simulation that put them in the hot seat running a business. This was peak! A business school scenario with an enterprise-wide mindset applied to it—team problem-solving and then getting judged and receiving feedback on their choices.

In the simulation, each team was presented with a situation, which began with, "*You're running a company.*" We crafted NetApp(ish) scenarios as case studies, with real-world challenges happening at the company right now. Maybe it's, like, GetApp, for example. Similar but not the same. They were told what the business did, what the problems were, and what the environment was. The directors made business decisions and got a scorecard around, say, dollars, sales, and employee experience. Let's say, they were presented with a challenge around financial investments (and playing team roles that may—or may not—have been based on real-world situations at the time) such as, "*All right, you made more money, but half of your people quit,*" "*You missed ten sales, but you kept your margins up,*" or "*You have to start a cross-functional team. There's a time limit. As the CFO, what's the first thing you'd do?*"

We tried to make the simulations have consequences. And they were sometimes given questions such as, "*What if someone in your team isn't holding up their end of the bargain? Would you call 'em out in the meeting? Talk to them one-on-one or try to switch them out?*" Managers would sometimes need to choose between multiple answers—we tried to make the decisions hard. With tradeoffs, gains, and consequences to each path. No clear black-and-white answers. Nothing obvious. It was like a mini business school, but no one functioned alone. Then they debriefed and assessed points. The pressure was on! The managers discussed their decisions as a director group. Pros, cons, and repercussions. Just as with senior leadership, at the end, I asked them how it had felt to wear an enterprise-wide hat. And

I followed with "*Your teams know you're here at the Directors' Immersion Experience. What goals are you going to take back to them?*"

After it was over, they started making more connections with each other. And continued meeting up. (Talk about silo-busting!) We heard nothing but great feedback, including comments such as, "*Just seeing these people and connecting with them was the best part about this.*"

56 · Inclusive Leadership

Well-being, balance, and leadership are all interconnected themes. A lot of lessons came out of the pandemic, a chief one being how to lead with grace, engagement, and authenticity. And by working together, collaboratively, greater success and greater health for each person as well as the business can be achieved. Our focus on well-being in Year Four catalyzed a leadership challenge that came at the right time in NetApp's growth.

At this point in my NetApp journey, I feel we accomplished so many of the concepts and transformation goals we started out hoping to achieve. It was time for a new personal direction, which is why I left to write this book and begin consulting.

EPILOGUE

We have finally arrived at the moment of true human and machine collaboration. For many years, emerging technology has been based on an "ask and answer" format. Do a search. Run a report. Now, with Generative artificial intelligence, we can literally collaborate with a machine. Many are already using ChatGPT (or one of its thousands of offshoots or competitors) to produce highly complicated results. Generative AI is poised to have a more profound and bigger impact on society than the internet.

But what is Generative AI, exactly? Vahed Qazvinian, Co-founder and CTO of Praisidio, offered a meaningful answer. *"Generative AI is a generationally transformative form of artificial intelligence that is capable of creating entirely new and original content, whether that's text, images, software, or music. Unlike traditional AI models that respond to specific inputs with predetermined outputs, Generative AI harnesses the power of neural networks and expansive datasets to generate novel ideas, solutions, or creations."*

Humanity's intelligence quotient just received a tremendous boost thanks to the power of these burgeoning tools. Does this mean we should be even more focused on our *emotional* quotient? Human empathy and resilience can be boosted just as powerfully by these creative, and super smart, partners. The balance between intelligence and emotion may indeed be the fulcrum around which human and machine collaboration is headed. Much of it will depend upon how we humans choose to engage with it.

Yes, we have a lot of decisions ahead of us; although these new technologies are at our fingertips, they will not replace most human interactions. Instead, they may simply bring us together more swiftly, with more actionable data. We will still have to choose how to interpret and engage with this data—and with each other in the face of it. In the context of ethics and consciousness, we have the exciting task ahead of us of deciding, collectively, what it all means. Talk about a transformation!

This brings excitement for the future and fear for today. The fear of missing out, of the unknown, and of robots taking our jobs, not to mention questions about how we should regulate. For now, these unknowns present a barrier to entry for many folks and companies. We will always have to strike a balance between ethics and advancement—as we always have at the dawn of every new generation of disruptive technologies. As James Courier, general founder of NFX recently wrote, "*Where we are today is just an on-ramp. It's now possible that most of our software and human-computer interfaces will be significantly augmented in the next 5 years after 14 years of near stasis. That opens up seams of opportunity for Founders.*"

Educational institutions and governments are at the forefront of our ethical concerns, and each day, we are seeing new, creative examples of how to find this balance between caution and innovation, between protection and risk-taking, between past methods and future pathways. Japan's education ministry, for example, recently introduced new guidelines allowing limited use of Generative Artificial Intelligence, such as ChatGPT, in elementary, junior high, and high schools. The guidelines emphasize caution for elementary school students and highlight the importance of discouraging cheating by passing off AI-assisted work as one's own.

Their decision is ingenious and instructive of how to harness artificial intelligence for future generations. And now, according to a recent *New York Times* headline, "Pressured by Biden, A.I. Companies Agree to Guardrails on New Tools." Huge AI companies are vying for good regulation while pushing forward. Amazon, Google, and Meta are among the companies that announced these guidelines as they race to outdo one another with competing versions of artificial intelligence.

And yet, right now, there are no speed limits. The horse is out of the barn and it's galloping away. As we see in the headlines every day, Generative AI is making a splash across various industries and at every level of human experience. I asked a few leaders in the Generative AI field, including Vahed, what their thoughts are about the future.

Q: What does this mean for leadership and organizations moving forward? What will we need to prepare ourselves for the future?

Envision an HR department transformed by Generative AI: automated personalized learning programs customized for each employee's unique career path, hyper-realistic job simulations for assessing candidates, instant and inclusive job descriptions, immediate access to automated people analytics, and the ability to predict and mitigate potential employee resignations. Such advancements, only now possible with this technology, empower HR professionals to be more proactive, informed, and attentive, ensuring they can prioritize the most vital aspect of any organization: its people. (Vahed)

Q: And what will leaders and organizations need to do to stay ahead in the age of Generative AI?

Thanks to generative AI, we've entered a world where access to information is ubiquitous and commoditized. Simply having the right answer won't be as impressive—the McKinsey job candidate will be able to pull up how many ping pong balls fit in a Boeing 747 within seconds (thanks to the AI system on their glasses, of course). Every car salesman will have the perfect pitch because they'll have your entire purchase history instantly available.

AI will be like social media, mobile apps, websites—table stakes for any modern company. What's going to differentiate outperformers from others is how they upskill their workforce on the more nebulous pieces such as soft skills. Because every job candidate and every salesman will have the right answer, winners will be determined by how they deliver that information, [meaning] their empathy and ability to relate to listeners. In some ways, the democratization of AI will force us to be more human and more creative. Leaders that recognize this

early will think of AI not as a means to an end but as an integral part
of their toolkit—like TurboTax for accountants, power drills for elec-
tricians, and medical reports for doctors. Ultimate success on the job
will come from how you use these tools. (Varun Puri, CEO at Yoodli
and AI Speech Coach)

So you've just completed a book on human-centered transformation.
You've built the muscles and acquired the insights to adapt not just to a
specific kind of challenge but to *any* business challenge. And here we are,
facing the biggest transformation we're *all* going to face since humans first
walked the earth.

My words for you? Use them. Apply them. Deploy these transformation techniques and mindsets with your organizations and leaders—or as
leaders yourselves. And get ready. And attack Generative AI as if it's your
partner, not your enemy. Because Generative AI is about to change every
aspect of your life. As we look to the future, getting ready with tools such as
these is how leaders and organizations are going to successfully adopt—and
build—with Generative AI.

As for me? My next challenge will be to navigate leadership and organizations to thrive in this new world. I couldn't be more excited. In some ways,
I could say I've been waiting my whole life for all these threads to come
together. These golden threads. Themes of authenticity. Being human-centered but tech-enabled. Believing in being democratic as a core leadership
principle. Being enabled and enabling others. Leading with grace. And not
just co-existing or collaborating with technology but also looking for all
the many new ways we can continuously co-create with it—and build new
worlds for people to work and create within.

The on ramp is here. Let's walk into the future together.

ACKNOWLEDGEMENTS

To my family, Cindy, Jasmine, and Brandon, you have been the uplifting and supportive engine that fueled my journey throughout this endeavor. Your unwavering encouragement and belief in me have been my greatest source of strength and inspiration.

Lisa Fitzpatrick, whose exceptional contributions went far beyond her duties to breathe life into this book with humor, intellect, and steadfast passion. Your dedication and creative brilliance have left an indelible mark on these pages, and I am truly grateful for our outstanding collaboration.

To the select few individuals whose unwavering dedication and expertise were pivotal in bringing this book to life, your fingerprints of success are unmistakably imprinted on every page. Your contributions have not only shaped this book but have left an indelible mark on its very essence. Thank you for your invaluable work: Elaine-Marie Bohen, "EM," Elise Graziano, Vicky Koutsis, Lisa Melsted, Christine Huntley, Michelle Mann, Avery Calman, Emily Miller, McKenna Daly, and Aman Musafar—"The Office of Transformation."

To George Kurian and Debra McCowan for their invaluable support and guidance, as well as for providing the runway and air cover that enabled us to lead a successful transformation.

To my incredible team of dedicated teammates, you are the heartbeat of this transformation. While I could name countless individuals who have contributed, it's your unwavering commitment that has truly made this journey possible. Thank you for your hard work and determination – together, we've achieved greatness: Stephanie Chalk, Trent Peterson, Nancy Ji, Thuy-Ly Nguyen, Rick Garbett, Jamhali Portus, Tammi Harris, Justin Tomlin, Tushar Dabral, Yu-Sun Hwang, Protima Achaya, Kathy Tyra, Tim Bonnet,

Kristine Lee Woldegiorgis, Karen Dammann, Chloe Zhou, Karen Matsueda, Anna N Schlegel, Lisa Northup, Joanne Glen, Calvin Lee, Anne-Marie Laster, Chinwe Abara, Sarah Soriano, Shreya Chaudhary, Priyanka Rao, Mike Tyler, Shawn Warn, Pamela Bess, Amy Powell, Anouk Snel, Manjari Gupta, the Global HR Team and CEO Staff.

To the Epic Author crew, thank you for the roadmap, inspiration, and execution: Trevor Crane, Samanatha Erbe, and Darwin Lopena.

ENDNOTES

1. BetterUp, LinkedIn, posted February 15, 2023, https://www.linkedin.com/posts/BetterUp_nearly-40-of-ceos-believe-their-organizations-activity-7026217041082605568-JDiI?utm_source=share&utm_medium=member_desktop.
2. Kotter, John P. *A Sense of Urgency* (Boston, MA; Harvest Business Press, 2008), vii-ix.
3. Concern for the "employee experience" is a recent and growing trend. In the hybrid work environment, it's replacing the term, and the idea, of culture a bit. As in, What is the employee experience going to be like when not everyone's in the office?
4. Effron, Mark. "Three Reasons HR Transformations Fail (and how to make sure yours doesn't)," The Talent Strategy Group, updated January 17, 2023, https://talentstrategygroup.com/three-reasons-hr-transformations-fail-and-how-to-make-sure-yours-doesnt/.
5. O.C. Tanner Institute, "Finding Fulfillment," 2023 Global Culture Report, 67, https://res.cloudinary.com/oct-corp/image/private/s--pTdZnnhF--/v1687983491/website/octanner-global-culture-report-2023.pdf.
6. Rock, David, Davis, Josh and Jones, Beth. "Kill Your Performance Ratings," Strategy + Business, Neuroleadership Institute, August 8, 2014, https://www.strategy-business.com/article/00275.
7. Ibid.
8. Ibid.
9. Shaywitz, Sally, Shaywitz, Jonathan. *Overcoming Dyslexia*, 2nd ed. (New York: Alfred A. Knopf, 2020), 143–24.
10. BetterUp.
11. BetterUp.
12. Wood, Adam, Leimgruber, Kristi, and Eatough, Erin. "Coach Your People, Transform Your Business," BetterUp Global Insights Report 2023, 19, https://grow.BetterUp.com/resources/coaching-culture-insights-report.
13. Fulton, Anne. "Activating the Ecosystem: Taking Thrive to the Next Level," Career Week Keynote, a company-wide virtual event hosted by NetApp, February 9, 2021.

Made in the USA
Las Vegas, NV
26 January 2024

84941326R00177